ENEMIES OF
THE PEOPLE?

ENEMIES OF THE PEOPLE?

How Judges Shape Society

Joshua Rozenberg

BRISTOL
UNIVERSITY
PRESS

First published in Great Britain in 2020 by

Bristol University Press
University of Bristol
1-9 Old Park Hill
Bristol
BS2 8BB
UK
t: +44 (0)117 954 5940
pp-info@bristol.ac.uk
www.bristoluniversitypress.co.uk

North America office:
Bristol University Press
c/o The University of Chicago Press
1427 East 60th Street
Chicago, IL 60637, USA
t: +1 773 702 7700
f: +1 773-702-9756
sales@press.uchicago.edu
www.press.uchicago.edu

British Library Cataloguing in Publication Data
A catalogue record for this book is available from the British Library.

Library of Congress Cataloging-in-Publication Data
A catalog record for this book has been requested.

ISBN 978-1-5292-0450-6 paperback
ISBN 978-1-5292-0452-0 ePub
ISBN 978-1-5292-0451-3 ePdf

Cover design and cover image credit: blu inc, Bristol
Printed and bound in Great Britain by TJ International,
Padstow
Policy Press uses environmentally responsible print
partners.

Contents

About the Author

Joshua Rozenberg is the only full-time journalist to have been appointed Queen's Counsel *honoris causa*. After taking a law degree at Oxford he qualified as a solicitor. He is an honorary Master of the Bench of Gray's Inn and a non-executive board member of the Law Commission.

Joshua was the BBC's legal correspondent for 15 years before moving to newspapers. He presents the popular Radio 4 series Law in Action, which he launched in 1984, and appears regularly on other news networks in the UK and abroad.

Preface

'Enemies of the People' was the *Daily Mail* front-page headline on 4 November 2016. It referred to three senior judges who had ruled that government ministers did not have the power to give the European Union notice of the United Kingdom's intention to leave. In effect, the High Court had ruled that Brexit could not be triggered without an Act of parliament.[1]

The newspaper's headline and the government's inadequate response to it had a much greater impact on the judiciary than most people realised at the time. Judges in the United Kingdom feared for their safety. Recruitment and retention became more of a challenge.

But did it change the way judges worked? Was judicial activism in the UK replaced with a degree of deference? Or were 11 senior judges emboldened to rule three years later – in the most far-reaching decision any of them had taken – that an order made by the Queen on the advice of her prime minister was no more than 'a blank piece of paper'?[2]

When John Roberts was nominated by President George W. Bush as chief justice of the United States in 2005, he was determined not to repeat mistakes made nearly 30 years earlier by Robert Bork – a candidate whose nomination was blocked by the Senate Judiciary Committee. Unlike Bork, Roberts avoided taking clear positions on contentious issues. But his masterstroke, according to one commentator,[3] came in the way he persuaded senators to believe that he was not the conservative ideologue that Bork had been.

'Judges are like umpires,' Roberts said. 'Umpires don't make the rules; they apply them.'[4]

This is nonsense, as Roberts was well aware. 'In our common law world,' said his UK counterpart Lady Hale in 2017, 'we cannot and do not pretend that the law is a clear and simple set of rules which can be readily applied to a given set of facts.'[5] Nor, in Lord Reid's classic metaphor, is the law to be found hidden in some Aladdin's cave in all its splendour.[6] Although judges do not believe in fairy tales any more, it seems that some senators are still willing to do so.

That's particularly surprising to find in the United States, where the Supreme Court can overturn legislation that it finds to be unconstitutional. In the United Kingdom, where the courts have no such powers, we find a much more realistic assessment of judicial law making from senior judges.

'It is accepted that judges have the power to make new law,' said Lord Lloyd-Jones, a justice of the UK Supreme Court, in 2018. 'But what is the proper role of judges in a common law system? To what extent is it appropriate for judges to develop the common law in accordance with general principles of law and justice, as they see them, and to what extent should they defer to parliament in the matter of law reform?'[7] As Lloyd-Jones observed, this was currently the subject of 'quite a heated academic debate' in the United Kingdom.

That debate had been revived by a lecture[8] that Jonathan Sumption QC delivered two months before he joined the Supreme Court at the beginning of 2012. In it, he argued that the courts had 'edged towards a concept of fundamental law trumping even parliamentary legislation'.

After retiring from the court Lord Sumption returned to the theme in his BBC Reith lectures. 'The courts have developed a broader concept of the rule of law which greatly enlarges their own constitutional role,' he said in 2019. 'They have claimed a wider supervisory authority over other organs of the state. They have inched their way towards a notion of fundamental law overriding the ordinary processes of political decision making, and these things have inevitably carried them into the realms of legislative and ministerial policy.'[9]

Claims that the courts had overreached themselves were highly contentious. Lord Dyson, a former Supreme Court justice, said he strongly disagreed with Sumption on this. Lord Falconer, a former lord chancellor, deprecated Sumption's conclusions.[10]

Whether you think judicial activism is a good thing will depend on whether you believe judges are better at taking some decisions than politicians are. But what can't be denied is that the judiciary has the power to shape society. How judges make law is the subject of this book.

★ ★ ★

I have many people to thank. Helen Davis of Bristol University Press conceived this book and commissioned it. Leonie Drake saw it through the press. The title comes from a lecture that the Northern Ireland Human Rights Commission invited me to deliver in May 2018.

My good friends Dr Natalie Byrom, Sir Martin Chamberlain, Baroness Deech DBE QC (hon), Rt Hon Lord Dyson, Professor Dame Hazel Genn DBE QC (hon), Sara Nathan OBE, Lord Pannick QC and Melanie Phillips (more than just a friend) very kindly read various drafts and saved me from a host of misjudgments. They are not to blame for the errors that remain.

This book, like the common law itself, owes a debt of gratitude to Her Majesty's judges for the judgments they deliver. Those judgments are reported by the British and Irish Legal Information Institute (BAILII),[11] an invaluable free resource that survives on charitable donations. Raw judgments are skilfully edited and enhanced by the Incorporated Council of Law Reporting for England and Wales, another not-for-profit organisation that has produced the most authoritative law reports for more than 150 years. Those reports – together with an up-to-date and annotated statute book – have reached me through the generosity of Thomson Reuters, which publishes the comprehensive online database Westlaw UK. The unfailingly helpful librarians at Gray's Inn filled in any gaps.

Readers should understand that my summaries of these judgments are necessarily incomplete. I have selected the points that seem relevant to my arguments, but anyone seeking to rely on these cases should read the original judgments – as well as checking whether they have been overturned by subsequent rulings or legislation. Many of the cases and statutes quoted apply only in England and Wales.

I dedicated an earlier book to my daughter's gerbils – asserting that, if nobody else did, they would consume it with enthusiasm. Sadly, these supposedly omnivorous rodents were deprived of that option by a nocturnal predator. So this book is dedicated instead to those litigants who prowl the public courts, fighting injustice as they see it. Some of them might not have wanted their stories to feature in this book. But without their willingness to trust the judges the common law would not continue to survive and thrive.

Joshua Rozenberg
October 2019

1

New Readers Start Here

What is the proper role of judges in a common law system? Should they strive for justice in each case before them, planting seeds that may take root and allow the common law to thrive? Or is judicial overreach a disfiguring aspect of our jurisprudence that threatens the rule of law and effective, democratic government?

Before we can answer these questions, we should explore how judges make law. First, though: a brief visit to parliament.

Parliament

In the United Kingdom (UK), we regard parliament as sovereign. 'What the Queen-in-parliament enacts is law,' said Professor Vernon Bogdanor, summarising an axiom of the British constitution.[1]

'Parliament can do everything except make a woman out of a man and the other way around,' wrote Jean-Louis De Lolme in the late 18th century.[2] The Geneva-born political theorist might not have been surprised to find that even this is no longer a limitation.[3]

But parliament is sovereign only in the sense that it makes binding laws. What it cannot do is govern. As Professor Robert Tombs explained, 'the role of parliament is to hold government to account, not to be the government'.[4]

And parliament cannot exercise its sovereignty while it is prorogued (suspended between sessions) or dissolved (for a general election). In September 2019 the UK Supreme Court decided that a decision to prorogue, or suspend, parliament for five weeks had been unlawful and of no effect because it prevented parliament from holding the government to account.[5] I shall have more to say about this remarkable ruling in Chapter 2.

There is also a view that 'the people' are sovereign – and that they 'lend' their sovereignty to members of parliament between public votes.[6] That theory was endorsed by the decision of members of parliament (MPs) to implement the result of the Brexit referendum held in 2016, even though most of them disagreed with it. But it does not help us to understand what limits there may be to parliamentary law making.

The judges fully accept that MPs and peers can amend or abolish laws made by the courts. In 1961, for example, parliament enacted legislation saying that 'the rule of law whereby it is a crime for a person to commit suicide is hereby abrogated'.[7] That's all it took: no court could question such a clear demonstration of parliament's power.

In addition to overturning long-standing principles, parliament can also choose to reverse the effect of specific court rulings.[8] In that sense, parliament always has the last word. Far from troubling the judges, this tends to reassure and fortify them.

Separation of powers

Parliament may be all powerful but the legislature is only one of three 'powers' in a modern democracy: the others are the executive and the judiciary. By 'executive' we usually mean the government, but the term may be used broadly, to include local authorities, or narrowly, to mean the prime minister and the secretaries of state who are members of the cabinet. The term 'judiciary' normally includes all who hold judicial office, full time or part time, including lay justices and tribunal members.

Lord Mustill summarised the relationship between the three powers in a judgment he gave in 1995:

> Parliament has a legally unchallengeable right to make whatever laws it thinks right. The executive carries on the administration of the country in accordance with the powers conferred on it by law. The courts interpret the laws and see that they are obeyed.[9]

The relationship between parliament, the executive and the judiciary is a subtle one. In the UK the powers are far from separate: most obviously, the executive is answerable to parliament and the government holds office only if the prime minister has the confidence of the House of Commons. By convention, government ministers are members of the legislature, which means they are given peerages if they do not already have a seat in parliament.

Parliament is more powerful than the government in the sense that it can vote down motions or bills supported by ministers. This happened in the spring of 2019, when, as prime minister, Theresa May failed on three occasions to secure a Commons majority for her Brexit deal. The government is more powerful than parliament in the sense that the prime minister can advise the Queen to prorogue parliament at a time of the government's choosing. But the courts are more powerful than the government in the sense that they can declare a prorogation unlawful in exceptional circumstances and quash it.

When the prime minister's decision to suspend parliament in September 2019 was challenged in the courts, the government argued that the judges 'should not enter the political arena but should respect the separation of the powers'. Not so, insisted the UK Supreme Court: 'by ensuring that the government does not use the power of prorogation unlawfully, with the effect of preventing parliament from carrying out its proper functions, the court will be giving effect to the separation of powers'.[10]

By convention, the government controls the parliamentary timetable. But, as we saw during the Brexit crisis, if the government cannot command a majority then MPs can take control of the agenda. The European Union (Withdrawal) (No 2) Act 2019, though initially opposed by the government, became law within less than a week.[11] No court would question the parliamentary procedures that led to its enactment.

It used to be possible for senior serving judges to speak and vote in the House of Lords.[12] But the Constitutional Reform Act 2005 introduced a greater degree of separation between the judiciary and the other two powers. Lord Irvine of Lairg, who held office from 1997 to 2003, was the last lord chancellor to sit simultaneously as a member of the legislature, the executive and the judiciary.

Keeping the legislature, the executive and the judiciary separate and distinct is intended to ensure that no arm of the state becomes too powerful. Allowing the powers to interlink and overlap, as they do in the UK, means that the government and parliament are not, in normal times, powerless.

Executive and judiciary

The most important separation we now have – and the most contentious – is between the executive and the judiciary. Each power must allow the other to do its job.

That means ministers must defend the independence of the judiciary (in Chapter 2 we shall see what happens when they fail to do so). It also means that the judges must allow the executive to govern. Courts must not interfere unless ministers have misused their powers.

But who's to decide? As Lord Justice Nolan said in 1992, 'the proper constitutional relationship of the executive with the courts is that the courts will respect all acts of the executive within its lawful province, and that the executive will respect all decisions of the court as to what its lawful province is'.[13]

In deciding whether ministers have kept within powers granted by parliament, the courts must interpret the words that parliament used. Often, definitions are provided. Sometimes, parliament simply leaves it to the judges to decide. The Constitutional Reform Act 2005 begins by saying that it 'does not adversely affect the existing constitutional principle of the rule of law'. But it makes no attempt to say what that principle means (nor does any other statute). Lord Bingham wrote a best-seller on it.[14]

Under the 2005 Act[15] each lord chancellor must swear to respect the rule of law.[16] Nobody has yet tested the effectiveness of that oath in court. But the day may come when the judges will have to decide what, if anything, it means in practice. That cannot be regarded as controversial, the Supreme Court insisted in 2019.[17]

Since 1992, when the case of *Pepper v Hart*[18] was decided, the courts have been able to resolve cases of ambiguity, obscurity or absurdity by looking up what the minister in charge of a bill said in the Commons or the Lords. But it is still for the courts to decide what parliament meant.

This is a very significant power. From time to time judges conclude that parliament 'cannot have intended' a particular outcome. They then insist that such an outcome could have been achieved by parliament, but only if it had used 'clear words'. Whatever words parliament has used, they never seem to have been quite clear enough.[19]

The principle of legality

There is a further limitation on parliamentary sovereignty, which Lord Hoffmann described, when giving judgment in 1999,[20] as the principle of legality. By this he meant that parliament must squarely confront what it is doing and accept the political cost:

> Fundamental rights cannot be overridden by general or ambiguous words. This is because there is too great a risk that the full implications of their unqualified meaning may have passed unnoticed in the democratic process. In the absence of express language or necessary implication to the contrary, the courts therefore presume that even the most general words were intended to be subject to the basic rights of the individual. In this way the courts of the United Kingdom, though acknowledging the sovereignty of parliament, apply principles of constitutionality little different from those which exist in countries where the power of the legislature is expressly limited by a constitutional document.

In his Reith lectures in 2019, Lord Sumption said this was better described as a principle of legitimacy:[21]

> Some things are regarded as inherently illegitimate: for example, retrospective legislation, oppression of individuals, obstructing access to a court, acts contrary to international law and so on. Now, that does not mean that parliament cannot do them. But those who propose these things must squarely declare what they are doing and take the political heat. Otherwise there is too great a risk that the unacceptable implications of some loosely worded proposal will pass unnoticed as a bill goes through parliament.

But this principle, Sumption argued, 'puts great power into the hands of the judges'. Whether it gives them too much power is one of the issues I shall be discussing.

To give effect to parliament's intentions, the courts may have to look beyond the statute they are interpreting. The Human Rights Act 1998[22] tells judges that 'so far as it is possible to do so … legislation must be read and given effect in a way which is compatible' with the European Convention on Human Rights. I shall have more to say about that later in this chapter.

Common law

Laws are made by parliament – but not by parliament alone. The uncodified British constitution allows courts to create law through the system of precedent: judges follow principles that have been applied in previous cases and develop new principles in the cases they decide. Their decisions are followed, in turn, by judges deciding similar disputes in the future.

We call this judge-made law the common law. Perhaps the best-known example is the modern law of negligence, which can be traced back to a single decision taken by three senior judges in 1932.[23]

Until the 1960s, judicial law making was regarded as controversial. Lord Reid, who sat as a law lord from 1948 to 1975 and was widely regarded as the outstanding judge of his generation, made the point in a much-quoted lecture[24] that I alluded to in the preface to this book:

> There was a time when it was thought almost indecent to suggest that judges made law – they only declare it. Those with a taste for fairy tales seem to have thought that in some Aladdin's cave there is hidden the common law in all its splendour and on a judge's appointment there descends on him knowledge of the magic words 'open sesame'. Bad decisions are given when the judge muddles the password and the wrong door opens. But we do not believe in fairy tales any more.

Murder

It is important to understand that judge-made common law is no less effective than Acts of parliament. Murder, for example, is a common-law crime. It has been a crime for as long as we have had a system of criminal justice. But parliament has never felt the need to pass a statute setting out its essential elements.

For these, we have to look at what the judges have decided over the centuries. Fortunately, there are textbooks that summarise the leading cases. One book used every day in the criminal courts of England and Wales says that 'murder is when a [person] ... unlawfully killeth ... any reasonable creature *in rerum natura* under the Queen's peace, with malice aforethought'.[25] In the many pages that follow, it explains what the judges currently understand this archaic language to mean.[26] But the source of this definition is not legislation: it is the writings of Sir Edward Coke, who served as chief justice under James I in the early 17th century. Coke (pronounced 'cook') recorded the common law as he then understood it to be in a four-volume work known as *Coke's Institutes*. His summary has been adapted to provide the definition just quoted.[27]

As we have seen, the common law can be amended or repealed by parliament. Coke said that the crime of murder could be committed 'within any county of the realm'. That suggests it would not be murder to kill someone outside the realm – in a foreign country. And the criminal law is not generally concerned with crimes committed in a place over which its courts have no jurisdiction. But legislation passed in 1861[28] makes it clear that a British citizen can be tried in England or Wales for a killing carried out abroad.

And there have been other reforms. In Coke's day you could not be charged with murder if the person you had attacked survived for longer than a year before dying. That arbitrary but pragmatic rule remained part of English law until as recently as 17 June 1996, when it was repealed to reflect advances in life-support systems.[29]

Narrow formalism or palm-tree justice?

The willingness of courts to develop the common law has varied over the decades. In the period immediately after the Second World War most judges followed the austere style of Viscount Simonds, a law lord from 1944 to 1962 (and lord chancellor 1951–54). His approach was later characterised by a judge of a very different stripe as 'legal literalism' and 'narrow formalism'.[30]

Lord Denning, who was in the Court of Appeal for much of that period, took a much more 'purposive' approach – although this became so unpredictable that it was derided as 'palm-tree justice'.[31]

Both judges were involved in a case in the early 1950s about local government boundaries. Denning set out his approach in a dissenting judgment:

> We do not sit here to pull the language of parliament and ministers to pieces and make nonsense of it. That is an easy thing to do, and it is a thing to which lawyers are too often prone. We sit here to find out the intention of parliament and of ministers and carry it out, and we do this better by filling in the gaps and making sense of the enactment than by opening it up to destructive analysis.[32]

When the case reached the House of Lords – at that time the UK's final court of appeal – Simonds made his disapproval of Denning very clear:

> The general proposition that it is the duty of the court to find out the intention of parliament – and not only of parliament but of ministers also – cannot by any means be supported. The duty of the court is to interpret the words that the legislature has used; those words may be ambiguous, but, even if they are, the power and duty of the court to travel outside them on a voyage of discovery are strictly limited.

Turning to Denning's policy of 'filling in the gaps', Simonds said this could not be supported either:

> It appears to me to be a naked usurpation of the legislative function under the thin disguise of interpretation. And it is the less justifiable when it is guesswork with what material the legislature would, if it had discovered the

gap, have filled it in. If a gap is disclosed, the remedy lies in an amending Act.[33]

Simonds was not the only senior judge to favour a declaratory principle. In 1951 Lord Jowitt, who was lord chancellor at the time, said the approach of the judges should be to expound the law as they believed it to be. At a conference in Australia he accused other speakers of confusing the task of the lawyer with the task of the legislator:

> It is quite possible that the law has produced a result which does not accord with the requirements of today. If so, put it right by legislation; but do not expect every lawyer, in addition to all his other problems, to act as Lord Mansfield did, and decide what the law ought to be. He is far better employed if he puts himself to the much simpler task of deciding what the law is.[34]

Proper development of the law

This ossified approach to law making could not survive a deceptively low-key announcement made in 1966 by the lord chancellor on behalf of himself and the law lords, the judges who then sat in the House of Lords as the UK's final court of appeal:

> Their Lordships regard the use of precedent as an indispensable foundation upon which to decide what is the law and its application to individual cases. It provides at least some degree of certainty upon which individuals can rely in the conduct of their affairs, as well as a basis for orderly development of legal rules.
>
> Their Lordships nevertheless recognise that too rigid adherence to precedent may lead to injustice in a particular case and also unduly restrict the proper development of the law. They propose, therefore, to modify their present practice and, while treating former decisions of this House as normally binding, to depart from a previous decision when it appears right to do so.

> In this connection they will bear in mind the danger of disturbing retrospectively the basis on which contracts, settlements of property and fiscal arrangements have been entered into and also the especial need for certainty as to the criminal law.
>
> This announcement is not intended to affect the use of precedent elsewhere than in this House.[35]

A report of this unexpected announcement was added at proof stage to the first legal textbook I bought as a student a couple of years later.[36] The book's editor welcomed the change of policy, while accepting that it made much of what he had written on precedent out of date.

At the time, though, a leading lawyer found it hard to see how the law lords could 'now depart from the law of the land'. Henry Fisher QC, vice-chairman of the Bar Council, said 'it might be thought that only an Act of parliament can give them the power to reverse their own previous decisions'.[37] Even a law student could see that he was wrong.

As things turned out, the UK's final court of appeal[38] has not overturned its previous decisions very often – although it happened three times in 2016.[39]

Even so, the 1966 'practice direction' was a dramatic change. What the law lords were saying was that, when they chose to do so, they would no longer declare what the law was. They would decide what it ought to be.

The politics of the judiciary

And how would they reach that decision? John Griffith was Professor of Public Law at the London School of Economics in 1977 when he published the first edition of his 'instant classic', *The Politics of the Judiciary*. Griffith's thesis was that the judges cannot act neutrally but must act politically. And their politics, he perceived, were conservative (if not Conservative). In his view, they acted in broadly similar ways when deciding 'political' cases – those arising from controversial legislation; or from controversial action initiated by public authorities; or cases involving moral or social issues:

Behind these actions lies a unifying attitude of mind, a political position, which is primarily concerned to protect and conserve certain values and institutions. This does not mean that the judiciary inevitably and invariably supports what governments do, or even what Conservative governments do, though that is the natural inclination ... They are protectors and conservators of what has been, of the relationships and interests on which, *in their view*, our society is founded.[40]

Times change. Griffith's book went through five editions over 20 years, and he revised his observations after the judges had failed to give the Thatcher government an easy ride.[41] But, in the last edition of his book, published in 1997, he still argued that the judges were acting politically:

If it is accepted, as I argue, that a judge, when sitting in his court, is frequently required to make decisions which involve an assessment of where the public interest lies and so make a political decision, then he cannot be said to act neutrally, although he may still be the person best suited to make that particular decision ... The falseness arises when judges are presented, or present themselves, as neutral arbiters capable of providing unpolitical solutions to political problems or of expressing unpolitical opinions on political issues. It is when the claim to neutrality is seen, as it must be, as a sham that damage is done to the judicial system.[42]

Finality good, justice better

Under our system of precedent, a judge is bound to follow the decision of a more senior court in a similar case unless that judge can 'distinguish' the earlier decision, which means finding a reason for saying it does not apply.[43] In addition, courts will normally follow earlier decisions taken by other courts at the same level. Appeal courts can overturn the decisions of lower courts.

The British brought their common law with them to the colonies they governed – and it remains dominant in the English-speaking world. Other countries have adopted a codified system, which means that you can expect to find the main legal rules written down in a comprehensive document known as the civil code. People in the UK sometimes refer to this as the continental system because it is used across the continent of Europe; lawyers usually refer to it as the civil law system, though that term has other meanings.[44]

What the law says on a particular issue can be harder to establish in a common law system because it may require lawyers to work through a series of decided cases. That may lead to more uncertainty than in a codified system. But the common law allows for greater speed and flexibility: it can be developed by the courts to deal with new technologies – such as cyber-assets – and adapted to reflect changing social attitudes. Common law judges start with the specific case before them; in civil law systems, the starting point tends to be an overarching principle.

The Bingham road-map

Lord Bingham, the greatest judicial figure in the UK since Lord Reid, explained in 1997 that the declaratory approach associated with Viscount Simonds in the 1950s was radically inconsistent with the subjective experience of modern judges:

> They know from experience that the cases which come before them do not in the main turn on sections of statutes which are clear and unambiguous in their meaning. They know from experience also that the cases they have to decide involve points which are not the subject of previous decisions, or are the subject of conflicting decisions, or raise questions of statutory interpretation which apparently involve genuine lacunae[45] or ambiguities. They know, and the higher the court the more right they are, that decisions involve issues of policy.[46]

Bingham, who was speaking at a conference in Auckland, suggested that making law was an entirely proper judicial function, provided it was exercised within certain limits. He identified a number of warning signs on the road to law making, ranging from *no entry* and *stop* to *give way* and *slow*. Bingham listed five cases in which one or other of these signs should be heeded by judges who were considering making new law:

1. where reasonable and right-minded citizens have legitimately ordered their affairs on the basis of a certain understanding of the law;
2. where, although a rule of law is seen to be defective, its amendment calls for a detailed legislative code, with qualifications, exceptions and safeguards which cannot feasibly be introduced by judicial decisions;
3. where the question involves an issue of current social policy on which there is no consensus within the community;
4. where an issue is the subject of current legislative activity;
5. where the issue arises in a field far removed from ordinary judicial experience.

This was a typically thorough checklist – although it still leaves individual judges to decide which signs to heed.

Striking the balance

How should the courts strike the balance between justice and certainty – between actively developing the law and deferring to past rulings? Delivering the Atkin Lecture in 2001, Sir Stephen Sedley restated the problem without resolving it:

> Many judges believe, not without reason, that certainty is the law's greatest virtue, and that to counterpose it to justice is to miss the point that uncertainty in the law is injustice on the grand scale. Others hold that where justice and precedent come into conflict it is precedent which ought to give way in the interests of the very justice which it is there to serve. Finality, said Lord Atkin, is a good thing; but justice is a better.[47] The two positions are locked forever in an arm-wrestling contest which neither possesses the strength to win outright. What one sees in the daily life of the law is their constant lurching to and fro.[48]

Something similar had been said nine years earlier by Lord Goff of Chieveley when giving judgment in the House of Lords, at that time the UK's highest court. He was responding to the argument that a particular outcome would overstep the boundary separating legitimate development of the law from unacceptable law making:

> I feel bound however to say that, although I am well aware of the existence of the boundary, I am never quite sure where to find it. Its position seems to vary from case to case. Indeed, if it were to be as firmly and clearly drawn as some of our mentors would wish, I cannot help feeling that a number of leading cases in your Lordships' House would never have been decided the way they were.[49]

Delegated legislation

The Westminster parliament can make or unmake any laws it chooses. But for it to pass all the laws needed to govern a modern society would be both undesirable and impractical. Parliament has therefore delegated powers to other law-making bodies.

The European Communities Act 1972 devolved powers to what became the European Union (EU). As a matter of law, it was always possible for those sovereign powers to be repatriated.

Under the Labour government elected in 1997 powers were delegated by Westminster to the devolved assemblies: the Scottish Parliament, the Welsh Assembly and the Northern Ireland Assembly. In areas of law covered by the devolution legislation, these legislatures can create laws that apply only in their own parts of the UK. But the ultimate authority remains with parliament at Westminster. We can see this from the fact that laws governing Northern Ireland have been passed by parliament during the years when its own assembly was not sitting.[50]

The most important powers – such as defence and the conduct of foreign relations – have never been devolved, and remain at Westminster. The UK government is also responsible for the external security of the Channel Islands and the Isle of Man, self-governing dependencies that are within the British Isles[51] but not part of the UK.

NEW READERS START HERE

Powers to make by-laws have also been devolved to local authorities and other public bodies. And law-making powers have been delegated by parliament to government ministers. You will often see a statute that says 'the secretary of state' may do this or that. These powers can be exercised by any cabinet minister or, in practice, by junior ministers acting on the secretary of state's behalf.[52]

Often the secretary of state is given the power to make regulations governing the way a statutory power is exercised. These regulations are known as delegated legislation because the power to make them has been delegated to ministers. They are also referred to as secondary legislation, in contrast to the primary legislation made by parliament.

The Human Rights Act 1998

The Human Rights Act 1998 took effect in 2000. Since then, it has been possible to challenge public authorities in the courts of the UK for failing to comply with rights guaranteed by the European Convention on Human Rights.

The following strike me as among the most important of them:

- the right to life – and, the judges have decided, the right to an impartial investigation into a death at the hands of the state (article 2);
- freedom from torture and inhuman or degrading treatment (article 3);
- the right to liberty (article 5);
- the right to a fair trial (article 6);
- the right to respect for one's private and family life (article 8);
- freedom of thought, conscience and religion (article 9);
- freedom of expression (article 10);
- the right to peaceful enjoyment of one's possessions (article 1 of protocol 1);[53]
- the right to education (article 2 of protocol 1);
- the right to free elections (article 3 of protocol 1);
- the right to enjoy all these rights without discrimination (article 14).

Some of these convention rights may conflict with each other in an individual case: for example, respect for an individual's private life may be inconsistent with a news organisation's freedom of expression. Similarly, freedom of religion may clash with restrictions on discrimination. Ultimately, these conflicts must be resolved by the courts.

The Human Rights Act – like the British constitution itself – is finely balanced.[54] It does not allow the courts to overturn Acts of parliament. But it does give the higher courts two very important powers.

One is to make what is called a 'declaration of incompatibility'. If the court considers that a statute does not comply with the European Convention on Human Rights it can say so.[55] Parliament may then change the law if it wishes to – and in the past it almost always has. I shall explain how declarations of incompatibility work in Chapter 4.

The other is known as 'reading down'. In many ways, this is even more revolutionary. Declaring that the legislation is incompatible with the convention should be seen as a last resort, a former president of the UK Supreme Court has argued, because judges must try to 'interpret' the legislation so that it does comply. As Lord Neuberger explained, 'judges are positively encouraged to rewrite statutes to comply with the convention and therefore to act as legislators rather than interpreters'.[56]

Neuberger was referring to section 3 of the Human Rights Act. This says that, 'so far as it is possible to do so, primary legislation and subordinate legislation must be read and given effect in a way which is compatible with the convention rights'. Of course, a great deal turns on what the judges regard as 'possible'. But if there is more than one possible way of interpreting a piece of legislation, the courts must choose the one that complies with the European Convention on Human Rights.

Reading down

A very simple example from the early days of the Human Rights Act may help to explain how judges can 'read down' a statute.

In 1983 Hugh Wallwyn-James became the tenant of a basement flat in Earl's Court, London. When he died in 2001 the landlord,

Ahmad Ghaidan, wanted the property back. If Wallwyn-James had been married, then his 'surviving spouse' – his widow – would have been allowed to continue renting the flat. But marriage, as such, was not required: if someone had been living with the tenant 'as his or her wife or husband', then that person would also have been allowed to stay.

In fact, the person Wallwyn-James had been living with was another man, Juan Godin-Mendoza – in what the court quaintly described as a stable and monogamous homosexual relationship. Could he succeed to the protected tenancy?

Godin-Mendoza's lawyers argued that it would be discriminatory to refuse him a statutory tenancy on the grounds of his sexual orientation. And the courts agreed. In the days before civil partnerships and same-sex marriage, they interpreted the phrase 'surviving spouse' in the Rent Act 1977 to include the survivor of a long-term same-sex partnership.[57]

So Godin-Mendoza was allowed to stay.[58] As Neuberger's successor, Lady Hale, commented some years later, the case established that the interpretative route in section 3 should, wherever possible, be preferred to making a declaration of incompatibility under section 4. 'What was possible under section 3 went further than either a literal or a purposive interpretation of what parliament had said,' Hale explained. But there were limits: courts 'must not adopt an interpretation which went "against the grain" or contradicted some fundamental principle of the legislation'.[59]

Judicial review

Long before the judges were given new powers and duties under the Human Rights Act, they were taking steps to ensure that ministers and others who had been given law-making responsibilities by parliament keep within their powers.

When the courts first started reviewing the legality of decisions taken by public bodies they used Latin names for the orders they granted. In 1977 these confusing and overlapping remedies were replaced with the simpler term 'judicial review'.[60] You challenged the validity of a decision by seeking judicial review of it. If your challenge was successful, you were granted judicial review. Judicial review was the outcome, not the process.

But judicial review is a phrase that is often misunderstood. Nowadays people talk of applying for *a* judicial review. That causes confusion because it suggests that *any* decision can be reviewed by a court and then overturned if a judge disagrees with it. As a matter of law, the courts have no such power. It is not their job to assess the merits of a decision.

Nor should it be. In a judgment which he delivered in 2007 Lord Bingham said that 'the democratic process is liable to be subverted if, on a question of moral and political judgment, opponents of the Act achieve through the courts what they could not achieve in parliament.'[61] He was referring to the Hunting Act 2004, passed just three years earlier by the House of Commons[62] and challenged by those affected by it.

The courts can quash a decision only if it is taken unlawfully. In judicial review 'unlawful' means contrary to the principles currently applied by the courts. People sometimes refer to a decision maker acting 'illegally'. But this term is best reserved for breaches of the criminal law.

Judicial review applies only to public bodies or bodies that exercise public powers. The law governing these principles is called public law. It is also known as administrative law, and the main court that hears judicial review applications is the administrative court.

Before you can apply for judicial review you need permission from a judge. This may be granted without an oral hearing.[63] Judges will grant permission only if they consider that the claim is arguable; it has not been delayed; and the claimant has sufficient 'standing'. That requirement, which is designed to deter busybodies and others who are not directly affected by a decision, is often interpreted generously. But in Chapter 3 we shall encounter a case where, on pragmatic grounds, the courts denied standing to an elected official.[64]

Permission is needed because judicial review cases harness the powers of the state. We can see that from the way cases are referred to. A claim for judicial review is listed as *Between the Queen on the application of [claimant] and [defendant]*. This is usually abbreviated to *R ([claimant]) v [defendant]*.

Unreasonable Wednesbury

Back in 1947 – before cases were named in this way – a case called *Associated Provincial Picture Houses Ltd v Wednesbury Corporation* established the need for decision makers to act reasonably and fairly. This is how Lord Greene, who was then master of the rolls,[65] summed up the responsibilities of someone who had been granted an executive discretion by parliament:

> The discretion must be exercised reasonably. Now what does that mean? ... A person entrusted with a discretion must, so to speak, direct himself properly in law. He must call his own attention to the matters which he is bound to consider. He must exclude from his consideration matters which are irrelevant to what he has to consider. If he does not obey those rules, he may truly be said, and often is said, to be acting 'unreasonably'. Similarly, there may be something so absurd that no sensible person could ever dream that it lay within the powers of the authority.[66]

Lawyers call this the '*Wednesbury* principle' or '*Wednesbury* unreasonableness', after the case decided by Lord Greene. It used to strike me as unfortunate that a harmless West Midlands town should be stigmatised as the epitome of unfairness, particularly as its local authority was found to have behaved entirely reasonably. However, Sir Stephen Sedley, a former appeal judge, rightly described the council's decision to exclude children under 15 from Sunday film shows as a 'textbook abuse of power which would not have got past any High Court judge a generation later'.[67]

Judicial review reviewed

In 1984, shortly before I first wrote about this topic,[68] the principles of judicial review were helpfully redefined by the distinguished judge Lord Diplock in a leading case.[69] Instead of *Wednesbury* unreasonableness, he used the term 'irrationality' as a test of whether a decision should be overturned. Unfairness was recategorised as 'procedural impropriety'. And the long-standing duty of a decision maker to keep within the powers delegated by parliament was described by Diplock as a duty not to act 'illegally' – though, as I say, I prefer the term 'unlawfully'.

Diplock used 'irrationality' to mean a decision that was 'so outrageous in its defiance of logic or of accepted moral standards that no sensible person who had applied his mind to the question to be decided could have arrived at it'. Taken literally, that is an extraordinarily high standard to be met. In practice, as Mr Justice Sedley said in 1996, it refers to 'a decision which does not add up – in which, in other words, there is an error of reasoning which robs the decision of logic'.[70]

As Lord Dyson observed in 2015, a far more nuanced approach emerged during the 30 years that followed Diplock's redefinition of judicial review. 'This has not been the direct result of any legislation,' the then master of the rolls said in a lecture. 'It has been the product of judicial activity in developing the common law.'[71]

Dyson gave some examples. In 1995 the Court of Appeal had to consider a long-standing Ministry of Defence policy that now seems outrageous. It was that homosexuality was incompatible with membership of the armed forces. Personnel who were found to be homosexual or were engaging in homosexual activity could no longer serve.

This policy was challenged as irrational by former service personnel who had been discharged because of their sexual orientation. Dyson's predecessor, Sir Thomas Bingham, dismissed their application. The government's policy had not been irrational at the time when the applicants were dismissed, he said. 'The threshold of irrationality is a high one. It was not crossed in this case.'

But Bingham then went on to approve a summary of the case law put to him by David Pannick QC, representing the applicants. In judging whether a decision maker has exceeded the range of responses reasonably available, said Bingham, the human rights context was important. 'The more substantial the interference with human rights, the more the court will require by way of justification before it is satisfied that the decision is reasonable.'[72]

Proportionality

In addition to illegality, irrationality and procedural impropriety, Diplock had suggested in 1984 that further grounds might be added in future cases. 'I have in mind particularly the possible adoption in the future of the principle of "proportionality" which is recognised in the administrative law of several of our fellow members of the European Economic Community,' he said. It was a far-sighted observation.

By 2003 the Court of Appeal could say that 'the *Wednesbury* test is moving closer to proportionality' and that in some cases it was not possible to see any daylight between the two of them. There might no longer be any justification for *Wednesbury*, the judges added, though it was not for them to perform its burial rites.[73]

Also in 2003, appeal judges said they had developed an 'issue-sensitive scale of intervention'. They still drew the line at reviewing the merits of a decision – in effect, retaking the decision themselves – but in appropriate cases they would 'look very closely at the process by which facts have been ascertained and at the logic of the inferences drawn from them'.[74]

Those comments reflected the implementation of the Human Rights Act in 2000. When the gay service personnel took their challenge to the Court of Appeal in 1995 they were unable to rely on the European Convention on Human Rights. At that time their only option was to bring a claim before the European Court of Human Rights in Strasbourg. They did so, and, in 1999, the court ruled in their favour.[75] Perhaps relieved that responsibility for the decision had been taken out of its hands, the government quickly changed its policy.

If the claimants had brought their claims a few years later they would not have needed to go to Strasbourg. Instead, they could have relied on the European Convention on Human Rights in the UK's own courts. The Human Rights Act 1998 came into force across the UK on 2 October 2000. Its effect was profound.

In deciding human rights claims, the UK courts must take into account the case law of the European Court of Human Rights.[76] Proportionality is one of the concepts developed by the Strasbourg court. However, the courts of England and Wales have not yet accepted that lack of proportionality, as such, is a ground for granting judicial review.

A uniform policy

Let us take an example of proportionality from 2006. The law lords were still the UK's final court of appeal. Under the leadership of Lord Bingham they had to consider a claim by Shabina Begum, a girl aged nearly 14 who had arrived on the first day of term at Denbigh High School in Luton dressed in a long, coat-like garment known as a jilbab. She was sent home and told to return wearing school uniform, and lost nearly two years' schooling before she joined a school where the jilbab was permitted.

Shabina Begum had challenged her 'exclusion' from Denbigh High, relying on article 9 of the European Convention on Human Rights. This says, in essence, that everyone has the right to freedom of religion, but that freedom to manifest one's religion is subject to such limitations as are necessary to protect the rights of others. So, the issue in the case was whether it was proportionate for the school to insist that all pupils wore uniform – which included the option for girls of a hijab (headscarf) and shalwar kameeze (tunic worn over shirt and trousers).

Bingham explained that the purpose of the Human Rights Act had been to allow people to enforce their rights without going to Strasbourg. The European Court of Human Rights had never assessed the decision-making process in the way that the English courts had when dealing with judicial review. It simply considered whether an applicant's rights had been violated.

As a result, courts in the UK would have to take an approach to proportionality in human rights cases that went beyond what was usual in judicial review. 'There is no shift to a merits review,' Bingham said carefully, 'but the intensity of review is greater than was previously appropriate.'

In the event, the law lords concluded that Denbigh High had been fully justified in acting as it did. 'It had taken immense pains to devise a uniform policy which respected Muslim beliefs but did so in an inclusive, unthreatening and uncompetitive way,' Bingham said.[77]

But where did this leave the question of proportionality in judicial review? In the lecture from which I have been quoting, Lord Dyson said the courts must now consider four questions.

- Is the objective of the measure under challenge sufficiently important to justify limiting a fundamental right?
- Are the measures which have been designed to meet that objective rationally connected to it?
- Are they no more than are necessary to accomplish the objective?
- Do they strike a fair balance between the right of the individual and the interests of the community?

It is the fourth question that is the most difficult. It looks as if the courts were being asked to decide the merits of the case – something they have always resisted.

How far should they go?

Back now to the question from Lord Lloyd-Jones that I quoted in the preface: 'to what extent is it appropriate for judges to develop the common law in accordance with general principles of law and justice, as they see them, and to what extent should they defer to parliament in the matter of law reform?'[78]

The Judicial Power Project, a group of academic lawyers supported by the think-tank Policy Exchange, had asserted that 'judicial overreach increasingly threatens the rule of law and effective, democratic government'.[79] But Lloyd-Jones was unpersuaded.

'There are, no doubt, limits to the judicial function in this regard,' he said, 'although they are difficult to formulate with any precision. It does seem to me, however, that recent criticism in this regard of the conduct of the judiciary in our jurisdiction has been considerably overblown and the dangers of judicial activism greatly exaggerated.'[80]

We see here a stark difference of opinion. A judge says it is his job to make law. There are limits, of course, but he believes that his colleagues have not gone beyond them. By contrast, a group of academics see a need to 'correct the undue rise in judicial power by restating ... the nature and limits of the judicial power within our tradition'. [81]

Who is right? This is how I plan to tackle that question in the pages that follow.

Now read on

Chapter 2 will explain why three judges were accused by a newspaper of being 'Enemies of the People'. When the case that had provoked that headline reached the Supreme Court, its justices got off much more lightly. One of them told me why:

> Quite apart from the outcome being less unexpected than it was in the divisional court, above all people had seen that what we were discussing was not politics. There was no discussion of whether Brexit was a good idea or a bad idea. What we were discussing was the limits of prerogative power to change the law – referring to the previous occasions on which the courts have had to consider that question, going back to the days of Charles I. People could see what we were doing might be considered boring. But it wasn't a case of judges playing politics – which I think was part of the reason for the animus behind some of the newspaper headlines.[82]

Chapter 3 deals with the criminal law. Here is a High Court judge in 1990, modestly but decisively overturning the 250-year-old principle that a man could not be convicted of raping his wife:

> I accept it is not for me to make the law. However, it is for me to state the common law as I believe it to be … I cannot believe that it is part of the common law of this country that where there has been withdrawal of either party from cohabitation, accompanied by a clear indication that consent to sexual intercourse has been terminated, that that does not amount to a revocation of that implied consent.[83]

Chapter 4 is about marriage and divorce. Here, we see a much more cautious approach from the Supreme Court. 'It is not for us to change the law laid down by parliament,' said Lady Hale, the court's president, in 2018. 'Our role is only to interpret and apply the law that parliament has given us.'[84] As we shall see, that deference paid off.

Chapter 5 considers assisted suicide and end-of-life decisions. Lord Neuberger explained in 2014 why he had refused to declare the law incompatible with human rights:

> First, the question … raises a difficult, controversial and sensitive issue, with moral and religious dimensions, which undoubtedly justifies a relatively cautious approach from the courts. Secondly … whether, and if so how, to amend [the law] would require much anxious consideration from the legislature … Thirdly … this is a case where the legislature is and has been actively considering the issue.[85]

But campaigners were not so easily thwarted.

Chapter 6 looks at questions of discrimination. These are particularly difficult because parliament tends to lay down general principles without explaining how they should be applied in practice. If a bus has room for either a wheelchair or a pushchair, which should have priority? Does a law intended to benefit surviving spouses or civil partners discriminate lawfully or unlawfully against former cohabitants? Lord Hodge argued in the Supreme Court that 'questions of social and economic policy fall within the remit of the democratically elected legislature and are beyond the remit of the courts'.[86] But who is to say whether a question meets this definition?

Chapter 7 discusses a high-profile case that was seen as a battle between gay rights and freedom of religion. It is one where the judges' views of society may have governed their view of what the law should be.

That should come as no surprise. In 2017 Lady Hale gave a lecture about judicial appointments. Once we acknowledged that the law was contestable, she said, we had to accept that views might legitimately differ about the outcome of many cases heard by a final court of appeal. So it mattered who the judges were:

I used to be rather sceptical about the idea that women brought something different to the business of judging ... But in fact we all bring something different to the business of judging. We bring our experiences of life, our values, our philosophies of judging, our inarticulate major premises, our unconscious biases ...

We like to think that the outcome of any particular case is determined by the law and the evidence and not by the predilections of the individual judge. We like to think that we are not predictable in the way in which we will decide the hard cases where the outcome is not clear. But we cannot have it both ways – we have already accepted that it matters who the judge is.[87]

Chapter 8 charts the creation of a new judge-made law protecting personal privacy. 'In English law there is no right to privacy,' a judge noted in 1990. 'If legislation is not forthcoming,' another judge predicted in 1996, 'I do not think the courts will be found wanting.' Was that a judicial threat to legislate?

The judges saw it differently. In their view, a much greater threat to the rule of law was legislation that allowed a member of the government to thwart the decision of a tribunal.

Chapter 9 explores access to justice. It shows how the judges are willing to overturn regulations made by ministers if they prevent people from asserting their rights in court. But was it right, as critics of the decision claimed, for the judges 'to second-guess and overturn political policy decisions' by reference to how they had turned out in practice?

Chapter 10 questions the Judicial Power Project's assertions that 'the decisions of parliament ought not to be called into question by the courts and that the executive ought to be free from undue judicial interference'. It challenges claims by Lord Sumption that the judges have over-extended their powers. Finally, it answers the question posed in the title of this book.

2

The Miller Tale

Shortly after the Brexit referendum result was declared early on Friday 24 June 2016, David Cameron emerged from the front door of 10 Downing Street to make two important announcements.

The first was that he would be resigning as prime minister. That was inevitable: he had campaigned for the UK to remain a member of the EU and yet 52% of the electorate had voted to leave.[1]

His second announcement was arguably more important. It was that the government would not immediately be notifying the European Council, under article 50 of the Treaty on European Union, of its intention to withdraw from the EU.[2]

'A negotiation with the European Union will need to begin under a new prime minister,' he said, 'and I think it is right that this new prime minister takes the decision about when to trigger article 50 and start the formal and legal process of leaving the EU.'[3]

That was not what Cameron had said four months earlier. 'If the British people vote to leave,' he told MPs in February, 'there is only one way to bring that about – and that is to trigger article 50 of the treaties and begin the process of exit. And the British people would rightly expect that to start straight away.'[4]

Article 50

Article 50 of the Treaty on European Union says that a member state can withdraw from the EU 'in accordance with its own constitutional requirements'. But what were they? The UK's constitution is 'uncodified' – largely unwritten – and there was nothing in the referendum legislation to say what should happen next.

In a newspaper article published a few hours after the result was declared, I suggested that giving effect to Brexit would require parliamentary approval. 'One might have argued,' I wrote, 'that a kamikaze prime minister could have triggered article 50 immediately after the referendum result was declared, using his prerogative powers. Those powers are used to sign treaties but not, I would argue, to put them into effect in the UK.'[5]

That proved to be correct – although I did not go so far as to say that it would be unlawful for the government to trigger article 50 without first obtaining an Act of parliament. The credit for that argument must go to three constitutional lawyers: Nick Barber, Tom Hickman and Jeff King. In a blog published the following Monday, they argued that ministers could not use their prerogative powers to overturn a statute.[6] And yet, judging by his announcement, that was just what Cameron seemed to think his successor could do.

Barber, Hickman and King explained that the royal prerogative is a collection of executive powers held by the Crown since medieval times and exercised on the monarch's behalf by ministers of the Crown. But these inherent powers were never granted or approved by parliament. So they are quite different from the law-making powers that ministers are sometimes given by statute: orders, regulations and other types of delegated or secondary legislation.

However, just as they did with delegated legislation, the judges have stepped in over the years to ensure that prerogative powers are properly exercised.[7] For that reason, the three academics predicted that the courts would not permit prerogative powers to be used to overturn rights granted by legislation, such as the European Communities Act 1972, which took the UK into what was then the Common Market. 'Before an article 50 declaration can be issued,' they wrote, 'parliament must enact a statute empowering … the prime minister to issue notice under article 50 of the Treaty of Lisbon.'[8]

That was an important proposition that needed to be tested in the courts. Mishcon de Reya was one of several law firms that took up the challenge. Its lawyers signed up a public-spirited investment manager named Gina Miller[9] and argued on her behalf that triggering Brexit would require primary legislation.[10] On 3 November 2016 the High Court agreed.[11]

Miller: the High Court decision

Judgment in the *Miller* case was delivered by Lord Thomas of Cwmgiedd, Sir Terence Etherton and Lord Justice Sales. 'The sole question in this case,' said the three senior judges, 'is whether, as a matter of the constitutional law of the United Kingdom, the Crown – acting through the executive government of the day – is entitled to use its prerogative powers to give notice under article 50 for the United Kingdom to cease to be a member of the European Union.'

The judges' answer was unflinching. Without specific authority from parliament, they ruled, 'the Crown cannot through the exercise of its prerogative powers alter the domestic law of the United Kingdom and modify rights acquired in domestic law under the European Communities Act 1972 … We hold that the Secretary of State does not have power under the Crown's prerogative to give notice pursuant to article 50 of the Treaty on European Union for the United Kingdom to withdraw from the European Union.'

In reaching this decision, the High Court accepted the argument put by Miller's counsel, Lord Pannick QC (as he had become). Pannick likened giving notice under article 50 to firing a gun. Pulling the trigger, by itself, was something that ministers might be able to do under their prerogative powers. But once the trigger had been pulled, it was inevitable that it would hit its target – even if it took two years.[12] And, when that happened, people in the UK would lose rights granted by parliament.

It was a fundamental principle of the UK constitution, argued Pannick, that the Crown's executive powers could not be used by ministers to diminish or abolish existing rights, whether conferred by common law or by statute. Counsel for the government had no answer to this point. His submission was 'flawed at this basic level', the court said.

If ministers could not use their inherent powers to trigger Brexit, then how could they give effect to the referendum result? To anyone who had been following the case, the answer was obvious. Ministers would have to ask parliament to pass legislation. Theresa May, who had inherited Cameron's Commons majority along with his job, would surely have no difficulty getting a simple bill passed.

But some of those who had voted to leave the EU saw the political landscape rather differently. The Brexiteers didn't want MPs to have anything to do with the article 50 notification. If parliament had to give its approval, Brexit might never be triggered. On this argument, the judges could be seen as trying to obstruct the referendum result.

What went wrong?

Viewed from a constitutional perspective, the High Court judgment was entirely supportive of democracy. In what amounted to a choice between government and parliament, the lord chief justice, the master of the rolls and a lord justice of appeal had come down on the side of the legislature.

Unfortunately, they chose not to spell any of this out. That might have been out of an abundance of caution: perhaps the judges feared they would be straying into parliament's territory by telling it what it could do. It might have been because the courts do not usually say 'what happens next'.

Perhaps the way forward was seen to be implicit. And perhaps, deep down, at least one of the judges secretly hoped that the government – which at that time had a comfortable majority – might have found its proposals blocked by parliament. But the judges have never expressed such view in public. If asked, they said they were applying the law as they saw it to the facts that they found.

According to one leading academic, the courts 'handed parliament a golden opportunity to shape Brexit' which was 'squandered almost immediately'. Parliament could have set conditions on triggering article 50.[13] Members could have required the government to negotiate from a position of strength before setting the clock running. But this view ignores the political realities as they were at that time: quite apart from the fact that MPs did not want to be seen to be thwarting the popular vote, their political careers could have been at risk if they had not toed the party line.

The High Court missed a trick by making no effort to 'sell' its judgment to the people. It would only have needed another sentence – perhaps in a press summary – explaining that a simple Act of parliament would permit the government to do as it wished. At that time, a substantial majority of MPs supported triggering article 50.

Spelling this out would have helped to shape broadcast news coverage on the day of the ruling. But it might not have had much effect on the Brexit-supporting newspapers. Coverage the following day played to readers' prejudices.

News or views?

The *Sun* carried a picture of Gina Miller under the headline 'Who do EU think you are?' The *Daily Express*, in a front-page comment headlined 'We must get out of the EU', said that Britain was now facing 'a crisis as grave as anything since the dark days when Churchill vowed we would fight them on the beaches'. It asserted, without a hint of irony or self-doubt, that 3 November 2016 'was the day democracy died'.

The *Daily Telegraph*, which used to be regarded as a serious newspaper, printed official photographs of the three judges in monochrome – with a blue tint to make them look more sinister. Its headline read: 'The judges versus the people'.

But the *Daily Mail* could be relied on to top that. Its front-page story carried the by-line of James Slack, who later joined Downing Street as Theresa May's spokesman. But it was written by Paul Dacre, the then editor. This is how it began:

> MPs last night tore into an unelected panel of 'out of touch' judges for ruling that embittered Remain supporters in parliament should be allowed to frustrate the verdict of the British public. The Lord Chief Justice and two senior colleagues were accused of putting Britain on course for a full-blown 'constitutional crisis' by saying Brexit could not be triggered without a Westminster vote. The judgment by Lord Thomas – a founding member of the European Law Institute, a club of lawyers and academics aiming to 'improve' EU law – throws into chaos Mrs May's timetable for invoking article 50 in March next year.[14]

Above the story were slightly out-of-date photographs of the three judges, two of them in the full-bottomed wigs that are worn only on ceremonial occasions. The sub-heading was 'Fury over "out of touch" judges who defied 17.4m Brexit voters and could trigger constitutional crisis'. And the headline, dominating the page, was 'ENEMIES OF THE PEOPLE'.

As Thomas's successor noted nearly two years later, that was 'a phrase used by tyrants throughout history to justify the persecution and death of those who do not toe the line'.[15] Looking back, a former foreign editor of *The Times* said it was 'one of the most chilling headlines ever to appear in a British newspaper'.[16]

But it was only a headline. Do readers still take any notice of what they read in the papers? And the *Daily Mail*, which used to be respected for its supposed ability to know what its readers were thinking, had shown how out of touch it was when it tried to belittle Sir Terence Etherton in its online edition by describing him, accurately but irrelevantly, as an 'openly gay ex-Olympic fencer'.

Only a headline?

My first reaction was therefore to dismiss the *Mail*'s headline as something that would soon be forgotten: 'today's news – tomorrow's fish-and-chip paper', as we used to say. Does anyone still remember the uncannily similar *Daily Mirror* front page of 31 July 1987, in which pictures of three senior judges were printed upside down alongside the headline 'You fools'?[17]

The lord chief justice and his two colleagues were far less relaxed. Lord Justice Sales recalled his reaction when the *Daily Mail* hit the streets on 4 November 2016:[18]

> My main task that day was to slip round to my local newsagent to buy a copy for my scrap-book. I found once again that when handing down a controversial judgment it is usually a good idea for a judge to stay away from social media and the online comment pages of national newspapers. If filled with vituperation, they can make for unpleasant and depressing reading …
>
> I felt curiously detached from the press coverage. It was almost as though it was happening to someone else. Part of the reason for this was that the judgment had been finalised several days before the hand down, as is usual. From my perspective it was 'done and dusted' and

my attention had moved on to other cases I had been dealing with in the meantime.

Over the next few days I felt unusually exposed when moving round London on foot and on public transport. However, no one approached me. This allows me to be sanguine about the experience of being front page news. My sense of anxiety abated.

In fact, the sense of threat felt most real when I received a visit from two police officers of the anti-terrorism unit of the Metropolitan Police to conduct a security review at my home. Fortunately, they assured me that their review of online activity and social media did not indicate an especially heightened threat of physical attack. In due course, I did work at my house to improve security and upgraded the alarm system ...

Reflecting on the experience, I have to say that I was rather naïve in terms of what was likely to happen when we handed down our judgment. I have delivered judgments before which caused a bit of a fuss, but nothing to compare to the reaction in this case. The lord chief justice was better attuned to the political mood and I think was more aware of what the reaction might be. I am personally grateful to him for looking out for his colleagues sitting with him, ensuring that heightened security arrangements were put in place to protect us, should the need arise.

The three judges also looked to the government for support. In decades gone by, the lord chancellor would have spoken on their behalf. But that great office of state was then occupied by Liz Truss MP, who was something of a political lightweight. Nothing was heard from her for a couple of days, presumably because she was waiting for instructions from Downing Street and nobody in the prime minister's office grasped the dangers of delay. Eventually, Truss expressed the view that judicial independence was 'the foundation on which our rule of law is built'.[19] When pressed, she said it was not for her to condemn the newspapers.

A little too late

Indeed, it was not. But what Truss was being asked to do was to defend the independence of the judiciary, in line with the oath she had taken on her appointment. As the judges saw it, that meant explaining that they had been traduced in the media. Truss's response was condemned by Lord Judge, the former lord chief justice, as 'a little too late and … quite a lot too little'.[20]

A couple of years later, Lord Neuberger said that Truss had completely missed the point. She had been free to criticise the press and she should have done so. But Neuberger, who by then had retired as president of the Supreme Court, was in forgiving mood.

'In fairness to her, she was a very recent appointment. She had had no experience of the rule of law and of the judiciary,' he said. 'It was unfortunate, and she should have got it right, but I think there were … mitigating circumstances.'[21]

What Truss could fairly have pointed out was that, under the new constitutional settlement reached more than a decade earlier, she was no longer head of the judiciary.[22] That role had been transferred from the lord chancellor to the lord chief justice. 'The whole point of the 2005 reforms,' said Professor Graham Gee in 2019, 'was to standardise the role of lord chancellor – so that lord chancellors would take not an independent line but a governmental line on matters relating to the judicial system.'[23] Truss could have argued that Thomas should have been defending himself and his colleagues, self-serving though that would inevitably have appeared.

But there is no way round the fact that it is the duty of the lord chancellor to uphold and defend judicial independence.[24] Lord Dyson, who before his retirement was the most mild-mannered of judges, was still incandescent when he wrote, in a memoir published two years later, that Truss's 11 months in office had been 'disastrous':[25]

> Not the least of her shortcomings was her failure to discharge the statutory duty to protect the independence of the judges when [they] were pilloried by some of the media as 'enemies of the people' … Critics of the court's judgment said that the judges were seeking to undermine the will of the people as expressed in the

referendum. That was a disgraceful misrepresentation of a decision which did no more than resolve a question of statutory interpretation. The judges could not have stated more clearly that they were saying nothing about the merits or demerits of Brexit.

It was one of Truss's successors who assessed the true damage caused by that notorious headline. David Gauke, in a valedictory speech to the judges in July 2019,[26] observed that the 'forces of populism' had become much stronger. Institutions such as the judiciary had become guardians of our democratic ideals. 'They do not work against the people: they share power in the best interests of everyone,' he said:

> Those grappling with complex problems are not viewed as public servants but as engaged in a conspiracy to seek to frustrate the will of the public. They are 'enemies of the people'. In deploying this sort of language, we go to war with truth; we pour poison into our national conversation …
>
> We must all have the courage to disagree on the facts and the good sense to appreciate that language can have powerful effects. That is why I deprecate the careless use of language which can undermine our admired and renowned institutions.

Gauke rightly received a standing ovation.

Drexit

The judges had been unlucky: less than two years later, Dacre ceased to be editor of the *Daily Mail*.[27] His coverage of the judgment and his strident support for Brexit were seen as contributory factors, being no longer to the taste of Lord Rothermere, the newspaper's proprietor.[28] Dacre's personal assistant insisted that he had not been sacked over his handling of the story. 'Apart from the fact that he stood down a long time after that headline,' she told me, 'he retired at the age of 70 after 28 years as editor.'[29] But Dacre's successor, Geordie Greig, lost no time in shifting the newspaper's editorial line.[30] When history repeated itself, his own headline was more muted.[31]

After standing down, Dacre seemed to accept that he might have gone too far. In a speech to the Society of Editors in November 2018 he still maintained that newspapers should have the freedom to write a headline like 'enemies of the people':[32]

> The title of an Ibsen play,[33] it was meant to be a distillation of the views of Brexit MPs angry that the High Court was becoming involved in the political process. In retrospect, the *Telegraph*'s banner *The Judges Versus The People* was, to coin a phrase, a tad more judicious.
>
> But what the hell. The point needed to be made. And it was the *Mail*'s headline, not the almost identical *Telegraph* one, that, as happens so often, put an issue on the agenda.

And, one might add, that did all the damage.

Miller: the Supreme Court

It was not until some months after the *Mail* headline was published that its impact could be properly understood. By then, the High Court ruling had been upheld in a majority ruling by an 11-judge Supreme Court.[34] Within minutes of the judgment, Truss praised the justices as 'people of integrity and impartiality' – a tacit acknowledgment by the lord chancellor that she had got it wrong the first time round. The worst that the *Daily Mail* could throw at the eight justices in the majority was an assertion that they came from 'almost identical rarefied backgrounds' – as if to imply that the three dissenters were somehow men of the people.[35] Nobody claimed that democracy had died another death.

Why the reticence? Partly because the judgment was less newsworthy: nothing changed. Partly because it was now clear that the government could solve the problem through legislation. And partly because the hearing had been televised: anyone who watched the proceedings online – and over 300,000 did – could see the justices grappling with law rather than politics. 'Our decision didn't come as any surprise to people,' one of them told me, 'because commentators had all been watching the proceedings; they had been able to see the way we were reacting. They could see that some were favouring the government's position but the majority were evincing signs of scepticism.'[36]

The law moves on

Theresa May accepted the Supreme Court judgment and introduced the necessary legislation in parliament. Lord Judge, a former lord chief justice, was sure it had not crossed her mind that she could disobey it.[37] 'The judges continued in office,' he continued. 'There are no proposals to alter the way in which the judiciary is appointed. In many countries that would be remarkable. In this country we take it for granted – when we should remember it with pride.'

The European Union (Notification of Withdrawal) Act 2017 was passed unamended by parliament in March of that year. MPs voted at third reading by a majority of 494 to 122 in favour of the legislation. At one level, this took the heat out of the controversy. But it also allowed the lord chief justice to speak more freely.

Lord Thomas had not taken kindly to Truss's assertion that the judges should have responded to the newspaper criticism themselves. That was what she seemed to be saying when she told the House of Lords constitution committee that there was still a 'myth' surrounding the so-called Kilmuir rules. 'Those rules about judges not being able to speak out in public were abolished in the 1980s,' she reminded them, 'and yet there is still sometimes a reticence to do so.'[38]

Three weeks later, it was Thomas's turn to give oral evidence. 'The idea that we do not realise that the Kilmuir rules have gone is quite frankly fanciful,' he told the peers. What Truss had not understood, the chief justice implied, was that no serving judge could have responded to the *Daily Mail* at that time without plunging the judiciary into political controversy. And some readers had believed what they read. 'The circuit judges were very concerned,' he added, 'because litigants in person were coming and saying, "You're an enemy of the people".'

These threats had been taken very seriously: Thomas confirmed that the Miller hearing was the only occasion in the whole of his judicial career when he had felt the need 'to ask the police to give us a measure of advice and protection in relation to the emotions that were being stirred up'.

Asked about Truss's insistence that it was not her job to censor or direct the press, Thomas insisted that she was under a duty to defend the judiciary from unwarranted attacks. 'I regret to have to criticise her as severely as I have, but to my mind she is completely and absolutely wrong about this,' he said. 'It really is absolutely essential that we have a lord chancellor who understands her constitutional duty.'[39]

Truss moves too

It was, I suggested at the time, 'hard to see how Truss can survive measured and devastating criticism like this from the most senior judge in England and Wales'.[40] Sure enough, she was moved to another post after the general election in June 2017. Unfortunately for the judges, this turned out to be chief secretary to the Treasury, the minister who holds the government's purse-strings. Having been criticised so publicly by the then lord chief justice, Truss showed no enthusiasm for recommendations made by the Review Body on Senior Salaries in October 2018 that judges who had suffered pay cuts by being required to join a new pension scheme should receive compensatory pay rises.[41]

Despite this, the lord chancellor, David Gauke, managed in June 2019 to secure a temporary recruitment and retention allowance of 25% for High Court judges and 15% for Circuit and Upper Tribunal judges who were eligible for the new pension scheme. This was significantly less than the Review Body's recommendation of a 32% permanent salary increase for High Court judges and 22% for Circuit and Upper Tribunal judges who had been caught by the new pension arrangements.[42] But it was sufficient to persuade the judges that the lord chancellor was now on their side.[43] He achieved this by going over Truss's head and appealing to Philip Hammond, chancellor of the exchequer and an old friend, before both men resigned from the government.[44]

Gauke also made a point of supporting the judges in October 2018 after Lord Hain, a backbench Labour peer, deliberately thwarted an order of the Court of Appeal. Protected by parliamentary privilege,

Hain had named Sir Philip Green as a claimant whose identity had been withheld by the courts.[45]

Freedom of speech, Gauke said, was 'an important constitutional principle' but 'so, too, is respect for the rule of the law and the jurisdiction of the courts. Therefore, I have serious concerns about the use of parliamentary privilege to undermine the rulings of our independent judiciary. Where judges have seen fit to make a court order, their rulings should be respected. It is particularly hard to justify using parliamentary privilege when the court process is ongoing.'[46]

This was not only a reprimand for Hain. It was a sign of the lord chancellor's support for the master of the rolls, Sir Terence Etherton, who had upheld the injunction that Hain then undermined and was also one of the *Daily Mail*'s three 'enemies of the people'.

Miller: the impact

The short-term effects of Gina Miller's first Brexit-related challenge are clear. We know that recruiting and retaining suitable judges to the High Court, already difficult at the time of the article 50 challenge, reached crisis point in the years that followed. Senior judges said that candidates for the judiciary were well aware that their decisions would be criticised. But words matter and, at a time of low judicial morale, it cannot have been much of an incentive to see one's potential colleagues condemned in such resonant language.

Lord Hodge, a Supreme Court justice, noted in February 2018 that the response to the Miller judgment had 'done nothing to encourage lawyers to give up legal practice for a judicial career at a time when recruitment and retention of senior judges has become a very serious problem'.[47] Lord Sumption, shortly before he retired as a justice of the Supreme Court, said that a major factor in the decline of applications for judicial appointment among the bar's high-flyers was 'the perception that the work of judges is no longer valued as much as it was, by the government or by the public at large'.[48]

Before Miller brought her claim, I had been sceptical about its chances of success: surely the judges, well aware of the public mood, would be reluctant to rule against the will of the people? If that reticence did have any effect on their thinking, though, it may have been countered by the view that they were handing power back to the people's representatives – who, according to a widely held view, should never have surrendered it to the voters.

Senior judges said that their judicial colleagues were not likely to be swayed by public opinion, particularly in a case where views were divided. Nor were they influenced by their own opinions on Brexit. Lord Reed mentioned a media analysis of how pro-EU each member of the UK Supreme Court was thought to be, based on their backgrounds and social media postings by their families.[49] In the event, he said, 'predictions of which way we were each likely to decide the case proved to be hopelessly wrong. What some of the media had not understood was that the fact that a judgment has political implications does not mean that the judges are deciding a political question.'[50]

And that view was endorsed in 2018 by Lord Burnett, who was not involved in Gina Miller's first challenge:

> A newspaper ran a story, with pictures of all the Supreme Court justices who were to hear the appeal, exploring their supposed European links. The simplistic, indeed facile, point apparently being made was that the judges in question could be expected to decide the case in line with the strength of those links. The way in which the majority and minority opinions lined up, in the result, did not support that analysis.
>
> It took moral courage in the face of such comments before and after the various hearings to apply the law without fear or favour. Without it, the decisions made would not have been based on an application of the law. Justice would not have been done. And the institutional independence of the judiciary, and of our democratic structures would have been weakened. As an institution the judiciary would have been seen to be capable of being swayed by public and political opinion; along that road lies arbitrary justice – which is no form of justice at all.[51]

It was Burnett's colleagues who took those words to heart a year later.

Proroguing parliament

At the end of August 2019 the Queen ordered parliament to be prorogued – suspended – from 9 September to 14 October.[52] The order, approved at a meeting of the Privy Council in Balmoral, was made on the advice of her prime minister, Boris Johnson.

Proroguing for five weeks was exceptional. The government argued that parliament was due to go into recess for the party conferences and so only seven working days would be lost. But its opponents feared that reducing the time for debate would increase the risk that the UK would leave the EU without a withdrawal agreement. The prime minister, it seems, thought the opposite: if MPs could not block 'no-deal' there would be greater pressure on the EU to make the concessions he had demanded – since no EU leader really wanted the UK to leave without an agreement.

Supporters of no-deal saw it as the only pure and effective form of Brexit. Opponents believed it would lead to short-term chaos and long-term economic damage. But, as things then stood, the UK would leave the EU on 31 October 2019 with or without a deal.

As soon as the government's prorogation plans were announced Gina Miller lodged a claim for judicial review. Similar proceedings had already been started in the Scottish courts by Joanna Cherry QC MP, the Scottish National Party spokesperson on justice and home affairs, with the support of other parliamentarians and campaigners.

Once again, Miller's challenge was heard by a high-powered divisional court, headed by the lord chief justice of England and Wales. Lord Burnett was joined by the master of the rolls, Sir Terence Etherton, and the president of the Queen's Bench division, Dame Victoria Sharp. Neither Burnett nor Sharp had been in post in 2016 when Etherton was defamed as an enemy of the people. But nobody could forget how the earlier judgment had been received.

Once again, Miller was represented by Lord Pannick QC, instructed by the law firm Mishcon de Reya. Pannick argued that Johnson had been acting unlawfully: the prime minister could not advise the Queen to prorogue parliament when that would seriously impede its work.

For the government, Sir James Eadie QC argued that Miller's claim was simply non-justiciable – not something the courts would look at. 'The exercise of this prerogative power is intrinsically one of high policy and politics,' said Eadie, 'not law'.

The High Court took the Eadie way out.[53] Johnson's decision and his advice to the Queen 'were inherently political in nature', said the judges, and there were 'no legal standards against which to judge their legitimacy'. Arguments that five weeks was too long 'face the insuperable difficulty that it is impossible for the court to make a legal assessment of whether the duration of the prorogation was excessive by reference to any measure'.

That was not the view taken by the Inner House of the Court of Session. Overturning an earlier ruling by one of their colleagues, three Scottish appeal judges looked at the available evidence and concluded that the prime minister's advice had been unlawful.[54]

Lord Carloway, who as Lord President was Scotland's senior judge, said that the prime minister's reasons for proroguing parliament would not be challengeable if they had been based on legitimate political considerations. Johnson had said he wanted to prorogue parliament during the party conference season, when it would normally have been adjourned, and then prepare for a new legislative session. But Carloway did not believe these were the prime minister's real reasons:

> The circumstances demonstrate that the true reason for the prorogation is to reduce the time available for parliamentary scrutiny of Brexit at a time when such scrutiny would appear to be a matter of considerable importance, given the issues at stake.

Lord Brodie agreed. He inferred from the evidence that

> the principal reason for the advice to the Queen ... was to prevent or impede parliament holding the executive politically to account in the run-up to exit day; to prevent or impede parliament from legislating on the United Kingdom's exit from the European Union; and to allow the executive to pursue a policy of no-deal Brexit without further parliamentary interference.

The third judge, Lord Drummond Young, took a similar view:

> The effect of the prorogation under consideration, in particular its length, is that proper parliamentary scrutiny is rendered all but impossible ... The inference must inevitably be drawn, on a strictly objective basis, that that was the purpose of the prorogation. In my opinion, that is not a proper purpose.

For a while, Downing Street seemed to be briefing privately against the judges. And one minister, Kwasi Kwarteng, went public in suggesting that the courts had been acting politically. 'Many people are saying that judges are biased, the judges are getting involved in politics,' he told the BBC. 'I think they are impartial but I'm saying that many people, many leave voters ... are beginning to question the partiality of the judges.'[55]

But the lord chancellor, Robert Buckland, came to their defence. 'Our judges are renowned around the world for their excellence and impartiality,' he tweeted, 'and I have total confidence in their independence in every case.'[56]

Three senior judges in England had thought that prorogation was an issue best left to the politicians. Three senior judges in Scotland had thought they could – and should – intervene.[57] To resolve the issue, 11 justices of the Supreme Court – the maximum number who could sit – heard appeals by Gina Miller and the advocate general for Scotland, representing the UK government.

There was huge interest in the three-day hearing, which was livestreamed millions of times. One newspaper[58] reported it under the front-page headline 'Judges warned to stay neutral', which implied that the government was trying to put improper pressure on the judiciary. The only basis for this tendentious claim was the prime minister's argument, already upheld by the High Court, that Gina Miller's claim was non-justiciable.[59]

From prorogue to no rogue

Judgment was delivered on 24 September 2019,[60] just four days (including a weekend) after the hearing. Contrary to their normal practice, the justices did not trust either the parties or reporters with advance copies of the 21-page ruling. The prime minister, on a visit to New York, had to get up at 5.30am to watch Lady Hale read a summary of the decision on television.

After setting out the background and emphasising that the case was not about when or on what terms the UK would leave the EU, Hale announced that the court's judgment was unanimous. This was a remarkable achievement, given the number of cases in this book where judges disagreed. Unanimity gave the judgment huge moral authority.

The first question was whether the case raised a legal question on which the courts could adjudicate – in other words, whether the lawfulness of the prime minister's advice to the Queen was justiciable. 'The court holds that it is,' said Hale.

As she explained, the courts have exercised a supervisory jurisdiction over the lawfulness of government actions for centuries. That covered the use of prerogative powers – powers recognised by the common law and exercised by the Crown, usually on the advice of ministers.

There was no doubt that the courts had jurisdiction to decide whether a particular prerogative power existed and, if so, what its extent was. If it did exist, and had been exercised within its limits, the next question was whether its exercise was challengeable in the courts according to the normal principles of judicial review. That depended on the nature and subject matter of the particular prerogative power being exercised: some could be challenged and others not.

This case was about the limits of the power to advise the Queen to prorogue parliament. There had been disagreement over whether that power was reviewable by the courts. But an unlimited power of prorogation would be incompatible with the legal principle of parliamentary sovereignty. It would also undermine the principle that ministers are accountable to parliament. The power to prorogue was limited by the constitutional principles with which it would otherwise conflict.

What, then, were its limits? They could be expressed like this, said the court:

> A decision to prorogue parliament (or to advise the monarch to prorogue parliament) will be unlawful if the prorogation has the effect of frustrating or

> preventing, without reasonable justification, the ability
> of parliament to carry out its constitutional functions
> as a legislature and as the body responsible for the
> supervision of the executive. In such a situation, the
> court will intervene if the effect is sufficiently serious
> to justify such an exceptional course.[61]

And did the prime minister's action have the effect of frustrating or preventing the constitutional role of parliament in holding the government to account? 'Of course it did,' said the 11 justices. 'This was not a normal prorogation in the run-up to a Queen's speech [which starts a new parliamentary session]. It prevented parliament from carrying out its constitutional role for five out of a possible eight weeks between the end of the summer recess and [EU] exit day on 31 October.'

It followed that, unlike the Inner House of the Court of Session, the Supreme Court had no need to consider whether Boris Johnson's motives or purpose were unlawful. Far from finding that the prime minister had lied to the Queen – as some reporters imagined – the court said it did not know what the Queen had been told and could not draw any conclusions.

One of the most striking aspects of this case was that the government had not provided a witness statement explaining the prime minister's reasons for seeking a prorogation. There was some speculation on what such a statement might have revealed. But all the court said was that 'no reason was given for closing down parliament for five weeks'.

As the justices noted, a memorandum from the prime minister's director of legislative affairs, written in August, had not addressed the competing merits of a prorogation and a recess (during which most parliamentary business continues as usual). Indeed, it wrongly gave the impression that they were much the same.

But that was not all:

> Nowhere is there a hint that the prime minister, in
> giving advice to Her Majesty, is more than simply the
> leader of the government seeking to promote its own
> policies; he has a constitutional responsibility ...

It is impossible for us to conclude, on the evidence which has been put before us, that there was any reason – let alone a good reason – to advise Her Majesty to prorogue parliament for five weeks ...

We cannot speculate, in the absence of further evidence, upon what such reasons might have been. It follows that the decision was unlawful.

There were gasps in court. Boris Johnson had lost. But what was to happen on the other side of Parliament Square, where the Palace of Westminster was virtually empty apart from workmen and tourists?

The prorogation had been announced in the House of Lords by three royal commissioners. According to the government, those proceedings could not be challenged because the Bill of Rights 1688 says that 'freedome of speech and debates or proceedings in parlyament ought not to be impeached or questioned in any court or place out of parlyament'.

The Supreme Court was not having any of that. It concluded that the actions of the royal commissioners were not proceedings in parliament at all. Although they had taken place in the House of Lords with peers and MPs in attendance, their announcements were not decisions of either house. It followed that there was nothing to stop the court from deciding that this prorogation was 'unlawful, null and of no effect'. It was 'as if the commissioners had walked into parliament with a blank piece of paper'.

And then, as Lord Pannick QC had asked them to, the justices explained what this really meant. As far as they were concerned, the Speaker of the House of Commons and the Lord Speaker could simply make arrangements for MPs and peers to resume their proceedings. That was all it needed. And, an hour later, the Commons Speaker, John Bercow, told reporters he would do just that: MPs would sit the following day. Among them was the prime minister, who took a red-eye flight to London.

In the records of the House of Commons for 9 September 2019, 'prorogued' was amended to 'adjourned'. The uncodified but supremely flexible British constitution had no difficulty in coping with an entirely unprecedented development. It was deeply moving to see the law in action.

More enemies of the people?

Reaction to Gina Miller's second Brexit-related victory was largely polarised. Those who supported Boris Johnson thought the judgment would make it more difficult for him to pursue his Brexit strategy. His opponents welcomed the opportunity of increased parliamentary scrutiny. Johnson's supporters were critical of the Supreme Court – even though restoring the last word to judges in the UK was seen as an aim of Brexit. There were rowdy scenes in parliament.

Hale was much praised, but also the subject of personal abuse. In the *Sun* a day later, she was described by Quentin Letts as 'the beady-eyed old nanny goat who read yesterday's verdict in the court. Brenda Hale has long been seen as a quintessential liberal blue-stocking. If she's a leaver, I'm a Martian.'[62]

Even though the court had said, in terms, 'we are not concerned with the prime minister's *motive* in doing what he did',[63] Letts wrote:

> Her Supreme Court questioned Boris's motives in proroguing parliament. The British people can now question her motives in reaching that verdict.
>
> They might be interested, for instance, to learn that she has just been given a cushy position at an Oxford college run by Alan Rusbridger, former editor of the left-wing *Guardian* newspaper.
>
> Rusbridger is a prominent remainer and he is a supporter of Gina Miller, who brought the Supreme Court case against the government.
>
> Corrupt? No. But it doesn't look great, does it?

Rather more seriously but just as disingenuously, unnamed sources in the prime minister's office were reported as saying 'the effect of this is to pose the question, who runs the country?' And Jacob Rees-Mogg MP, leader of the House of Commons, was said to have described the ruling as a 'constitutional coup'.[64]

A few hours later, the attorney general, Geoffrey Cox, tried to reassure MPs:

The government accept the judgment and accept that they lost the case. At all times, the government acted in good faith and in the belief that their approach was both lawful and constitutional. These are complex matters, on which senior and distinguished lawyers will disagree. The divisional court, led by the lord chief justice, as well as Lord Doherty in the outer house of Scotland, agreed with the government's position, but we were disappointed that, in the end, the Supreme Court took a different view. Of course, we respect its judgment.

Rejecting calls that he should resign because he had advised the government that prorogation would be lawful, Cox said the advice had been sound at the time. 'The court of last resort ultimately disagreed with it but in doing so it made new law, as it was entirely entitled to do.'[65]

Cox was right to say that the Supreme Court was entitled to make new law – although, as we shall see in Chapter 10, there are differing views on whether the justices created something new or merely extended the existing law to an area they had not previously reviewed.

But Professor John Finnis, of whom we shall hear more, said that 'as well-intentioned but constitutionally unauthorised law making, this judgment undermines the rule of law and the constitutional settlement'.[66]

In my view, the exact opposite is true.

3

Creating Crimes

You might think that cases involving criminals would not give the judges much scope to develop the law. We have to go back to 1961 for the last occasion on which senior judges created a brand-new crime. As Lord Bingham confirmed in 2006, 'there now exists no power in the courts to create new criminal offences'.[1] But creating or extending defences is quite another matter.

The Ladies' Directory

Shortly after the Street Offences Act 1959 made it unlawful for sex-workers to solicit in the street, a man named Frederick Charles Shaw had the idea of publishing an illustrated booklet in which they could advertise their services. Nowadays, of course, he would have built an app. Shaw was charged with conspiracy 'to induce readers thereof to resort to the said advertisers for the purposes of fornication and of taking part in or witnessing other disgusting and immoral acts and exhibitions, with intent there by to debauch and corrupt the morals as well of youth as of divers other liege subjects of Our Lady The Queen and to raise and create in their minds inordinate and lustful desires'.[2]

According to the charge sheet, this was a conspiracy to corrupt public morals. That was said to be a common law misdemeanour, or common law offence as we would now call it. Prosecutors pointed to a number of cases from the 17th century onwards which were said to recognise the crime of corrupting public morals. But none, of course, covered the publication of a booklet with telephone numbers.

Shaw was convicted and sentenced to nine months' imprisonment. His appeals against conviction and sentence were dismissed by the Court of Appeal. In 1961 he appealed to the House of Lords, at that time the highest court in the land.

Viscount Simonds was the senior law lord, and readers will remember from Chapter 1 that he professed to support a much narrower approach to law making than his colleague Lord Denning. 'Need I say,' asked Simonds, 'that I am no advocate of the right of the judges to create new criminal offences?' But he went on to do just that:

> In the sphere of criminal law I entertain no doubt that there remains in the courts of law a residual power to enforce the supreme and fundamental purpose of the law, to conserve not only the safety and order but also the moral welfare of the state, and that it is their duty to guard it against attacks which may be the more insidious because they are novel and unprepared for.

Simonds then gave an example of a new offence that he hoped he might find an opportunity to create:

> Let it be supposed that at some future, perhaps early, date homosexual practices between adult consenting males are no longer a crime. Would it not be an offence if even without obscenity, such practices were publicly advocated and encouraged by pamphlet and advertisement? Or must we wait until parliament finds time to deal with such conduct? I say, my Lords, that if the common law is powerless in such an event, then we should no longer do her reverence. But I say that her hand is still powerful and that it is for Her Majesty's judges to play the part which Lord Mansfield pointed out to them [in 1763].[3]

Three other law lords agreed with Simonds, with the result that Shaw's conviction was upheld. It was left to Lord Reid, aged 70, to recognise that, as society diversified, the judges could no longer be custodians of public morality. 'In my opinion,' said Reid firmly, 'there is no such general offence known to the law as conspiracy to corrupt public morals'. He went on:

> Even if there is still a vestigial power of this kind it ought not, in my view, to be used unless there appears to be general agreement that the offence to which it is applied ought to be criminal if committed by an individual. Notoriously, there are wide differences of opinion today as to how far the law ought to punish immoral acts which are not done in the face of the public ... Parliament is the proper place, and I am firmly of opinion the only proper place, to settle that ... Where parliament fears to tread it is not for the courts to rush in.

Reid lost the argument – but he carried the day.

Lord Lane

The first chief justice I knew was Lord Lane, who served from 1980 to 1992. He is remembered for dismissing the first appeal of six men who had been wrongly convicted of 21 murders arising from the bombing of two Birmingham pubs in 1974. 'The longer this hearing has gone on,' said Lane in 1988, 'the more convinced this court has become that the verdict of the jury was correct.'[4] Three years later, a differently constituted Court of Appeal set the Birmingham Six free.[5]

Lane and the judges of his generation were well aware that police officers concocted evidence against the suspects they arrested. But they believed – honestly, though unforgivably wrongly – that these suspects had committed the crimes of which they were accused (or, if not those crimes, others of equal seriousness). I suspect that Lane and his colleagues felt it was their duty to ensure, as far as they could, that the guilty were convicted. The flaw in this reasoning is that some defendants who appeared before them – such as the Birmingham Six – were simply not guilty.

We can learn more about social attitudes at the time from two cases that Lane dealt with in the last decade of the 20th century.

One was concerned with sado-masochism and the other involved marital rape.

Operation Spanner

At the end of 1990 a group of men pleaded guilty, on legal advice, to offences involving unlawful wounding and assault occasioning actual bodily harm. As Lane explained, they 'belonged to a group of sado-masochistic homosexuals who willingly and enthusiastically participated in the commission of acts of violence against each other for the sexual pleasure which it engendered in the giving and receiving of pain'.

I shall spare you the (painful) details, which are all in the law reports.[6] Everyone agreed to what was done to them and there were no complaints to the police. The acts were carried out in private and, although video recordings were made, there was no profit motive.

The question for the courts was a simple one: can an adult give valid consent to being injured in this way? This was not an issue that the courts had previously been asked to decide. A decade earlier, though, the Court of Appeal had said that a person who injured another during the course of a street brawl could be convicted of assault, even though both parties had agreed to fight each other. It was not in the public interest for people to cause each other actual bodily harm without good reason, the court concluded at the time.

But was it in the public interest to allow sado-masochistic activities? According to Lane and his two colleagues, it was not. The consent of those involved was no defence. So the men's appeals against convictions were dismissed. Their prison sentences were reduced, but one defendant was left with a three-year sentence and another with two years; both cases also involved an indecent photograph of a child.

Five of the defendants appealed to the UK's final court of appeal.[7] Lord Templeman, the senior of the five law lords who sat, rightly observed that the issue was not one of law at all. 'The question whether the defence of consent should be extended to the consequences of sado-masochistic encounters can only be decided by consideration of policy and public interest,' he said. But, he went on, 'I am not prepared to invent a defence of consent for sado-masochistic encounters which breed and glorify cruelty.'

Two other law lords agreed with Templeman, and so the appeal was dismissed. But from the two most junior members of the court we saw a very different interpretation of what the public interest required. Lords Mustill and Slynn were a decade younger than the two most senior law lords in the case. I remember them both as far less hidebound and conventional.

'These are questions of private morality,' said Mustill. 'The standards by which they fall to be judged are not those of the criminal law ... The state should interfere with the rights of an individual to live his or her life as he or she may choose no more than is necessary to ensure a proper balance between the special interests of the individual and the general interests of ... the populace at large.'

Slynn agreed. It was not for the courts, he said, 'in order to protect people from themselves, to introduce into existing statutory crimes relating to offences *against* the person concepts which do not properly fit there. If parliament considers that the behaviour revealed here should be made specifically criminal, then the [law] can be amended specifically to define it.'

All five judges had considered the relevant case law. But, in a difficult case, they reached different conclusions. They were honest enough to say that whether to criminalise behaviour of this kind was a matter of policy. They simply disagreed on what the policy should be.

So, Lane's approach was upheld on appeal and the European Court of Human Rights decided not to interfere.[8]

His ruling was also followed by the Court of Appeal in 2018 when it decided that consent could provide no defence to charges of wounding with intent to do grievous bodily harm brought against Brendan McCarthy, an unlicensed tattooist and body-piercer who added 'body modification' to his repertoire.

Again, I'll spare you the (even more painful) details. Lord Burnett of Maldon, the lord chief justice, struggled to find a principled distinction between tattooing, piercing and (male) circumcision – which were lawful – and the sort of modification McCarthy was accused of carrying out at his premises in Wolverhampton. But Burnett and the two judges sitting with him knew where to draw the line. McCarthy's argument, said Burnett, envisaged 'consent to surgical treatment providing a defence to the person performing the surgery whether or not that person is suitably qualified as a doctor, and whether or not there is a medical (including psychological) justification for the surgery. Even were we attracted by the argument, which we are not, such a bold step is one that could only be taken by parliament.'[9]

As a result, McCarthy pleaded guilty to three counts of grievous bodily harm in March 2019 and was jailed for three years and four months.[10]

Marital rape

Sir Matthew Hale, who was chief justice from 1671 to 1676, is presumed to have recorded the contemporary common law accurately in his *History of the Pleas of the Crown*, published decades after his death. 'The husband cannot be guilty of a rape committed by himself upon his lawful wife,' he wrote, 'for by their mutual matrimonial consent and contract the wife hath given up herself in this kind unto her husband, which she cannot retract.'

That principle remained largely unquestioned by the courts until 1990, although the courts had sometimes allowed exceptions in cases where initial steps had been taken to end a marriage.

But then came the case that changed the law. In 1989 a woman who had been married for five years left home with her four-year-old son and went back to live with her parents. She left her husband a note saying she wanted a divorce. About three weeks later, while her parents were out for the evening, her husband forced his way into their house and attempted to have sex with his wife against her will. In the course of a struggle he squeezed her neck with both hands.

The husband, known only by the initial R to protect the identity of his wife, admitted a charge of assault occasioning actual bodily harm. In a bold move, the Crown Prosecution Service in Leicester had also charged him with rape. His lawyers argued that, as a matter of law, a man could not be convicted of raping his wife. That submission was rejected by Mr Justice Owen. The defendant then admitted attempted rape and was sentenced to three years in prison.

His appeal came before a court of five judges rather than the usual three, often a sign that the court is considering whether to change the law. Lane, as chief justice, delivered a robust judgment:[11]

> The idea that a wife by marriage consents in advance to her husband having sexual intercourse with her whatever her state of health or however proper her objections ... is no longer acceptable ... It seems to us that where the common law rule no longer even remotely represents what is the true position of a wife in present day society, the duty of the court is to take steps to alter the rule if it can legitimately do so in the light of any relevant parliamentary enactment ...
>
> We take the view that the time has now arrived when the law should declare that a rapist remains a rapist subject to the criminal law, irrespective of his relationship with his victim.

Then came the crucial bit:

> This is not the creation of a new offence, it is the removal of a common law fiction which has become anachronistic and offensive and we consider that it is our duty having reached that conclusion to act upon it.

Later in 1991, the law lords agreed.[12] So did the European Court of Human Rights.[13]

Lane was rightly proud of changing the common law to reflect modern social attitudes. His decision in this case is likely to have had a much greater impact on society than his ruling on sado-masochists. But both were examples of policy-making by the senior judiciary.

Homicide

I explained in Chapter 1 that murder is a common law offence: it is a crime because the judges have always treated it as a crime. Murder is clearly the most serious type of homicide. But the judges have developed distinctions between murder and other types of unlawful killing.

In England and Wales a homicide that falls short of murder may amount to manslaughter. In Scotland and some Commonwealth countries the nearest equivalent is culpable homicide. In the US some states recognise degrees of murder in addition to manslaughter. What these offences have in common is that they may be punished less severely than murder itself.

Murder attracts a mandatory sentence in the UK. Until 1965[14] the penalty was death; since then, it has been life imprisonment. A life sentence may be passed on a defendant convicted of manslaughter – but the sentence is not mandatory.

It is well known that defendants sentenced to life imprisonment may be released during their lifetimes – although they remain on licence for the rest of their lives and are liable to recall if they commit further offences. What I suspect very few murderers realise is how long they are likely to serve before a decision is taken on whether they can be safely released.

Starting points range from 15 years[15] to the rest of the prisoner's life.[16] Having set a starting point, the court must take account of specified aggravating or mitigating factors in fixing the minimum term.

These provisions were initiated in 2003 by David Blunkett, the home secretary, after he lost the power to set tariffs himself: the courts had decided that the length of time a lifer should serve was a matter for the judiciary, not a politician.[17]

Mandatory and minimum sentences make it harder for judges to pass an appropriate sentence on an individual defendant. To avoid injustice in homicide cases, the courts have developed a number of 'partial' defences to murder. When these defences are allowed, a defendant charged with murder may be convicted of manslaughter. That avoids the need for the court to pass a life sentence.

Let us consider a couple of examples.

Kiranjit Ahluwalia

In 1989, Kiranjit Ahluwalia killed her husband by throwing petrol into his bedroom and setting it on fire while he slept. She was convicted of murder and sentenced to life imprisonment with a minimum term of 12 years.

Her defence was that she had not intended to kill her husband or cause him serious harm. There was a secondary defence of provocation: Ahluwalia had suffered severe violence and abuse from her husband during the ten years of their marriage. But, as the law then stood, provocation required acts by the deceased that would cause in any reasonable person 'a sudden and temporary loss of self-control'.

This was exactly what the courts thought might happen when a man discovered his wife in the act of adultery. But it was not typical of battered women who suffered years of abuse before killing their male abusers, choosing a moment when those men were unable to fight back.

Ahluwalia's appeal was heard in 1992. While insisting that a sudden and temporary loss of self-control remained essential to the partial defence of provocation, the Court of Appeal decided that a delayed reaction would not, it itself, exclude that partial defence – provided it was not delayed too long. But the court allowed Ahluwalia a retrial after deciding that new psychiatric evidence could support a defence of diminished responsibility: her experience of violence and abuse had led to a 'major depressive disorder'.[18] The Crown subsequently accepted her plea of guilty to manslaughter and she was released later that year.

Other battered women were freed on similar grounds, among them Sara Thornton.[19] In 2009 parliament replaced the defence of provocation with a new partial defence to murder called loss of control.[20]

Sally Challen

In 2009, after more than 30 years of marriage, Sally Challen left home and began divorce proceedings. She said she had suffered decades of emotional abuse. Although her husband, Richard, agreed to a reconciliation the following year, she believed he was being unfaithful to her. When she went to see him at their family home, she had a hammer in her handbag. As her husband was eating she repeatedly hit him over the head with it. After fracturing his skull she covered his body with blankets. The next day, she tried to kill herself. She left a note saying she could not live without him.

At her trial in 2011 defence lawyers argued that Challen was obsessively jealous and suffering from diminished responsibility. That would have amounted to a partial defence, reducing murder to manslaughter. But the jury was not persuaded by the psychiatric evidence and convicted her of murder.

As we have seen, provocation is also a partial defence. Defence lawyers took a tactical decision not to rely on provocation at Challen's trial. Even so, the judge found that she had been provoked by her husband and took this into account in setting her minimum term. Because she had brought a weapon with her, the starting point was 25 years. The judge reduced this to 22 years. Later in 2011, the Court of Appeal reduced Challen's minimum term to 18 years.

Quite separately, parliament created a new criminal offence of controlling or coercive domestic abuse.[21] It took effect at the end of 2015. The offence targets psychological abuse or mental cruelty in which one partner to an intimate or family relationship – other than a parent–child relationship – repeatedly or continually coerces or controls the life of the other. The perpetrator need not resort to physical harm or violence, though the behaviour must have a 'serious effect' on the victim for the offence to be proved. One victim whom I interviewed said she had been told what to wear, when she could go out of the house, what she was allowed to eat and even what exercise she should take.[22]

Clearly, a criminal offence cannot provide any sort of defence. But parliament had now recognised that coercive control can have a serious effect on victims. That led Challen's lawyers to argue that her case should be reopened. Her solicitor, Harriet Wistrich, told me that although coercive control was understood as a concept in certain academic circles and among domestic violence practitioners, it was not understood by most of the legal profession or the judiciary.[23]

Challen was given permission to appeal in March 2018. Almost a year later, the Court of Appeal quashed her conviction but ordered a retrial at which Challen's lawyers could argue that the killing was manslaughter rather than murder. In April 2019, after nearly nine years in custody, Challen was granted bail. Two months later, prosecutors accepted her plea of guilty to manslaughter. For this she was sentenced to nine years and four months, of which she would normally have served half in custody. As she had already been in prison for longer, Challen was released immediately.

Developing the criminal law

There is one more case I want to discuss in this chapter. It was not one in which the courts created a new defence, still less a new crime. But it demonstrates the flexibility of the common law in the hands of a judge with nearly 50 years' experience of the criminal courts.

In March 2009 John Radford was convicted of 19 serious sexual offences against 12 women. But these were only 'index', or specimen, charges. The civil courts subsequently concluded that between 2002 and 2008 he had carried out no fewer than 105 rapes and sexual assaults on women who were passengers in the London taxi he drove for a living.[24] Tried under his former name of John Worboys, he was referred to in the press as the black-cab rapist.

Radford was given a so-called indeterminate sentence for public protection, with a minimum prison term of eight years. That had expired in February 2016. It was then the responsibility of the Parole Board to decide whether he should be released. Before doing so, the board needed to be satisfied that it was 'no longer necessary for the protection of the public' to keep him in prison.

Should the black-cab rapist be freed?

At that time, cases were reviewed by individual members of the board. Armed with a dossier of information about the prisoner, the board member decided whether the case required an oral hearing. If so, the hearing was conducted by a panel of one, two or three members.

In Radford's case an unnamed three-person panel met in November 2017. It was chaired by a psychologist and included a lawyer who had no experience of sitting as a judge.

After considering reports on Radford, the panel concluded that the public would not be at risk from him. It seems they believed – incorrectly – that they were not allowed to take account of allegations against him that had not been tested in court.

In a letter from the Parole Board,[25] Radford was told that he would be released on licence. It was then up to the Ministry of Justice to make the necessary arrangements.

Call in the lawyers

There was huge public concern when news of Radford's imminent release emerged in the first week of 2018. By then, he had been in prison for nearly ten years. Given that offenders serving fixed sentences are normally released half-way through, that would have been the equivalent of a 20-year fixed sentence for one rape, four sexual assaults, two assault-related charges and 12 charges of administering a substance with intent. If those had been the only offences he had committed, it would have been hard to argue that he had got off too lightly. But that was not the case here.

Two of Radford's victims, known only as DSD and NBV to protect their identities, wanted to stop Radford being released. So did the Mayor of London, Sadiq Khan, given that Radford's crimes had been committed in the capital. But what could they do?

Rather than tell you straight away what the courts concluded, I want to give you a chance to decide what you would have done. Make notes if you like. You'll then be able to see whether the judges agreed with you.

This is quite a recent case, of course, and you will probably remember the outcome. But how do you think the judges reached their decision? They were particularly concerned not to 'open the floodgates', as the lawyers say. If DSD and NBV were successful, what was to stop another challenge the next time a prisoner was approved for release?

Let me tell you a bit more about the law before you make up your mind. When the Parole Board was set up by parliament in 1967 it was simply an advisory body. Since then, it has become much more like a court. The board, acting through panels, has to decide whether prisoners serving indefinite sentences – and some prisoners serving fixed sentences for serious offences – continue to represent a significant risk to the public. A prisoner serving a life sentence cannot be released unless the board is 'satisfied that it is no longer necessary for the protection of the public that the prisoner should be confined'.[26]

Parliament had never provided a right of appeal against the board's decisions. In those circumstances, you might have expected the judges to step in. And you would be right: prisoners who are denied parole regularly seek judicial review of the board's decisions. But DSD and NBV faced two problems. First, they were outsiders, not prisoners, and they were challenging a release decision, rather than continued detention. That had never been done before.

Their second problem was that they would be challenging a finding whose reasoning and evidence they had not seen. By law, Parole Board hearings were private, as were the board's reasons.[27] Nobody knew why the panel had thought it would be safe to release Radford.

Surely there must have been good reasons? In such a high-profile case as this you would have expected the board to have deployed its most experienced members and taken special care to assess the risk to the public. If it had followed its own rules, there was surely little that the judges could do. As you will remember from Chapter 1, it is not the job of the court in a case such as this to substitute its own decision for that of the decision maker.

In January 2018 the mayor and the two victims issued judicial review proceedings against the Parole Board and the justice secretary. While arrangements were made for the hearing in March 2018, Radford's planned release was put on hold. Sir Brian Leveson, the senior criminal appeal judge, decided to hear the case himself with two High Court judges.

What would they do? You be the judge.

The black-cab rapist: what the court said

At a preliminary hearing in February 2018 Leveson had taken steps to ensure that Radford would be legally represented when the case was argued in full. He was neither the claimant nor the defendant – but he certainly had an interest in the outcome. In the event, Radford was represented by Edward Fitzgerald QC, one of the leading lawyers in this area of the law.

The court also ordered that the claimants should be shown, in confidence, the dossier of evidence before the Parole Board as well as the panel's findings. Some of this material was published in the judgment that the court delivered in March 2018, though the names of those involved remained confidential.[28]

Unusually, the court decided that the Mayor of London did not have the necessary standing to bring a claim. 'There are situations where the court adopts a very liberal approach to the issue of standing,' the judges said, 'but this is not one of them.' Nobody regarded the mayor as a 'mere busybody', the judges stressed. It was just that DSD and NBV were better placed to bring the challenge. The mayor might have been allowed to do so if there had been nobody else.

Phillippa Kaufmann QC, for DSD and NBV, put two main arguments to the court. She submitted that the decision to release Radford had been irrational in the *Wednesbury* sense, as explained in Chapter 1. And, having seen how much information about Radford's past offending was missing from the Parole Board dossier, and its importance in assessing the risk of reoffending, she argued that this could not rationally have been ignored.

There was considerable force in some of her submissions on the first point, the court found. Radford was in a high-security Category A prison when he was recommended for release. That was extremely rare – prisoners are usually moved to lower-security conditions ahead of release – and so the decision required particularly strong justification.

Another surprising thing was Radford's approach to his offending. During his first six years in prison he had stoutly maintained his innocence and applied for his case to be considered as a miscarriage of justice. Then, about nine months before he was due to be considered for parole, he admitted the offences of which he had been convicted and told a psychologist that he wanted to take responsibility for his offending.

Leveson had spent a lifetime prosecuting, defending and judging criminals and he knew that some could be highly manipulative. So he and his fellow judges were rather more sceptical of Radford's apparent about-turn than were the Parole Board panel and its advisers. It seemed to the court that the independent psychologists who considered Radford's case had not 'thoroughly probed' the possibility that he was not being open and honest with them. It was possible, the judges said, that Radford had provided 'a carefully calibrated account, steering adroitly between admitting too much and too little, rather than one that is entirely open and forthcoming'. And yet, they acknowledged, 'the possibility that Mr Radford is devious, calculating and an expert manipulator could not have been lost on this panel'. Its members were experienced and must have taken the prisoner's proclivities into account.

Had it been irrational for the panel not to have probed Radford's answers? No, said the judges, that was a matter for the panel. Its reasons had been detailed and comprehensive. Whatever the court might have thought of the decision, it was for the panel to make it – not the judges. 'We are compelled to conclude that the decision of the panel must be respected,' they said. It followed that the irrationality charge must be dismissed.

Was that it? Not quite. Another of the *Wednesbury* grounds for judicial review is a failure to take account of relevant considerations. DSD and NBV argued that the panel should have considered Radford's other offences. True, these had not been proved against him in a criminal court. But questions could – and should – have been raised: 'the panel did not obtain any evidence bearing on the issue of possible wider offending, no questions were asked of Mr Radford about it, and the reasoning in the release direction is premised solely on the commission of the index offences on the terms admitted by Mr Radford'.

The judges accepted that it was not the job of the Parole Board to decide whether an offender had committed other offences. But the panel could still have considered evidence of wider offending as a means of probing and testing the truth of Radford's account. Was it irrational for the panel not to have made further enquiries? In the circumstances of this case, said the judges, it was.

It followed that the decision to release him had to be quashed. The court sent the case back to the Parole Board for a rehearing before a new panel. And, the judges added pointedly, 'we would encourage the Parole Board to ensure that the panel included someone with judicial experience'.

Not their decision?

The decision was widely welcomed. But were the judges overstepping the mark in telling the Parole Board what to do?

Certainly not, they insisted. 'We have not held, nor must we be understood as suggesting, that Mr Radford's present risk is such that his continued imprisonment is necessary for the protection of the public, or that the Parole Board should so find. Subject only to the review jurisdiction of this court, the assessment of all the available evidence, and all matters relevant to Mr Radford's risk, is for the Parole Board alone to make.'

Maybe – but it was pretty clear what the court expected of the Parole Board. Far from being handled with particular care, Radford's case had been dealt with particularly incompetently. Radford had been able to manipulate the board and its advisers, just as he had deceived the women he had assaulted.

It is perhaps unfair to blame the board for not finding someone with judicial experience to chair the original panel. Like every other body for which the Ministry of Justice is responsible, it has suffered budget cuts since 2010. That no doubt explains why the justice secretary was not represented at the Parole Board hearing by a barrister, who would have alerted it to unexplored lines of inquiry.

What Leveson and his colleagues had done was to find a legally respectable way of rescuing the board from its failures. In so doing, they restored a measure of public confidence in the criminal justice system as a whole.

For this was a very shrewd judgment. It identified the main weakness in the panel's handling of this case without trying to second-guess the decision itself. It made it more likely that Radford's punishment would reflect the totality of his offending – which is what the public had been led to believe would happen when he was convicted. And, by confining the grounds of challenge to circumstances that are likely to be very rare, it ensured that the floodgates were not thrown open to future claims.

The Parole Board took the hint. In November 2018 it told reporters that it had reconsidered Radford's request for parole. 'After considering the circumstances of offending, the progress made while in custody, and the evidence presented within the dossier,' it said, 'the panel was not satisfied that Mr Worboys was suitable for release or progression to the open estate.'[29]

Meanwhile, the justice secretary took steps to avoid the need for cases such as this to come to court in the future. In February 2019 David Gauke announced that victims of crime would be able to challenge the decision to release a prisoner on parole if they believed it was 'fundamentally flawed'. Applications would be considered by a named senior judicial member of the Parole Board, who would decide whether the case should be looked at again – either by the original panel or in an entirely new hearing before a fresh panel.

There would also be a 'tailored' review of the board to consider whether it should become a judge-led tribunal.[30]

Meanwhile, further charges were brought against Radford. In June 2019 he admitted two counts of administering a drug with intent to commit rape or indecent assault on four other complainants. The prospect of his release receded even further.

4

Families and the Law

We saw in Chapter 3 how the judges have adapted the criminal law and applied the principles of judicial review to fill in some of the deficiencies left by parliament. But no area of the law poses more challenges for an activist judiciary than that of the family.

Before we look at how some of these issues have been handled by the Supreme Court, it is worth reminding ourselves that the UK's most senior judges do not have the same powers as their counterparts in Washington, DC.

Can courts declare laws unconstitutional?

In the United States (US) the Supreme Court has the last word. It can declare legislation unconstitutional, and thereby overturn it. The US court's decisions cannot be reversed by the legislature without a constitutional amendment – which is very difficult to secure.

As Lord Reed observed in 2019,[1] this gives the US court power to bring about major and controversial changes to family life:

> For example, it was not congress that guaranteed abortion rights to all American women, or that allowed same-sex couples in every state to marry, but the Supreme Court.[2] In Britain, on the other hand, it was parliament that liberalised abortion law in 1967, and the UK and Scottish parliaments which passed laws permitting same-sex marriages. The UK Supreme Court does not have the power to change the law in that way and the justices would not want to have that power.

Lord Reed, who was the UK Supreme Court's deputy president at that time, noted that the court's critics had accused it of getting involved in political questions in some of the decisions it had taken under the Human Rights Act 1998. To the extent that this was true, parliament was to blame. 'EU law and the Human Rights Act have enabled individuals and companies to challenge legislation and administrative decisions on a range of grounds which did not previously exist,' Reed said, 'and it is the duty of the courts to decide those cases when they come before them.'

Whose house is it anyway?

How have our own courts dealt with family issues? Let's begin with a case decided in 2007, when the House of Lords was still the UK's highest court. Five law lords dismissed an appeal by a man who claimed that, after living with his partner for 27 years, he was entitled to a half rather than just over a third of the house that they had bought in joint names.[3]

Barry Stack was appealing against a judgment in favour of his former partner, Dehra Dowden. When the couple met as teenagers in 1975 he was a self-employed builder and decorator while she was training with the London Electricity Board – 'eventually rising to become the most highly qualified electrical engineer in the London area', as Lady Hale noted in her judgment.

Dowden put more money into the homes that they bought together, although Stack, understandably, carried out more of the improvements. The extra 15% that Stack was arguing over amounted to £111,000. 'This is a not inconsiderable sum,' said Hale, 'but the costs of pursuing the argument to this [court] will have been quite disproportionate.'

Not surprisingly, the couple had never agreed on how the value of their joint home should be divided if they were to split up. As business partners, they would have owned the property jointly. If they had been married, the court could have decided what division would be fair. But parliament had not decided what the consequences should be for a cohabiting couple: the government's law reform advisers had found it impossible to devise a scheme that would have been fair to all types of cohabitation.

'While this conclusion is not surprising,' Hale said in her judgment, 'its importance for us is that the evolution of the law of property to take account of changing social and economic circumstances will have to come from the courts rather than parliament.'

Really? The courts *had* to make new law? That view – Hale's most explicit endorsement of judicial activism – was not shared by Lord Neuberger, who dissented on this point but concurred in the result. The Law Commission had certainly described the law as 'unduly complex, arbitrary and uncertain'. But, in his view, that did not justify it being rewritten by the courts.

'A change in the law, however sensible and just it seems, always carries a real risk of new and unforeseen uncertainties and unfairnesses,' Neuberger said. 'That is a particular danger when the change is effected by the court rather than the legislature, as the change is influenced by, indeed normally based on, the facts of a particular case, there is little room for public consultation, and there is no input from the democratically elected legislature.'

This was wise advice. But the other law lords preferred Hale's pragmatic activism to Neuberger's principled caution.

The chained wife

Hale succeeded Neuberger and served as president of the UK Supreme Court from 2017 until the end of 2019. So long as she could win over enough of her colleagues, she should have been in a strong position to influence the development of family law.

This was, after all, her specialist subject when she was one of the government's law reform advisers from 1984 to 1993. Hale had initiated a highly critical report about divorce for the Law Commission in 1990.[4] And she made no secret of the fact that she favoured the introduction of no-fault divorce – effectively, divorce on demand. 'It may seem paradoxical to suggest that no-fault divorce is aimed at strengthening family responsibility,' she said in a lecture shortly before hearing the case I am about to describe, 'but I believe that it is.'[5]

Tini Owens and her husband Hugh were married in 1978 and had two children. Early in 2015 she left the matrimonial home and started living apart from her husband. Exactly why the couple's long marriage failed was not disclosed – neither party gave interviews – but in 2015 Tini Owens filed court papers seeking divorce.

At that time an application for a divorce was known as a 'petition', reminding us that until as recently as 1858 a man seeking a divorce from his adulterous wife had to begin proceedings in the Ecclesiastical Court.[6] The spouse who initiated the process was the petitioner and the other spouse was the respondent.

In her petition, Tini Owens asserted that her marriage had broken down irretrievably. That assertion was indispensable because irretrievable breakdown was – and remains – the only ground for divorce in England and Wales. But the law at that time – which had remained largely unchanged since the Divorce Reform Act 1969 came into force at the beginning of 1971 – did not allow divorce on demand. It said that a court could not hold that a marriage had broken down unless the petitioner established at least one of five specified 'facts'.[7]

One of those facts was that 'the respondent has behaved in such a way that the petitioner cannot reasonably be expected to live with the respondent'. This was the one Tini Owens relied on. If she wanted a divorce without delay, she had no alternative.

It was very common for a petitioner to base a divorce petition on the respondent's behaviour. Even in the closest of marriages, there are bound to be irritations and annoyances. It was not difficult for a spouse seeking a divorce to spin these into a pattern of behaviour. Objectively speaking, that behaviour might not be very bad. But it was normally sufficient to support a divorce petition because most respondents choose not to argue about the details. What would be the point?

Of course, the parties may deeply disagree about issues such as money and children. But most respondents took the view that, if the petitioner was determined, it was futile to defend the divorce petition itself. After all, it takes two to make a marriage.

If the divorce was not going to be defended, there was no point in stuffing the petition with the worst aspects of a respondent's behaviour. There was an overwhelming probability that no court would need to consider how bad it was.[8] Indeed, lawyers routinely advised their clients to reduce the level of acrimony by pulling their punches.

Tini Owens alleged that her husband had been moody, argumentative and embarrassingly critical of her in front of others. Hugh Owens disagreed. Although conceding that their marriage had never been emotionally intense, he thought they had learned to 'rub along'.

So he defended the petition in court. After considering his wife's allegations, a judge dismissed them in January 2016 as flimsy and exaggerated. [9] The judge's findings were upheld by the Court of Appeal in March 2017.[10] In 2018 Tini Owens appealed to the Supreme Court.[11] It was the first time the highest court in the UK had agreed to hear a defended divorce petition. It would also be the last.

Can the chains be loosened?

In the rather different context of Jewish law, Tini Owens could have been described as a 'chained wife' – a woman whose husband was refusing, for as long as he could, to allow her the option of remarriage.

When the Supreme Court gave judgment in July 2018, Tini Owens was 68 and Hugh Owens was 80. Giving the main judgment, Lord Wilson said he could not think of a decision that more obviously required to be informed by changing social norms than an evaluation of whether it was reasonable for a couple to continue living together.

After reviewing past cases, Wilson confessed that he had once fallen into the notorious 'linguistic trap' that ensnared family lawyers for 50 years. When discussing a claim of this sort, they routinely referred to allegations of the respondent's 'unreasonable behaviour'. But it was not the respondent's behaviour that had to be unreasonable for the petition to succeed. It was the expectation of continued life together. Tini Owens did not have to prove that her husband had behaved unreasonably. She had to show he had behaved in such a way that she could not reasonably be expected to live with him.

And that had simply not been established on the evidence. Why, then, had the Supreme Court agreed to hear the appeal?

It was, said Wilson, because Tini Owens's counsel had initially suggested that the key phrase in the statute should be reinterpreted.

On this basis, she would not have to prove that Hugh Owens's behaviour – viewed objectively – was so bad that she could not reasonably be expected to live with him. What she had to prove instead was that the *effect of it on her* satisfied that test.

That would have meant introducing a subjective element into what was primarily an objective test. By the time the case was heard, though, her counsel had conceded that this argument went too far.

Hale agreed. But what concerned her most of all was that the trial judge had failed to consider the cumulative effect of a great many humiliating incidents over a period of time. 'Those who have never experienced such humiliation may find it difficult to understand how destructive such conduct can be of the trust and confidence which should exist in any marriage,' said Hale, who was herself divorced in 1992 before remarrying shortly afterwards.

But the Supreme Court was not there to correct mistakes of this sort. It was not a 'court of error', Hale explained. 'If the law is clear, permission to appeal is not normally given … simply because the law may have been misapplied in the individual case.'

Given that the trial judge had not evaluated the petition as a whole, she thought the best thing to do would be to order a rehearing. But nobody wanted to go through all that again – quite apart from the cost. And why bother? Tini Owens had less than 20 months to wait before she could apply for a divorce based on an entirely different 'fact' – that the parties have lived apart for five years. That was clearly her preferred choice.

In the end, then, the judges decided that there was nothing that the courts could do for Tini Owens and others in her position, however sympathetic they might be. Hale, who found it a 'troubling' case, made the court's position very clear. 'It is not for us to change the law laid down by parliament,' she said. 'Our role is only to interpret and apply the law that parliament has given us.'

That's true, of course, but Wilson – and perhaps Hale – had thought that interpreting and applying the law might have produced the result Tini Owens had been hoping for. Once a majority of her colleagues agreed that this was a non-starter, Hale was 'reluctantly persuaded' that the appeal must be dismissed.[12]

Could the judges have done more?

Writing in the *Financial Times*, the legal commentator David Allen Green accused the justices of being unjust:

> Rather than take a liberal and thoughtful approach to the applicable law, the judges adopted – in my view – an illiberal and misconceived one. The justices held that the wife's own subjective view that it would be unreasonable for her to continue with the marriage, even with all her evidence in support, was not sufficient. It did not matter in any fundamental way that the marriage had broken down …
>
> In a perfect world, parliament would now act. But in a perfect world there would also not be divorces or a parliament clogged up with many other things. The appeal courts should not use cases to send messages to parliament. In a way, that is far more 'political' than any judicial activism.
>
> Justices should instead interpret and construct statutes so as to serve justice, in accordance with settled practice and practical common sense. This week, the Supreme Court judges failed this basic test with their very own unreasonable behaviour.[13]

I disagree. As the lord chief justice commented shortly afterwards, issues of this sort were best left to parliament. But Lord Burnett of Maldon knew how judges could be tempted into areas reserved for the government or the legislature:

> It can be particularly tempting when public opinion, or at least voluble parts of it, seems to suggest that a judicial view would be welcome. But that cannot justify a judge in going beyond the proper, constitutional, boundaries and straying into political matters. This may lead to criticism. But the damage that it can do to the judge – in terms of public confidence in his or her ability impartially to exercise the judicial function – and for the judiciary as a whole can be serious.

Judges inevitably hold opinions; and on many subjects of controversy our judicial work provides insights not widely available. Yet there may be times where the courageous thing to do is to remain silent.

A recent example arose in our Supreme Court concerning the availability of divorce to a separated couple where one refuses consent ... There has been a long running campaign to replace the current arrangements with no-fault divorce, the details of which have generated keen debate. The Supreme Court contented itself with suggesting that the time had come for parliament to look again at what is now rather antique legislation, given developments in society over the last 50 years, rather than prescribing a suggested policy solution.[14]

It is indeed temping to take a view, as Burnett demonstrated by his disparaging reference to 'rather antique legislation'. But his message to the judges was that, while it might be acceptable for them to criticise the law, they must apply it – in the words of their oath – 'without fear or favour'.

Parliament steps in

The judges' approach was vindicated a few weeks later when, to everyone's surprise, Theresa May's government announced that it would be introducing no-fault divorce.[15] Ministers proposed that irretrievable breakdown should remain the sole ground for divorce in England and Wales. But a spouse would no longer need to prove any of the five 'facts' that had previously been required. Instead, one party to the marriage – or both – would simply provide the court with notice of an intention to divorce. And it would no longer be possible for a respondent to defend the divorce in the way that Hugh Owens had done. Similar reforms would apply to the dissolution of a civil partnership.

The government consulted on its proposals with impressive speed. Far from being 'clogged up' with Brexit – as commentators had believed – parliament had time on its hands and the prime minister, in the last weeks of her premiership, seemed desperate for something she could point to as part of her legacy. So David Gauke, her justice secretary, brought a Divorce, Dissolution and Separation bill before the House of Commons in June 2019.[16] This was designed to:

- replace the requirement to provide evidence of conduct or separation facts with a new requirement to provide a statement of irretrievable breakdown. The court must take that statement to be conclusive evidence;
- remove the right to contest a divorce application;
- require parties to wait at least six months for a divorce, unless there are exceptional circumstances. This would comprise 20 weeks from the start of proceedings to the conditional order and a further six weeks from the conditional order to the divorce order.[17] The ban on divorce during the first year of marriage would remain;
- introduce a new option of a joint application for cases where the decision to divorce is a mutual one;
- update terminology, replacing terms such as 'decree nisi', 'decree absolute' and 'petitioner' with 'conditional order', 'final order' and 'applicant'.

When these reforms were first debated the Conservative MP Fiona Bruce said they would 'allow one party to walk away from the most important commitment they are likely to have made in their lifetime, without giving any reason at all and without their spouse being able meaningfully to object to their decision to do so'. Bruce, a solicitor, thought the bill would weaken family relationships, reducing the rate of marriage and the stability it gives to children. She wanted the government to promote reconciliation by providing better mediation services.[18]

These were admirable sentiments. But, as other MPs told Bruce, preserving the old law would do nothing to strengthen the institution of marriage. The law can give a lead to society, but there are limits to its reach.

A very civil partnership

In the same week as the Owens case, the Supreme Court heard a second appeal by a woman who did not want to be married. But this was a very different claim. It involved a woman and a man who wanted to formalise their relationship by registering as civil partners. Their problem was legislation which said that 'two people are not eligible to register as civil partners if they are not of the same sex'.[19]

Rebecca Steinfeld and Charles Keidan had two children together during the three years it took their case to reach the Supreme Court. Judges were persuaded that they had 'deep-rooted and genuine ideological objections to the institution of marriage, based upon what they consider to be its historically patriarchal nature'.[20] They could have had a register office wedding if they had not wanted a religious ceremony. But their view was that 'marriage does not reflect the way in which they understand their commitment to each other or wish their relationship to be seen'.[21] It was 'not disputed that their unwillingness to marry is based on genuine conviction'.[22]

Even so, they wanted their relationship to have formal public recognition and to provide a stable relationship in which their children could grow up. They also wanted the financial benefits of marriage, such as rights of inheritance and relief from inheritance tax on death.[23] These benefits are available to civil partners. But civil partnership was not available to two people of the opposite sex.

So the couple brought a claim for judicial review. But because they were challenging primary legislation, their claim inevitably depended on whether they could bring it within the Human Rights Act.

The first civil partnerships in the UK were registered in December 2005. They allowed same-sex couples to claim benefits that had previously been denied to them. These put them in pretty much the same position as a married couple. But same-sex partners were not formally 'married'. That did not become possible in England and Wales – or in Scotland, where the rules are slightly different – until 2014.[24]

When same-sex marriage was introduced, civil partnerships were retained. It became possible for civil partners in England and Wales to convert their partnerships into marriages and it became possible for civil partners in Scotland to marry without first dissolving their civil partnerships. But same-sex couples who preferred not to marry could continue to register as civil partners in England, Wales or Scotland.

The parliaments at Westminster and Edinburgh could have changed the law so that all civil partnerships were converted into marriages and no new civil partnerships could be registered. But this was not done.

By now, you may be able to work out the nature of Steinfeld and Keidan's challenge. It was really very simple. Same-sex couples who want to formalise their relationships now had two choices: to marry or to register as civil partners. Opposite-sex couples had only one option. That, said Steinfeld and Keidan, was discriminatory. In effect, the couple were being discriminated against on the grounds of their sexual orientation. And that, they argued, was a breach of their human rights.

The European Convention on Human Rights does not ban discrimination as such. What article 14 of the convention says is that 'the enjoyment of the rights and freedoms set forth in this convention shall be secured without discrimination'. So you have to look for another right that has been broken. Article 8 of the convention requires respect for a person's private and family life. So Steinfeld and Keidan argued that the legislation was in breach of article 14 taken together with article 8.

But there is one further point to consider before I ask how you would have decided their claim. Article 8, like most of the articles in the convention, is a qualified right, because there are a number of exceptions in its second paragraph. Governments are allowed to limit the exercise of the right to respect for private and family life if that is necessary for the protection of the rights and freedoms of others. In simple terms, the discrimination must be proportionate in order to be justified. The government insisted that it was. What do you think?

Was the discrimination justified?

Steinfeld and Keidan launched their claim in the High Court early in 2016. The government pointed out that it had been considering whether to retain civil partnerships ever since 2012, when it launched a public consultation on introducing same-sex marriage.

It had decided not to extend civil partnerships to opposite-sex couples but held a further review early in 2014. It now wanted to wait and see what effect the Marriage (Same Sex Couples) Act 2013 had on the take-up of civil partnerships.

Giving judgment in January 2016, Mrs Justice Andrews said that Steinfeld and Keidan's claim fell at the first hurdle. It did not 'come within the ambit' of article 8 (respect for family life), and so article 14 (discrimination) did not apply. That was because withholding public recognition of an unmarried opposite-sex couple's relationship did not impinge on the 'love, trust, confidence, mutual dependence and unconstrained social intercourse' that Lord Bingham had identified as the essence of family life.[25]

'The only obstacle to the claimants obtaining the equivalent legal recognition of their status and the same rights and benefits as a same-sex couple is their conscience,' the judge said. 'Whilst their views are of course to be afforded respect, it is their choice not to avail themselves of the means of state recognition that is open to them. The state has fulfilled its obligations under the convention by making a means of formal recognition of their relationship available.'

If that was wrong, she added, then she would have dismissed the claim on the ground that maintaining the existing position – in the short term, while the government took stock – was objectively justified. 'The government's decision to wait and see,' she concluded, 'serves the legitimate aim of avoiding the unnecessary disruption and the waste of time and money that plunging into a programme of legislative reform without waiting is likely to produce.'

So ministers won. But a shrewd government would not have rested on its laurels. It would have decided whether it wanted to extend civil partnerships, abolish them or let them lapse. Ministers can hardly have been surprised that Steinfeld and Keidan launched an appeal. When their case came before the Court of Appeal in November 2016 the government's position was still to wait and see what impact same-sex marriage had on civil partnership before making up its mind.

Judgment was given in February 2017 by Lady Justice Arden, Lord Justice Beatson and Lord Justice Briggs. When two or more judges of equal rank sit together, they are listed in order of seniority. The most senior – the judge who has served longest at that level

– takes the chair.[26] Arden had much greater seniority than the two men who sat on either side of her,[27] but she was outvoted by them.

In Arden's view, Steinfeld and Keidan should have won. Unlike Andrews in the lower court, she thought that their claim came within the ambit of article 8. And she also thought the government's wait-and-see policy could no longer be justified. She delivered a very lengthy judgment explaining her reasons.

Beatson and Briggs agreed with Arden that the claim came within the ambit of article 8. Like her, they based this on an analysis of recent case law. But they both thought the government's policy could be justified.

For the government's policy to be lawful, Arden had said, it needed to be proportionate. It also had to strike a fair balance between the interests of opposite-sex couples who wanted to register as civil partners and the rest of the community. But the wait-and-see policy did not do so. It was open-ended in time and did not address the 'important social question' of whether couples such as Steinfeld and Keidan should be granted the rights they were seeking.

Beatson thought it was legitimate for the government to say it needed time to make up its mind. Same-sex marriage had been available at that point for just under three years. So, 'at present', the minister's position was objectively justified. But the government would have to make up its mind 'within a reasonable timescale'.

Briggs said there was no 'general public consensus, or even majority view, as to whether to do away with civil partnership (or close it to new members) or to extend it' to opposite-sex couples. Most people – unaware that 'the current impasse cannot lawfully be allowed to continue indefinitely' – favoured doing nothing. He was certainly not saying that every aspect of the wait-and-evaluate policy was beyond criticism. But, like Beatson, Briggs did not regard 'micro-management of the government's detailed thinking about this policy as being part of the business of the courts'.

So, ministers had scraped through again. An astute government would have realised that there was likely to be a further appeal. But, with Brexit dominating their thoughts, ministers did nothing for more than a year.

The government then made a desperate last-minute plea for more time. Knowing that Steinfeld and Keidan's appeal was going to be heard by the Supreme Court on a Monday in May 2018, it published a policy paper on the previous Thursday.[28] This announced that a public survey would be launched that month and analysed in the summer of 2019. The government would then be able to launch a consultation exercise in 2020 'at the earliest'.

That was as far as the paper went. But, even if the government moved quickly after that, its response to the consultation would not be expected before 2021. That suggested that the necessary legislation would not be passed before 2022 or brought into force before 2023. Would that meet the concerns expressed by the Court of Appeal in 2017? You might think it was not so much kicking the can down the road as blasting it out of sight.

The Supreme Court rules

The five members of the Supreme Court who heard Steinfeld and Keidan's appeal in May 2018 agreed on the outcome and they were able to deliver a pithy judgment just six weeks later.[29]

Lord Kerr, who spoke for them all, noted that the government had now accepted that article 14 – prohibition of discrimination – was 'engaged'. That meant that the government would have to justify the unequal treatment in order to win. Ministers also accepted that they would need to justify the discrimination from the date the inequality arose: the date in March 2014 when same-sex couples in England and Wales were given the right to marry. And yet the government had taken a deliberate decision not to change the law – at that time or subsequently – on the basis that there was no public consensus on what to do.

There was very little that the government could say to justify its admitted discrimination. Its argument was that the courts should show a degree of reticence in the field of social policy. They should defer to the elected government on what changes should be made and when.

Kerr said that the government's wait-and-evaluate approach 'displayed, at best, an attitude of some insouciance'. He could understand why the government might have wanted to maintain the status quo while considering various options. 'But that is a far cry from saying that it is *necessary* to exclude different sex couples from the institution of civil partnership.' That necessity had not been established.

Indeed, the government should have eliminated the inequality of treatment immediately it allowed same-sex couples to marry – either by abolishing civil partnerships or by extending them to opposite-sex couples. 'Taking time to evaluate whether to abolish or extend could never amount to a legitimate aim for the continuance of the discrimination.'

Even if it had been, the government had not struck a fair balance between competing rights. It was hard to see what interests the community had in denying opposite-sex couples civil partnerships. By contrast, denying those rights to same-sex couples for an indefinite period might have far-reaching consequences for them.

Steinfeld and Keidan were at the Supreme Court to see the justices rule in their favour. Photographers were there to cover the hoped-for outcome. One wanted to follow the couple to the nearest register office and photograph them as they completed the legal formalities. But that betrayed a fundamental misunderstanding of the Human Rights Act.

Declaration of incompatibility

I mentioned declarations of incompatibility in Chapter 1. Now is the time to explain how they work. Let's start from first principles.

The European Convention on Human Rights is an international treaty that took effect in 1953. The Human Rights Act is a law passed by the UK parliament in 1998 that came into force in 2000.

Section 1 of the Act defines the 'Convention rights' covered by the legislation. I listed some of them in Chapter 2.

Section 2 of the Act says that the courts of the UK 'must take into account' decisions of the European Court of Human Rights. The court, based in the French city of Strasbourg, interprets the convention. It does this when it decides cases brought by individuals or organisations against any of the 47 European countries that have agreed to be bound by it. The court is run by the Council of Europe, to which all 47 states belong. The Council of Europe has nothing to do with the EU, and so none of this is affected by Brexit.

Section 3 of the Act says that 'so far as it is possible to do so, primary legislation and subordinate legislation must be read and given effect in a way which is compatible with the Convention rights'. This is an extraordinary power that allows the courts to reinterpret primary legislation passed by parliament and secondary legislation made by ministers or others. The judges call this 'reading down' legislation. It is up to them to decide how far they can stretch or bend the law to bring it into line with the convention rights. I gave an example of this in Chapter 2. But what if the judges decide that they cannot interpret legislation in a way that is compatible with the convention?

Section 4 of the Act says that 'if the court is satisfied that the provision is incompatible with a Convention right, it may make a declaration of that incompatibility'. And what effect does that have? First, it 'does not affect the validity, continuing operation or enforcement of the provision in respect of which it is given'. And, second, it 'is not binding on the parties to the proceedings in which it is made'.

Let me explain what that meant when Steinfeld and Keidan won their case in the Supreme Court.

First, there had been a breach of a Convention right, as defined by section 1 of the Human Rights Act. In this case, the government had breached article 14 (non-discrimination) taken together with article 8 (respect for family life).

That decision had been reached by the Supreme Court after it had taken into account decisions of the European Court of Human Rights, as it was required to do by section 2 of the Human Rights Act.

The Civil Partnership Act 2004 clearly defines a civil partnership as 'a relationship between two people of the same sex ... which is formed when they register as civil partners of each other'. There was no suggestion from the couple's lawyers that it might be possible for the judges to interpret 'same sex' as meaning 'same or opposite sex'. So, section 3 of the Human Rights Act could not be used to reinterpret or read down the legislation.

That left the justices with the option of making a declaration of incompatibility under section 4 of the Human Rights Act. They certainly did not have to do so and there have been cases where courts have favoured reticence.[30] But in this case they did, declaring that sections 1 and 3 of the Civil Partnership Act 2004 – 'to the extent that they preclude a different sex couple from entering into a civil partnership' – were incompatible with article 14 of the convention taken together with article 8.

What effect did that have? In an earlier case, Lord Neuberger said it enabled the courts to send a message to parliament. But in doing so the judges were not usurping the role of parliament or offending against the separation of powers:[31]

> A declaration of incompatibility is merely an expression of the court's conclusion as to whether, as enacted, a particular item of legislation cannot be considered compatible with a convention right. In other words, the courts say to parliament, 'This particular piece of legislation is incompatible, now it is for you to decide what to do about it.' And under the scheme of the Human Rights Act 1998 it is open to parliament to decide to do nothing.[32]

It was, as Neuberger remarked in a subsequent interview, 'a curious and, I think, not unattractive typical British middle way' between senior judges changing the law – as they would have done in the US – and saying that these were not matters for the judiciary at all.[33]

But there is more to it than that. Finding that the law is incompatible with human rights must surely put ministers under moral pressure to change it. And there must be an expectation that parliament will act quickly to put things right. Why else would section 10 of the Human Rights Act have provided ministers with special powers to remedy incompatibilities identified by the courts?

A declaration of incompatibility is also a warning. If the law remains unchanged, claimants are likely to apply to the European Court of Human Rights. The Strasbourg court will be told that judges in the UK have identified breaches of the convention. European judges are likely to follow the lead of their UK colleagues in ruling against the government. In that event, ministers would be under a treaty obligation to bring the law into line with human rights. It was to shortcut this process that the Human Rights Act was introduced.

See what you can do

In this case, the government moved with what Lady Hale called 'astonishing' speed.[34] Just ahead of her speech to the Conservative party conference in October 2018, Theresa May told a newspaper that civil partnerships would be extended to opposite-sex couples.[35] Rather than introducing legislation of its own, the government supported a private member's bill which became the Civil Partnerships, Marriages and Deaths (Registration etc) Act 2019.

Instead of changing the law directly, this legislation gave a secretary of state power to amend the Civil Partnership Act 2004 so that two people 'who are not of the same sex are eligible to form a civil partnership in England and Wales (provided that they would be eligible to do so apart from the question of sex)'. That power had to be exercised before the end of 2019.

This is a pretty unattractive way of law making. Although it gave the government more time to draft the necessary amendments, these would not be debated by parliament in the normal way.

Even so, it showed how quickly the government could move if it wanted to. Penny Mordaunt MP, who at that time was minister for equalities as well as secretary of state for defence, published a detailed policy paper in July 2019.[36] This said that the Civil Partnership Act 2004 would be amended to allow an opposite-sex couple to register as civil partners of each other. 'We have no intention of extending eligibility to form a civil partnership to family members (such as siblings),' the government added firmly.

When it became clear that parliament would be dissolved in November 2019 so that a general election could be held a month later, the Civil Partnership (Opposite-sex Couples) Regulations 2019 were rushed through parliament. These enabled the first opposite-sex civil partnerships – including Steinfeld and Keidan's – to be registered on 31 December 2019.

A judge torn in two directions

The civil partnership reforms stemmed from the declaration of incompatibility made by the Supreme Court in the Steinfeld and Keidan case. But some claimants do not even get that far. Three weeks before its decision on opposite-sex civil partnerships the

Supreme Court had delivered a judgment that was both frustrating and revealing.[37]

Seven justices were ruling on a claim brought by the Northern Ireland Human Rights Commission, a statutory body set up after the Good Friday Agreement of 1998. The commission was challenging provisions in the Offences against the Person Act 1861 that make it illegal to procure an abortion. Those provisions were modified in the rest of the UK by the Abortion Act 1967. In Northern Ireland, though, termination of pregnancy was still punishable with life imprisonment unless done 'for the purpose of preserving the life of the mother'.

Because the 1861 Act is primary legislation, the Supreme Court cannot overturn it. Instead, the commission wanted the court to declare the legislation incompatible with the right to respect for private and family life guaranteed by article 8 of the European Convention on Human Rights.

The court was shown harrowing statements from women from Northern Ireland whose babies had failed to develop properly and would inevitably be stillborn. In other cases, women had become pregnant through rape. A child under the age of 13 was carrying a baby as a result of sexual abuse by a member of her family. None of them could have abortions unless they left Northern Ireland to do so.

Instead of helping one of these women to bring a claim, the commission decided to bring proceedings in its own name. Courts in Northern Ireland decided that it had the power to do so. The commission said that it would have been difficult to find a claimant who was seeking an abortion for one of the specified reasons at the precise time when proceedings were commenced.

Four of the seven justices – Lady Hale, Lord Mance, Lord Kerr and Lord Wilson – thought that the existing law was incompatible with the right to family life in article 8.[38] But four of the justices – Mance, Lord Reed, Lady Black and Lord Lloyd-Jones – held that the commission did not have the necessary standing to argue, in the abstract, that primary legislation was incompatible with human rights. As you will have spotted, Mance was in both groups.

By a majority, the court had decided that the commission had no grounds for bringing a case because it had not identified any unlawful act or any actual or potential victim. If the commission had no standing to request a declaration of incompatibility, the court could not make it.

This was not merely a question of statutory construction, according to Mance: he thought it implausible that parliament had intended to give the public body carte blanche to challenge any UK primary legislation of its choosing. On this vital point, the courts of Northern Ireland had been wrong.

It took the justices more than seven months to produce a judgment of 143 pages – the longest in a single case. The result could be summed up in a phrase: the court had no jurisdiction because the commission had no standing.

You can imagine the fights that must have been going on behind the justices' closed doors. Surely the whole point of the commission is to challenge legislation that violates human rights? The minority judges thought it would be anomalous to treat the Northern Ireland commission differently from its counterparts in Great Britain. Kerr and Wilson accused Mance, Reed, Black and Lloyd-Jones of rejecting an interpretation that 'gives effect to the ascertainable will of parliament', preferring instead a 'literal construction which will frustrate the legislation's true purpose'.[39]

Hale went further. Compatibility was not a matter on which a democratic legislature enjoyed unique competence, she maintained. 'In some ways, the courts may be thought to be better qualified because they are able to weigh the evidence … in a dispassionate manner.' In a speech about judicial decision making some months later, she said: 'it certainly takes moral courage of a high order to adopt an interpretation which means that you cannot make the order which you think should be made'.[40]

Cynics sometimes accuse judges of reaching a decision on the merits of a case and then contriving the law to produce the desired result. But that was not the case here. Far from supporting the current law in Northern Ireland, Mance was satisfied that it was 'untenable and intrinsically disproportionate in excluding from any possibility of abortion pregnancies involving fatal foetal abnormality or due to rape or incest'. That opinion was shared by Hale, Kerr and Wilson, making it the majority view.

Should they have said so, given that they had no jurisdiction to make the declaration requested? Mance's answer was that the law clearly needed radical reconsideration and it was inevitable that a challenge brought in the name of a victim would result in a declaration of incompatibility. But why would he, and three other justices, take the trouble to say that the current law in Northern Ireland was disproportionate, and so in breach of article 8? These remarks were clearly *obiter dicta* – comments made 'by the way' that were not necessary to the decision and therefore not binding.

What's the point?

It is not uncommon for the lower courts to say what they would have done if they could. A judge might say how a case would have been decided on a different view of the law, just in case an appeal court finds on some future occasion that the judge's preferred analysis was wrong. But that cannot be the case in the final court of appeal.

The only point of a court saying it would have granted a declaration of incompatibility to an individual claimant must be to put pressure on ministers. And Reed, the recently appointed deputy president, expressed understandable concern. Having found that the commission had no standing to bring a challenge, 'it would ordinarily follow that the court should express no view' on compatibility. He thought that the court should steer clear of politics, leaving these issues to be debated in 'democratically accountable institutions'.

But what's wrong with giving them a bit of a push? Karen Bradley, secretary of state for Northern Ireland at the time, promised in November 2018 that the government would introduce legislation 'at the earliest opportunity, before the end of 2019', to give the Northern Ireland Human Rights Commission the power to bring cases in its own name before courts in the UK.[41]

Far from being a plausible policy decision, as Mance had thought, preventing the commission from litigating had been a mistake. 'We have now discovered there was an error in the explanatory memorandum in 1998 when the Northern Ireland Act was enacted,' Bradley told MPs three months later. 'It was not clear, unlike for other human rights commissions across the United Kingdom, about whether the Northern Ireland Human Rights Commission had legal standing. That is something we have committed to rectifying.'[42]

An obscure paragraph in the government's EU withdrawal legislation was designed to do this[43] – although the bill lapsed when parliament was dissolved in November 2019. And, speaking some months earlier, Lord Kerr felt vindicated by the government's promise. 'I like to believe,' he said, 'that this is, at least in part, due to the common-sense conclusion that to deny the commission (the obvious agency to take this type of proceedings) was plainly an example of the law of unintended consequences.'[44]

Kerr denied my suggestion that he and the justices who agreed with him had been putting pressure on the government. The courts had been given the job of deciding whether legislation was compatible with the European Convention on Human Rights. It was for parliament to decide what to do about it. 'People can call us activist,' he told me, 'but we are doing no more than parliament has asked us to do.'[45]

Progress

In July 2019 backbench MPs seized the initiative and parliament passed the Northern Ireland (Executive Formation etc) Act 2019. The 'etc' in the title is crucial: section 9 of the Act made major changes to the law on abortion in Northern Ireland on 22 October 2019 – because a power-sharing executive government had not been restored by then. The broad effect of these changes was that criminal charges could no longer be brought against women or girls who had abortions or against healthcare professionals who assisted them.

The secretary of state was also required to make regulations permitting abortion if there was a threat – which did not have to be 'long-term or permanent' – to a pregnant woman's physical or mental health; in cases of rape or incest; and in cases of severe foetal impairment. Those regulations had to be in force by the end of March 2020.

Section 8 of the Act required the secretary of state to make regulations by January 2020 permitting same-sex marriage and opposite-sex civil partnerships in Northern Ireland. Again, that power would not have come into force if an executive government had been restored.

These reforms were clearly controversial. But it was universally accepted that they should be resolved by a legislature rather than by the courts.

More conservative than we thought?

The Northern Ireland abortion challenge was exactly the sort of case in which an activist court would have contrived to change the law. The fact that it did not even make a declaration of incompatibility – albeit by a majority of one vote and on what surely must be seen as a technicality – suggested that Hale's Supreme Court was far more conservative than some people had expected.

But that broad assessment can be seen as an oversimplification. Brice Dickson, Professor of Law at Queen's University Belfast, offered a more nuanced view immediately after the ruling. 'The court's decision provides further evidence,' he wrote, 'that while Lady Hale, Lord Kerr and Lord Wilson are amongst the most liberal of the 12 justices, Lords Reed and Lloyd-Jones are amongst the most conservative.'[46]

I can offer partial confirmation of this view. Lord Reed, speaking to me in 2019 as deputy president of the UK Supreme Court, acknowledged that some of his colleagues were more willing to develop the law than others – though there were limits:[47]

> We are all within a band. Nobody here is going to start thinking that we can start making up the law – however we like. Equally nobody thinks that the common law should stand still. It's existed for about 900 years and clearly it's not the same now as it was in the 12th century. But, within that band, I think whether you are more or less adventurous, more or less cautious, what view you take of how far we should become involved in developing the law, to what extent we should leave it to the Law Commission, the government and parliament, varies to some extent from one justice to another.

And did Reed have a particular view of his own? Or did it depend on the case he was deciding?

It does depend to some extent on the case because you can have cases which are in areas of the law where parliament has shown an interest and has already become involved. You can have cases concerned with areas of the law which are really only of technical interest to the lawyers. I'm much more inclined to develop the law in that sort of technical area where there's going to be no controversy – beyond perhaps the legal profession – about how we develop the law of contract or unjust enrichment or tort. But if we're dealing with areas of controversy in society, I'm much more inclined – and I think more inclined than some of my colleagues – to stand back and leave it to the political branches of government to decide on the appropriate policy.

It was a frank and revealing comment from a lawyer who was destined to become the UK's most senior judge.

5

The Right to Death

In the last chapter we looked at how the courts have dealt with questions of personal status. These are important to those involved, but not as important as the issues I am about to discuss. It is no exaggeration to say that people's lives depend on them.

Our starting point is that all of us have the right to choose how and when we may end our lives. In the summer of 1961 suicide ceased to be the crime of 'self-murder' in English law.[1] The European Court of Human Rights ruled subsequently that the right of an individual to decide how and when to end his or her life is an aspect of the right to respect for private life protected by article 8 of the European Convention on Human Rights.

Fortunately, suicide is not a choice most of us wish to take. Some will regard it as immoral. Those of us who are of sound mind should surely recognise that – however bad life may be – death by one's own hand is deeply painful to our family, friends and even to those who never knew us. In most cases, of course, the time and nature of our death is decided by illness, accident or simply the passing of time. But, as we shall see later in this chapter, for some people the prospect of suicide is the only thing that makes life worth living.

The defence of necessity

Though suicide is not a crime, homicide certainly is. And yet the courts have sometimes been willing to condone homicide if they regard it as 'necessary'. When might that be?

In 1884 the defence of necessity to murder was rejected by the judges in the remarkable case of *R v Dudley and Stephens*,[2] celebrated a century later by Professor Brian Simpson in his unforgettably named book *Cannibalism and the Common Law*.[3] Thomas Dudley and Edward Stephens were shipwrecked sailors who had survived by killing and eating their cabin boy. Once rescued, the two sailors were convicted of murder and sentenced to death – although their sentences were later commuted to six months' imprisonment.

By the start of the new millennium, however, judicial attitudes had changed: in 2000 a hospital in Manchester was allowed to end the life of one conjoined twin in order to save the other.[4] Without medical intervention, both would have died. Lord Justice Ward saw it as a case of self-defence: doctors were 'removing the threat of fatal harm to [one twin] presented by [her sister] draining her lifeblood'. But the operation had been opposed by the children's parents, who were devout Roman Catholics.

Advances in medical science have posed new dilemmas. In 1993 the courts were confronted with the case of Tony Bland – a young man whose injuries in the Hillsborough stadium disaster of 1989 had left him in what was then described as a persistent vegetative state. Bland's father could see no point in continuing his life support, adding that his son 'wouldn't want to be left like he is'. The courts decided that doctors would not violate the sanctity of life by withdrawing invasive medical treatment and care, to which Bland had not consented and which conferred no benefit upon him.[5]

At that time, life-sustaining care for patients who would otherwise have died was relatively new. The courts struggled to find a principled justification for what they saw as a pragmatic outcome. As the Supreme Court noted 25 years later, 'it was not a foregone conclusion that the withdrawal of artificial life support measures could be tolerated at all by the criminal and civil law'.[6]

Since then, more cases have come to court. Withdrawal of life support used to be approved by the Court of Protection on a case-by-case basis. In July 2018 the Supreme Court ruled that a court order would no longer be needed before clinically assisted nutrition and hydration was withdrawn from a patient suffering from what is now described as a 'prolonged disorder of consciousness'. But the provisions of the Mental Capacity Act 2005 must be followed, the relevant guidance must be observed and there must also be agreement on the best interests of the patient.[7]

That case involved an unnamed financial analyst working for an investment bank in London. Though he worked long hours in a stressful environment, he had a healthy diet, regular health checks and exercised at a gym. In June 2017, at the age of 52, he had a heart attack and for more than ten minutes could not be resuscitated. During that time, lack of oxygen caused extensive damage to his brain. His family agreed with doctors that it would be in his best interests for food and water to be withdrawn, as a result of which he would die within two or three weeks. A High Court judge ruled in November 2017 that a court order would not be needed for this to be done. Nutrition and hydration were maintained, pending an appeal by the official solicitor – who looks after the interests of those who cannot look after themselves – but the patient died of an infection before the case could be heard by the Supreme Court.

Tony Nicklinson

Although Bland's case and the application to separate the conjoined twins raised profound ethical concerns, there was no attempt by the government to change the law as interpreted by senior judges. Ministers must have been relieved that decisions such as these had been taken out of their hands. As Lord Neuberger noted in 2014, 'the courts have been ready both to assume responsibility for developing the law on what are literally life and death issues, and then to shoulder responsibility for implementing the law as so developed … Despite pleas from judges, parliament has not sought to resolve these questions through statutes but has been content to leave them to be worked out by the courts.'[8]

Neuberger, as president of the Supreme Court, was giving judgment in an appeal brought on behalf of Tony Nicklinson, a man who remained paralysed for seven years after suffering a catastrophic stroke when he was 51. Communicating via an eye-blink computer, Nicklinson said his life was 'dull, miserable, demeaning, undignified and intolerable'. He wanted to end it at a time of his own choosing but had no way of achieving this other than by self-starvation. His preference was for someone to kill him by injecting him with a lethal drug – in effect, euthanasia. If that was unlawful, he wanted access to a machine that would be designed to deliver the drug to him when he activated it. But section 2 of the Suicide Act 1961 says that anyone intentionally encouraging or assisting a suicide faces up to 14 years in prison.

Nicklinson had previously asked three judges in the High Court to declare that it would be lawful for a doctor to kill him or to help him kill himself. Failing that, he sought a declaration that the current law was incompatible with the European Convention on Human Rights. But both those arguments were dismissed by a divisional court. The judges ruled that altering the common law so as to create a defence to murder in the case of voluntary euthanasia would introduce a major change in an area where there were strongly held conflicting views, where parliament had rejected attempts to introduce such a change and where the result would create uncertainty.

That ruling was delivered in August 2012.[9] As soon as he heard that his claim had failed, Nicklinson began refusing all nutrition, fluids and medical treatment. He died of pneumonia later that month.

Nicklinson's widow wanted to challenge the High Court decision. She was allowed to become a party to the proceedings but her appeal was dismissed in 2013.[10] The Court of Appeal judges agreed that it was for parliament to decide whether to create a defence of necessity in cases of murder. Any defence provided to those who assisted someone to die would have to apply not merely to euthanasia but also to assisted suicide, which remains a serious criminal offence. Although suicide is no longer a crime, the court explained, that meant only that people who tried to kill themselves would not face prosecution. Since there was no right to kill yourself, there could be no right to require the state to let others kill you or assist you to die.

What about the human rights issues? According to the Court of Appeal, a blanket legal ban on providing assistance to those wishing to die was not a disproportionate interference with the right to private life under article 8 of the European Convention on Human Rights.

Lord Dyson was one of the judges in the Court of Appeal. Writing six years after the judgment,[11] he said that the court had held 'that the time had not come for the common law to be developed to recognise a defence of necessity to murder in certain cases of euthanasia, such as where a doctor gave effect to the settled wish of a competent person to end his life'. Note the careful phrasing: Dyson could conceive of a judge-made law at some future time permitting doctors to kill their patients.

'My view as a private citizen is that assisted suicide should be permitted, subject to stringent safeguards,' Dyson wrote in his memoirs. 'But that did not influence my conclusion that, as a matter of law, decriminalising assisted suicide was not a matter for the judges.'

The Supreme Court rules

As I say, the Supreme Court ruled on Nicklinson's final appeal – together with two others – in 2014. By then, the main question before the court was whether the ban on assisted suicide in section 2 of the Suicide Act 1961 – as amended by parliament in 2009 – was incompatible with article 8 of the European Convention on Human Rights: respect for a person's private life. If the justices found that it was, they would have to decide whether or not to make a declaration of incompatibility.

As we saw in Chapter 4, that would not change the law: it would merely send a message to parliament that the law needed to be changed. And a declaration was the most that Nicklinson's supporters could have hoped for: nobody suggested that the courts could 'read down' section 2 of the Suicide Act under section 3(1) of the Human Rights Act and create a defence of necessity to murder.

Neuberger gave the first judgment, reviewing past cases and noting that the possibility of relaxing the statutory prohibition on assisting suicide had been debated by MPs or peers at least six times in the past nine years. Parliament had approved the general prohibition on assisting suicide some five years earlier, when it redrafted – rather than abolished – section 2 of the 1961 Act.

That was seen as supporting the government's argument that reforming the law on an issue as difficult, sensitive and controversial as assisted suicide was best left to parliament. But, as Neuberger explained, the fact that the law had been changed recently would not prevent the courts from ruling that it was in breach of the European Convention on Human Rights. 'Difficult or unpopular decisions which need to be taken are, on some occasions, more easily grasped by judges than by the legislature,' he said. 'Although judges are not directly accountable to the electorate, there are occasions when their relative freedom from pressures of the moment enables them to take a more detached view.'

All this led its president to conclude that, if it chose to, the Supreme Court could declare the Suicide Act incompatible with article 8 of the European Convention on Human Rights. As it was recognised that the court might overturn its earlier decisions, nine judges had sat instead of the normal five. Four of them agreed with Neuberger, meaning that the majority regarded a declaration of incompatibility as possible in this case. However, only two of those – Lady Hale and Lord Kerr – would have gone further and made the declaration. So they were in the minority.

Neuberger, by contrast, did not think that it would be appropriate to make a declaration before Parliament had been given the opportunity to consider whether to change the law. This was unusual: courts normally decide cases on the law as it is, not as it might become. But Neuberger offered four reasons:

> First, the question whether the provisions of section 2 [of the Suicide Act 1961] should be modified raises a difficult, controversial and sensitive issue, with moral and religious dimensions, which undoubtedly justifies a relatively cautious approach from the courts.
>
> Secondly, this is not a case ... where the incompatibility is simple to identify and simple to cure: whether, and if so how, to amend section 2 would require much anxious consideration from the legislature; this also suggests that the courts should, as it were, take matters relatively slowly.
>
> Thirdly, section 2 has, as mentioned above, been considered on a number of occasions in parliament, and it is currently due to be debated in the House of Lords in the near future; so this is a case where the legislature is and has been actively considering the issue.
>
> Fourthly, less than thirteen years ago, the House of Lords in *Pretty v DPP*[12] gave parliament to understand that a declaration of incompatibility in relation to section 2 would be inappropriate, a view reinforced by the conclusions reached by the divisional court and the Court of Appeal in this case: a declaration

of incompatibility on this appeal would represent an unheralded *volte-face*.[13]

Hale explained later why she disagreed. 'Some of us see no constitutional reason not to exercise the power which parliament has given us,' she said. 'It is always for government and parliament to decide what, if anything, to do about it.'[14]

The four justices who did not think a declaration of incompatibility was even possible in this case believed that parliament was inherently better qualified than the courts to assess the issues it raised. Lord Sumption said the prohibition on assisted suicide involved a choice between 'two fundamental but mutually inconsistent moral values upon which there is at present no consensus in our society'. The choice was bound to be influenced by a decision maker's personal opinions. 'This is entirely appropriate if the decision-makers are those who represent the community at large. It is not appropriate for professional judges. The imposition of their personal opinions on matters of this kind would lack all constitutional legitimacy.'[15]

What we see here is the most senior judges in the UK struggling with the issues at the heart of this book. Lord Wilson said he and his fellow justices had spent six months deliberating on the Nicklinson case and related appeals 'with an intensity unique in my experience'.

The courts could have provided a remedy for people like Tony Nicklinson. But the effect on others would be controversial. There are moral objections to euthanasia: it fails to respect the sanctity or supremacy of human life. There are also pragmatic objections: the elderly might be made to feel they were a burden on their families or on society as a whole. So the courts hold back. But governments find these issues far too difficult, even in normal political times, because any reforms are bound to be criticised by one side or the other.

What the judges tend not to spell out is that changing the law is not, for them, a risk-free process. Nobody suggests that they would lose their jobs if they got it wrong. But an out-of-touch decision can – and sometimes does – damage public confidence in the judiciary. If the public really believe that judges are enemies of the people, democracy itself will come under threat.

The law should be broken

The request by Nicklinson's family for a declaration of incompatibility was dismissed by a majority of seven to two. But, while allowing MPs and peers time to consider whether the law should be changed, Neuberger said that if the issue was not satisfactorily addressed there was 'a real prospect that a further, and successful, application for a declaration of incompatibility may be made'.

Was that a threat? Or merely a prediction? This was how Lord Sumption referred to it in his 2019 Reith lectures:

> Over the years, parliament has considered proposals to change the law but has always decided against it. Yet five of the nine judges who sat on this appeal thought that the question was ultimately one for the courts. Two of the five would have declared the Suicide Act to be incompatible with the convention. The other three decided not to do that, but only because it would be premature until after parliament had had an opportunity to consider the matter. One of the three even threatened that, unless this was satisfactorily addressed, the courts might do it for them. If this threat meant anything, it meant that the courts should be prepared to exercise legislative powers in place of the legislature. I am not alone in questioning the constitutional propriety of all this.[16]

This is surely disingenuous. The most that the five justices of the Supreme Court felt they could do was to make a declaration of incompatibility – and three of those five decided that they should not even do that. Neuberger had been predicting that such a declaration might be made in the future. But that would not be the court exercising legislative powers, as Sumption put it. It would merely be sending a message to parliament.

At the end of his first Reith lecture Sumption took questions from the audience. One came from Ann Whaley, a woman who had been questioned under caution by Thames Valley police before she helped her terminally ill husband, Geoff, travel to the Dignitas facility in Switzerland, where he died in February 2019.[17] She thought that the law should permit assisted suicide.

Sumption told her that he did not support changing the law on assisted suicide. But people did not always need to obey that law. 'I think that the law should continue to criminalise assistance in suicide,' he said, 'and I think that the law should be broken … from time to time.'

He went on:

> We need to have a law against [assisted suicide] in order to prevent abuse. But it has always been the case … that courageous relatives and friends have helped people to die. And I think that that is an untidy compromise, of the sort that I suspect very few lawyers would adopt. But I don't think there is necessarily a moral obligation to obey the law. And, ultimately, it is something that each person has to decide within his own conscience.[18]

It was extraordinary to hear a former Supreme Court justice arguing that the law should be broken. Intentionally encouraging the commission of a crime is itself a criminal offence.[19] Of course, there was no chance that Sumption would be charged with encouraging assisted suicide: he was speaking generally rather than encouraging the commission of a particular offence. And a prosecution would not be in the public interest – just as it had not been in the public interest to prosecute the woman who had asked him the question. But, as Sir Stephen Sedley wrote, 'to meet the injustice a bad law may generate by absolving people of a moral obligation to obey it is a remarkable stance for anyone, let alone a judge, to take'.[20]

In any case, the main reason why this issue has been before the courts in recent years is that 'courageous relatives and friends' did not want to face even the possibility of prosecution. It is all very well for Sumption to imply that charges of assisting in suicide will be used only against those who act abusively – for example, by encouraging the suicide of people who are not terminally ill. But the way to deal with a bad law is not to break it; it is to change it. And that must be a decision for parliament.

Noel Conway

In the Nicklinson case Lord Neuberger had said that there was a real prospect of a further challenge if the issue of assisted suicide was not addressed by parliament. He was speaking in 2014 and it did not take long for another case to come along. But, again, the judges disagreed on whether it was a matter for them or for parliament.

Noel Conway was diagnosed with motor neurone disease in 2014 at the age of 65. The neurological illness is degenerative and terminal, attacking the nerve cells responsible for controlling voluntary muscle movement so that the muscles gradually weaken and waste away.

Nobody knew how long Conway would have to live, but he expected to be told, at some point, that it would be less than six months. At that point, while he still had the capacity to make the decision, he wanted to be given medical help so that he could end his own life before he became, as he put it, 'entombed in my own body'.

There were significant factual differences between the Nicklinson case and the Conway case. Nicklinson was not terminally ill. He could continue living in his paralysed state. Or he could end his life by refusing nutrition, hydration and treatment – as he eventually did. But this was slow, painful and distressing. The Supreme Court had been sceptical about the possibility of a suicide machine operated by an eye-blink. What Nicklinson had been seeking was, in reality, euthanasia.

By contrast, Conway was indeed terminally ill. He was being kept alive by 'non-invasive ventilation' – in other words, an oxygen mask. By the summer of 2018 he needed this for 23 hours a day. The law permitted him to ask for that ventilation to be removed at any time. That would lead to his death, probably within hours. There was evidence that medication could be given to ensure that he was not aware of the ventilation being withdrawn and to manage breathlessness, discomfort and distress.

But Conway did not regard that as a dignified death. He feared the drowning sensation he had already experienced when his ventilation was temporarily withdrawn. Conway wanted assistance from a medical professional so that he could ingest medication that would end his life. If he could no longer drink, he wanted to activate a switch. Alternative methods would be distressing for his loved ones, he said.

Unlike Nicklinson, Conway's lawyers said he was not arguing for euthanasia: this would merely be assisted suicide – accelerating a death that was imminent. But, again, section 2 of the Suicide Act 1961 stood in his way. So, like Nicklinson, he relied on article 8 of the European Convention on Human Rights.

Conway's lawyers applied for permission to seek judicial review and, in view of its importance, the application was heard in March 2017 by a three-judge divisional court. Lord Justice Burnett summed up Conway's argument:

> The inflexible nature of section 2(1) of the 1961 Act, which admits of no carefully crafted and policed exceptions to criminality for those who assist suicide, is a disproportionate interference with the article 8 rights of someone who wishes to end his life but is unable to do so without assistance. The essential question in this application is whether the circumstances which led the Supreme Court to refuse to grant the declaration [of incompatibility] in June 2014 have changed so that a different outcome could be possible today.[21]

Burnett, who was promoted to lord chief justice some months later, refused Conway permission to seek judicial review. His reason was that both houses of parliament had debated reforms to the Suicide Act since the Nicklinson judgment and had decided not to change the law. Parliament had done precisely what the Supreme Court had suggested was necessary. It was, Burnett added, 'institutionally inappropriate for a court to make a declaration of incompatibility, whatever our personal views of how the underlying policy issues should be resolved'. Mr Justice Jay agreed; and so permission was refused.

But there was also a dissenting judgment from Mr Justice Charles. He thought it would have been right to grant Conway permission, since the majority in Nicklinson's case had thought an application might be appropriate in the future. And Charles's dissent was upheld by the Court of Appeal a month later. Two senior judges said that, because the issue was no longer under active consideration in parliament, 'Conway should be entitled to argue that it is no longer institutionally inappropriate for the court to consider whether to make a declaration of incompatibility, whilst giving due weight to parliament's recent decision'.[22]

So the case went back to the High Court for a substantive hearing. It came before a new divisional court of three judges headed by Lord Justice Sales.

At issue was the interpretation of the European Convention on Human Rights. The government's counsel accepted that that the prohibition against assisting suicide in section 2 of the Suicide Act was an interference with the right to respect for a person's private life contained in article 8(1) of the convention. Indeed, the European Court of Human Rights had previously decided that the right of an individual to decide how and when to end his or her life was an aspect of the right to life. But, said the government, this interference with Conway's rights under article 8(1) was justified by the exceptions in article 8(2). The ban on assisted suicide was 'necessary in a democratic society' as a proportionate measure 'for the protection of health', 'for the protection of morals' and 'for the protection of the rights of others'. It therefore followed, the government argued, that section 2 was compatible with article 8.[23]

In October 2017 the High Court agreed with the government and refused to grant the declaration of incompatibility that Conway had been seeking. Section 2 of the Suicide Act was necessary to protect the weak and vulnerable, the court said. It also promoted trust between patients and doctors. And the government was entitled to rely on the sanctity of life as a moral issue, even though the court said it was not deciding the case on this ground.

Above all, and following Lord Sumption's judgment in the *Nicklinson* case, the High Court said that the parliamentary process was a better way of resolving issues involving controversial and complex questions of fact arising out of moral and social dilemmas:

> Parliament has considered the matter with the benefit of the judgments of the Supreme Court in *Nicklinson* and has decided to maintain section 2 in place, after taking all relevant countervailing arguments into account. In those circumstances, we consider that there are powerful constitutional reasons why parliament's assessment of

the necessity of maintaining section 2 in place should be respected by this court.[24]

Conway appeals

The High Court turned down Conway's application for permission to appeal. That's unusual in an important case such as this but it shows that the court thought Conway's chances of success were slim. However, he was subsequently granted permission to appeal by two appeal judges.[25]

In the Court of Appeal Conway's lawyers argued that the court was at least as well-placed as parliament to decide whether the blanket ban on assisted suicide in section 2 of the Suicide Act was necessary and proportionate. Conway was not advocating a free-for-all. He had put forward a number of safeguards designed to ensure assisted suicide would be available only for adults of sound mind with no more than six months left to live. By simply adopting the balance set by parliament, the High Court judges had effectively abdicated their constitutional responsibility under the Human Rights Act to make the proportionality assessment for themselves.

The appeal was heard by three judges, including the master of the rolls, Sir Terence Etherton, and the president of the Queen's Bench division, Sir Brian Leveson. They gave judgment in June 2018.[26]

Their starting point was that section 2 of the Suicide Act interfered with our right to end our lives at a time of our own choosing. Under article 8(2) of the European Convention on Human Rights that interference could be justified only if it was necessary – in this case, for the protection of morals or for the protection of rights of others. It also needed to be proportionate, striking a fair balance between the rights of the individual and the interests of the community.

Permitting assisted suicide, the court said, would be 'a statement about the way in which, as a society, we draw the line between two important but, on this issue, competing values: the concept of the sanctity of life, reflected in article 2 of the convention, and the right to personal autonomy in choosing the time and manner of our death, protected by article 8'.

The judges then reviewed the difficulties of prognostication – predicting how long a patient will survive – and concerns among doctors at the effect a change would have on their relationships with patients. The court found a distinction between this case and those mentioned at the beginning of this chapter. The cases of Tony Bland and the conjoined twins were ones in which parliament had not intervened and was not proposing to intervene. In order to reach a decision in those cases the courts had no option but to tackle the difficult moral, ethical and social considerations involved. That was not the position here, the appeal judges said:

> There is no common-law right to assisted suicide and parliament has expressed a clear position, not only by the terms of the 1961 Act itself, but by subsequently and relatively recently rejecting legislation along the lines of Mr Conway's scheme. What is in issue is not the application of well-established principles to new facts but the possible legalisation of conduct that was criminal at common law and is now criminal as a matter of statute ...
>
> There can be no doubt that parliament is a far better body for determining the difficult policy issue in relation to assisted suicide in view of the conflicting, and highly contested, views within our society on the ethical and moral issues and the risks and potential consequences of a change in the law and the implementation of a scheme such as that proposed by Mr Conway.

As before, Conway's appeal was dismissed. The Court of Appeal also refused him permission to appeal to the Supreme Court. His last chance was to ask the Supreme Court itself for permission to appeal.

Conway's last hope

Normally, an application to the Supreme Court for permission to appeal is dealt with in writing and the court's reasons for granting or refusing permission are perfunctory. In Conway's case, three justices, led by Lady Hale, held an oral hearing to decide whether they should hear a full appeal at a later date. As she explained, 'whether this is the right case and the right time ... is the reason we asked for this hearing'.

Conway's solicitors briefed Lord Pannick QC to represent him at the permission hearing. If Pannick could not persuade the justices, nobody could. Too ill to attend court, Conway watched the proceedings online.[27]

Pannick told Hale and her fellow justices that the government needed to show a compelling justification if it wanted to stop an individual with full mental capacity securing assistance to end his or her life when that individual believed that remaining alive was incompatible with personal dignity.

Conway recognised the need to balance his interests against the need to protect the vulnerable. But those concerns could be met if a court decided, in each case, whether an individual's consent to assisted suicide was voluntary.

Parliament could devise the procedure to be followed. Parliament would also have to draw the line by deciding which cases should be covered by an exception to the Suicide Act. But, Pannick argued, it was unlawful for parliament to do nothing.

For the government, Sir James Eadie QC argued that the Court of Appeal had reached the right decision. He was closely questioned by Lord Kerr about his assertion that Conway could bring about his death swiftly and painlessly by refusing ventilation and accepting palliative care.

In the event, the panel of three justices decided in November 2018 that this was not, after all, the right case and the right time.[28] Conway's chances of success were simply too slim:

> Ultimately, the question for the panel is whether the prospects of Mr Conway's succeeding in his claim before this court are sufficient to justify our giving him permission to pursue it, with all that that would entail for him, for his family, for those on all sides of this multi-faceted debate, for the general public and for this court. Not without some reluctance, it has been concluded that in this case those prospects are not sufficient to justify giving permission to appeal.

Note the clumsy phrase 'it has been concluded' instead of the more natural 'we have concluded'. The panel was clearly split. As the court said, it had been asked three questions: whether the 'adamantine' – or hard-and-fast – rule banning assisted suicide was a justified interference with human rights; if so, whether the court should make a declaration to that effect; and, in particular, whether a declaration was appropriate in this case. 'These are questions upon which the considered opinions of conscientious judges may legitimately differ,' the court said. 'Indeed, they differ amongst the members of this panel.'

We may infer that one of the three justices would have given permission to appeal. Since Hale and Kerr would both have made a declaration of incompatibility in the Nicklinson case, the dissenter is likely to have been one of them. Given the concerns he expressed in argument, my money is on Kerr. But if it had been two–one the other way and permission had been granted, I am still not sure that Conway would have won the declaration of incompatibility he sought. And even if he had, changing the law would still have been a matter for parliament.

Speaking a week or so after the judgment, Conway told the BBC that he was 'bitterly disappointed, bewildered, and felt cheated'. He complained of a 'medieval mindset which overrides more modern ways of thinking, like the Human Rights Act'.

But he was not yet ready to remove his ventilator. He was too busy finishing a memoir – using voice recognition software because he had no movement below the neck.

Conway did not know how long he would survive without his ventilator. 'If it's removed, I should have only a few minutes to live, but it could be hours or even days.' He acknowledged that he would receive pain relief but believed that it would leave him in a semi-conscious state and deny him a dignified death: 'It would be terrible for my wife and family, not knowing whether I could hear them or how long it would take before I expired.'

Somebody in that position deserves our deepest sympathy. But allowing him to die at a time of his own choosing does not need a change in the law. He simply needed to tell his carers to remove (or not replace) his oxygen mask. They would inevitably have administered palliative care and, despite his fears, there was no reason to suppose his death would be undignified. He would simply fall asleep and not wake up.

Noel Conway regarded suffocation under sedation as 'unacceptable'. But the availability of that option – at least in theory – explains why this was not a suitable case for the Supreme Court.

Philippe Newby

Specialist lawyers acknowledged that Conway had 'available to him a lawful means of ending his own life that would involve a relatively minimal degree of suffering' and that this had been a relevant factor in the courts' decision to refuse a declaration of incompatibility.[29] The next claimant to seek a declaration of incompatibility was a motor neurone disease sufferer whose disease was progressing much more slowly. But Philippe Newby was refused permission to bring judicial review proceedings in January 2020.

6

Discerning and Discriminating

We all oppose unlawful discrimination. None of us should be put at a disadvantage because of personal characteristics that cannot be changed. But this is a particularly difficult area of the law for the judges to develop. Courts may have to choose between two parties who may both be the victims of discrimination. Applying past judgments to current problems may be far from straightforward.

Wheelchair or pushchair?

If a bus has enough room for either a wheelchair or a pushchair, which should have priority? That was more or less what the Supreme Court was asked to decide in 2016. Let's see if you can come up with a better answer than the seven justices who gave judgment early in 2017.

The case was brought by Doug Paulley, who relies on a wheelchair for mobility. In 2012 he tried to board a bus from Wetherby to Leeds, only to find that the designated wheelchair space was occupied by a child sleeping in a buggy. The driver asked a woman accompanying the child to fold down the chair and move. She refused, insisting – somewhat implausibly – that her buggy would not fold.

Paulley offered to fold down his wheelchair and sit in an ordinary seat. But the driver said it would not be possible to secure his chair safely on the winding roads of West Yorkshire. Paulley waited 20 minutes for the next bus, missed his train at Leeds and arrived at his destination an hour late.

With the support of the Equality and Human Rights Commission, Paulley sued the bus operator, FirstGroup, for unlawful discrimination against him on the ground of his disability. The company's policy in 2012 was to ask other passengers to move if they were preventing a wheelchair user from occupying the dedicated area opposite the exit doors. But wheelchairs did not have priority over buggies. That policy had changed by the time the case came to court and wheelchairs were said to have priority. But the effectiveness of this policy depended on the goodwill of passengers: the driver had no power to compel anyone to move.

Under the Equality Act 2010, a service provider must not discriminate against a customer on the grounds of a protected characteristic, such as disability. In addition, the provider must make reasonable adjustments if a provision, criterion or practice[1] puts a disabled person at a substantial disadvantage.[2]

Paul Isaacs, a part-time judge sitting at Leeds County Court, found that there were reasonable adjustments that FirstGroup could have made to its conditions of carriage, allowing the driver to order a non-disabled person to move out of the wheelchair space or, if necessary, to leave the bus. He found that the bus company had discriminated against Paulley and awarded him £5,500 damages.

FirstGroup successfully appealed.[3] Giving the leading judgment, Lord Justice Lewison said the case was not about whether other passengers should make room for a wheelchair user: of course they should, if possible. Nor was it about whether parents in the wheelchair space with a child in a folding buggy should fold their buggies in order to make way for a wheelchair user: of course they should, if possible.

What was at issue, said Lewison, was whether a bus company needed to have a policy requiring other passengers to vacate the wheelchair space if told to do so by the driver, regardless of why they were using it. That, the appeal judge concluded, was a step too far. A policy requiring other passengers to make room for wheelchair users – rather than merely requesting them to move – would be unfair as well as impractical. One could imagine circumstances in which others might have a better claim to the space (for example, a sick baby in a pram or a guide dog accompanying a blind passenger). But it would be unreasonable to expect the driver to judge between competing priorities.

Lady Justice Arden agreed that a bus company must take all reasonable steps, short of compelling passengers to move from the wheelchair space. Requiring passengers to move – or get off the bus if it was full – would require legislation.

Lord Justice Underhill accepted that the court's finding meant that wheelchair users would occasionally be prevented by other passengers from using the wheelchair space on a bus. 'I do not, however, believe that the fact that some passengers will – albeit rarely – act selfishly and irresponsibly is a sufficient reason for imposing on bus companies a legal responsibility for a situation which is not of their making and which they are not in a position to prevent.'

So, Paulley won in the county court. FirstGroup won in the Court of Appeal. It was now Paulley's turn to appeal to the Supreme Court. Would you have found in his favour and restored his damages?

A difficult balancing act

Doug Paulley had to wait six months for a judgment. When it finally arrived, it seemed to take him up hill and down dale.

Four of the seven justices allowed Paulley's appeal but decided he should not receive damages. The three remaining judges agreed that his appeal should be allowed and would also have restored his damages. So the court was unanimously on his side – but it decided, by a majority, that he should not receive any compensation.[4]

Lord Neuberger, who gave the first judgment in the Supreme Court, described the original decision made by the part-time judge in Leeds as a 'require and enforce' policy: non-wheelchair users would be required to vacate the wheelchair space and the driver could enforce this policy by ordering them off the bus. Such a decision, said Neuberger, was 'likely to involve confrontation at best and violence at worst'.

But there was another option, described as 'require and pressurise'. It was 'not enough', said the Supreme Court president, 'for FirstGroup to instruct its drivers simply to request non-wheelchair users to vacate the space and do nothing further if the request was rejected'. More needed to be done. 'In particular, where there is some other place on the bus to which a non-wheelchair user could move, I cannot see why a driver should not be expected to rephrase any polite request as a requirement, and, if that does not work and especially if the bus is ahead of schedule, why the driver should not be expected to consider whether there was any reason why the bus should not stop for a few minutes with a view to pressurising or shaming the recalcitrant non-wheelchair user to move.'

Not even the most senior judges in England and Wales have full-time official cars. Some may drive to court in London, but most use buses or trains and quite a few cycle. So Neuberger, like everyone else who travels by bus, was familiar with the driver who turns off the engine and refuses to budge until a recalcitrant passenger gives in to popular pressure. The Supreme Court president thought that a more pragmatic approach would produce positive results in cases where FirstGroup's 'more pallid' policy would not. But his convoluted language suggests that he felt uncomfortable telling drivers what to do.

Because the company's current policy did not go far enough, Neuberger agreed that the appeal should be allowed. But Paulley's lawyers had not argued for the 'require and pressurise' policy in the Court of Appeal – though it had been part of his original case in the county court. The judge at Leeds had not decided whether Paulley would still have been disadvantaged if that had been the company's policy. For that reason, thought Neuberger, it would not be fair for the Supreme Court to award him any damages.

Lord Toulson concurred, noting that the risk that a bus might be full when it arrived was one shared by all travellers. 'The risk may be greater for wheelchair users because there is likely to be only one wheelchair space, but if that space is occupied ... I do not see that it would be reasonable to require the occupier to leave the bus midway through their journey.'

Lord Sumption had misgivings about the Neuberger driver whose 'polite request' was rephrased as a requirement when, in reality, it was no such thing. But Sumption was still willing to stay on board. 'In a situation where there is no ideal solution but only more or less unsatisfactory ones,' he said, 'I think that the approach of Lord Neuberger and Lord Toulson comes as close to giving effect to the policy of this legislation as a court legitimately can.'

Sumption recognised that there were limits to what the law could achieve in dealing with lawful but inconsiderate behaviour. Like the other justices, he recognised the need for a pragmatic solution. But was this, as he suggested, the court doing its best to give effect to parliament's intention? Was it the sort of judicial law making that he opposed? Or was it an unprincipled compromise dreamed up by the judges to deal with a problem that ought not to arise very often?

More to the point, can we really justify the cost of three hearings before 11 judges just to establish that the law requires drivers to show common sense when faced with difficult customers? You would hope that most bus drivers do that already.

The Equality Act

As I mentioned, Doug Paulley brought his claim under the Equality Act 2010. This was not the first statute of its kind: anti-discrimination laws in England and Wales date back to the 1970s, when legislation was introduced to ensure equal pay for work of equal value. Discrimination on grounds of sex or race was also banned. Subsequent laws outlawed discrimination on grounds of disability, religion and sexual orientation. In 2010 these laws were consolidated into a single statute.[5]

The Equality Act 2010, which implements an EU equal treatment directive, begins by defining nine 'protected characteristics':

- age
- disability
- gender reassignment
- marriage and civil partnership
- pregnancy and maternity
- race
- religion or belief
- sex
- sexual orientation

The Equality Act 2010 then defines conduct that is prohibited in relation to these characteristics. We shall discuss just two of the types of conduct defined: direct and indirect discrimination.[6]

Direct discrimination

The law says that 'a person (A) discriminates against another (B) if, because of a protected characteristic, A treats B less favourably than A treats or would treat others'.[7] This is 'direct discrimination'.

The prohibition on direct discrimination aims to achieve formal equality of treatment; one person must not be treated less favourably than another because of a protected characteristic. Apart from age discrimination and discrimination arising from disability, direct discrimination can never be justified.

Indirect discrimination

The law also bans 'indirect discrimination'. This applies when an apparently neutral provision puts people who have a protected characteristic at a disadvantage compared with those who do not share that characteristic.[8]

The prohibition on indirect discrimination aims to achieve substantive equality. In the words of Lady Hale, it is 'an attempt to level the playing field by subjecting to scrutiny requirements which look neutral on their face but in reality work to the comparative disadvantage of people with a particular protected characteristic'.[9] It is subject to a defence of justification.

Indirect discrimination is easier to understand through a simple example. Imagine that an employer requires all staff to work night shifts and some weekends.

On the face of it, this is not discriminatory: it applies to all workers regardless of their protected characteristics. In reality, it puts women at a disadvantage. They are more likely than men to have child-care responsibilities that make shift-work impossible.

What the law says[10] is that 'a person (A) discriminates against another (B) if A applies to B a provision, criterion or practice which is discriminatory in relation to a relevant protected characteristic of B's'.

Let's apply this to our example. Person A is the employer. Person B is the female employee. The 'provision, criterion or practice' is the requirement that staff must work night shifts. And the protected characteristic is B's sex.

As the statute explains,[11] a provision, criterion or practice is discriminatory in relation to a relevant protected characteristic of B's if

> (a) A applies, or would apply, it to persons with whom
>   B does not share the characteristic,
> (b) it puts, or would put, persons with whom B shares
>   the characteristic at a particular disadvantage when

> compared with persons with whom B does not
> share it,
>
> (c) it puts, or would put, B at that disadvantage, and
>
> (d) A cannot show it to be a proportionate means of
> achieving a legitimate aim.

Person A, the employer, applies the shift-work requirement to men
– people who do not share B's protected characteristic. That puts
all women working for person A at a particular disadvantage when
compared with men. Person B herself suffers that disadvantage.

So it all depends on whether person A can show that putting all
staff on shift-work is objectively justified: to avoid discrimination,
person A must show that the shift-work provision is a proportionate
means of achieving a legitimate aim. In some circumstances, it
might be. In others, it will not be.

As we have seen, the Equality Act specifies nine protected
characteristics. There are other grounds on which people suffer
discrimination – because they are overweight, for example, or poor
– but these are not covered by the legislation.[12] It would have been
possible to make the list of protected characteristics open-ended.
That would have given the judges more scope to develop the law.
Parliament chose not to do so and the judges have respected that.
But the Human Rights Act 1998 gave judges the power – indeed,
a duty – to do something similar.

Article 14

Under the Human Rights Act,[13] courts in the UK must give
effect to legislation in a way that is compatible with the European
Convention on Human Rights. Article 14 of the convention says
that:

> The enjoyment of the rights and freedoms set forth in
> this convention shall be secured without discrimination
> on any ground such as sex, race, colour, language,
> religion, political or other opinion, national or social
> origin, association with a national minority, property,
> birth or other status.

Two things stand out. First, the examples listed are just that: the phrases 'any ground such as' and 'or other status' make it clear that the provision covers types of discrimination that are not listed. And, second, this is not a free-standing right. The only rights that must be secured without discrimination are those to be found elsewhere in the convention.

Let's consider an example. It comes from Northern Ireland, where discrimination law is slightly different from the law in England and Wales. But it relies on the Human Rights Act, which is in force throughout the UK.

Just a bit of paper?

Siobhan McLaughlin never married her partner John Adams during the 23 years that they lived together in Belfast. 'I naively thought that the longer you were together as a couple the more rights you had,' she told a reporter after he died in 2014. 'Our four children had their dad's name. To me it was just a ring and a bit of paper – the commitment was the same.'

But of course it was not, as McLaughlin discovered when she applied for a social security benefit called widowed parent's allowance.[14] Her claim was rejected by the Northern Ireland Department for Social Development because she was not a widow. The couple had not formalised their relationship because Adams had promised his first wife that he would never remarry. By the time McLaughlin became aware that she and Adams would cease to be regarded as a couple for social security purposes after his death, he was terminally ill and heavily medicated.

In 2016 a High Court judge in Belfast dismissed McLaughlin's argument that the word 'spouse' in primary legislation could be 'read down', under the Human Rights Act, to mean 'cohabitant'. That was not what parliament had intended, Mr Justice Treacy held, and McLaughlin was not entitled to a bereavement payment.[15]

But, as the judge noted, bereaved parents have to bring up their children whether or not they were married. He quashed the decision to refuse McLaughlin widowed parent's allowance, finding that the government had discriminated against her.

That decision was overturned by the Northern Ireland Court of Appeal later in 2016.[16] The government had argued that the current law promoted the institution of marriage and avoided arguments in individual cases about whether a couple were cohabiting. The appeal judges agreed: it was for parliament, not the courts, to decide what benefits unmarried partners should receive.

McLaughlin had one last chance and appealed to the Supreme Court in 2018. That court normally sits in Westminster but, as a sign that it serves the entire UK, it decided to hear McLaughlin's appeal – and one other – in Belfast.

Her argument before the Supreme Court was that she had been the victim of discrimination. Article 14 – which deals with discrimination – has been interpreted by the courts over the years. As we have seen, it is not a free-standing right. To decide whether it had been breached, the judges had to ask themselves four questions.[17]

1. Do the circumstances of this case fall within the ambit of another, substantive, convention right?
   There does not have to be a breach of that substantive right because otherwise there would be no need for article 14. But the breach has to be connected with one of the other rights. In this case, McLaughlin relied on article 8 (respect for private and family life) and article 1 of the first protocol to the convention (the right to peaceful enjoyment of one's possessions). Either would do.
2. Has there been a difference of treatment between two people who are in an analogous situation?
   McLaughlin argued that her status was analogous to that of a widow or the survivor of a civil partnership. But the government argued that Strasbourg case law was against her on this.
3. Was the person treated differently on one of the grounds listed in article 14 – which includes the person's 'other status'?
   That was an easy one to answer because the courts have previously said that being unmarried is a status.
4. Is there an objective justification for that difference in treatment?
   McLaughlin said there was not. But the government argued that the objective justification for treating unmarried people differently from those who were married or civil partners was to support the long-term stability of family relationships. There

were also administrative difficulties in establishing whether the deceased and the survivor were cohabiting.

The Supreme Court delivered its ruling in August 2018.[18] What do you think it said? Did it agree with the High Court judge in Belfast that McLaughlin had been the victim of discrimination? Or did it side with the Court of Appeal and respect the views of parliament?

I'll make it easier for you by telling you that the answers it gave to questions 1 and 3 were both 'yes': it was clear that the denial of a contributory social security benefit falls within the ambit of article 1 of the first protocol, and there was no doubt that McLaughlin had been treated differently because she was unmarried. So, all you have to decide is whether her situation was analogous to that of a widow and, if it was, whether you think there was an objective justification for treating her differently from a woman who had been married.

Paper matters

The Supreme Court was divided. To begin with, I shall tell you how Lady Hale answered question 2.

The High Court had found that the relevant 'facet of the relationship' between McLaughlin and her partner was not their public commitment but the co-raising of children. Hale agreed. Widowed parent's allowance was paid only if the survivor is responsible for the care of children who were, at the date of the deceased's death, the responsibility of one or both of them. So, she reasoned, its purpose must be to benefit the children.

It followed that McLaughlin was in an analogous position to that of a widow. Both had to bring up children on only one income. It made no difference to the children whether their mother had been married.

Lord Hodge disagreed. Even if the relevant facet of the relationship between the deceased and the survivor was raising children together, it did not follow that the widowed parent's allowance was there to benefit children. On the contrary, the money is no longer payable if the mother dies, retires, cohabits with a partner of either gender or remarries – regardless of whether the new partner accepts any responsibility for the children. What's more, he said, the sums payable are not related to the children's needs.

They depend on whether the deceased made sufficient National Insurance contributions.

What about question 4? For discrimination to be justified there has to be a 'legitimate aim' and, in relation to the difference in treatment, 'a reasonable relationship of proportionality' between the aim and the means.[19] The promotion of marriage and civil partnerships was indeed a legitimate aim. But unmarried cohabitants were generally treated as a couple for the purpose of means-tested benefits. In such cases, said Hale, it was hard to see why people and their children should be paid any less simply because the adults were not married to each other.

This case was about non-means-tested benefits. But was it a 'proportionate means of achieving the legitimate aim of privileging marriage' to deny McLaughlin and her children the benefit of Adams's contributions because they were not married to one another?

In Hale's view, the answer was manifestly 'no' – at least on the facts of this case:

> The allowance exists because of the responsibilities of the deceased and the survivor towards their children. Those responsibilities are the same whether or not they are married to or in a civil partnership with one another. The purpose of the allowance is to diminish the financial loss caused to families with children by the death of a parent. That loss is the same whether or not the parents are married to or in a civil partnership with one another.

Again, Hodge disagreed. Widowed parent's allowance was a survivor's benefit, he said, not one aimed at the children. They benefitted only indirectly from it. It could be terminated while the survivor was responsible for them. There might be 'good policy reasons for a benefit which is directed at bereaved children, as the Child Poverty Group submits and commentators in the press have argued when this appeal was heard'. But, said Hodge, 'such questions of social and economic policy fall within the remit of the democratically elected legislature and are beyond the remit of the courts'.

Hale thought there had been unjustified discrimination. Hodge thought it was not disproportionate to treat a surviving cohabitant differently from a surviving spouse or civil partner. Hale thought she was merely interpreting legislation. Hodge suggested that she was making new law, usurping the role of parliament. Which of them was right?

Before you make up your mind, let's look at some of the factors that may influence your decision. McLaughlin had already lost her partner to cancer. He had paid his National Insurance contributions in good faith. Should she really have to work all hours just to feed her children?

On the other hand, who do you think should decide on eligibility for social security payments? A democratically elected parliament led by a government accountable to the voters? Or unelected and unaccountable judges?

Perhaps you have strong views about marriage, on one side or the other. These may not be faith based, but you may think that society is right to privilege marriage and civil partnership because they tend to strengthen society. Or maybe you think that a voluntary relationship that was ended only by death after nearly a quarter of a century was stronger than many marriages.

Perhaps you think that living together *should* have the same legal consequences as marriage, despite the difficulty in establishing whether or not a couple are cohabiting. And that if parliament has not quite got round to saying this, it needs a nudge from the courts.

Or possibly you think that McLaughlin's partner behaved unreasonably in not marrying her, even after his former wife had died. Perhaps you thought she herself had behaved unreasonably in telling herself that, as a matter of law, cohabitation was the same as marriage. Surely everyone knows by now that 'common-law marriage' is a myth – however long you live together. Or maybe you think that this misapprehension is so widespread that the judges ought to bring the law into line with popular belief.

Whatever your view, you can see that two different judges – faced with the same legal arguments at the same time on the same case – disagreed on whether there had been a breach of the European Convention on Human Rights. Why might they have reached different conclusions in interpreting what seems to be a pretty straightforward provision? Because one of them was a woman?

Because the other had practised and then sat in the courts of Scotland? Because one was regarded as more activist and the other more conservative? Or because passing judgment is not an exact science and the cases that reach the Supreme Court are inevitably the most difficult?

The point was well made by Justice Robert H. Jackson, sitting in the US Supreme Court in 1953:

> Whenever decisions of one court are reviewed by another, a percentage of them are reversed. That reflects a difference in outlook normally found between personnel comprising different courts. However, reversal by a higher court is not proof that justice is thereby better done. There is no doubt that, if there were a super-Supreme Court, a substantial proportion of our reversals of state courts would also be reversed. We are not final because we are infallible, but we are infallible only because we are final.[20]

On that test, Hale was final and therefore infallible: she was supported by the three other justices who heard the appeal, Lord Mance, Lord Kerr and Lady Black.

So McLaughlin's appeal was allowed by a majority of four to one. The Supreme Court declared that section 39A of the Social Security Contributions and Benefits (Northern Ireland) Act 1992 was incompatible with article 14 of the European Convention on Human Rights, read with both article 8 and article 1 of protocol 1, to the extent that it precluded any entitlement to widowed parent's allowance by a surviving unmarried partner of a deceased person.

It used to be unusual for serving judges to talk about cases they have decided. It was even more unusual for judges to disclose personal circumstances that may have affected their approach. But Hale did just that in a subsequent lecture:[21]

> This [case] was about widowed parents' allowance – now superseded but at the relevant time a national insurance benefit for a surviving spouse left with dependent children. It was meant to compensate for the loss of a breadwinner. So it depended upon the national

insurance contribution record of the deceased. And it was not means-tested so it was particularly valuable if the survivor was in work and not in receipt of means-tested benefits. (My own mother, for example, benefitted from its predecessor, widowed mothers' allowance, when my father died while my sister and I were children and she went back to work as a teacher.) But it was limited to married couples.

If it is seen as for the benefit of the survivor, then that might be justified. Couples who are married (or in a civil partnership) have mutual obligations of support. So it is reasonable for the contributions of one to go to compensate for the loss of support to the other. Couples who are not married or in a civil partnership do not have that obligation.

But if it is seen as a benefit for the children, the position is quite different. Children should not suffer because their parents are not married to one another. Indeed 'very weighty reasons' are required for drawing distinctions between them.

So where – as in this case – the children involved were the children of the deceased and the survivor, it was not justifiable to distinguish between them. It might be different if the connection between the children and the deceased was looser but that was not this case. As the rules were in primary legislation, we made a declaration of incompatibility.

If the rules had been made by a minister as secondary legislation, Hale implied, the court might have found that the minister had acted unreasonably. In that event, judicial review might have been granted and the minister would have been told to think again.

But, unless it was possible to 'read down' the legislation under section 3 of the Human Rights Act 1998, the most the court could do was to declare, under section 4 of the Act, that it was incompatible with the European Convention on Human Rights.

I explained in Chapter 4 that this puts ministers under pressure to seek legislative changes. The government accepted that these would be needed across the UK. But there seemed to be little sense of urgency.

'We recognise that we have incompatible law on the statute book,' a minister at the Department of Work and Pensions told MPs in July 2019.[22] 'I want to make a decision as quickly as possible but, because of the complexity, every time I think I am looking at a potential solution, there are more unintended consequences of that that then lead to more issues.'

More than a year after winning her declaration of incompatibility, Siobhan McLaughlin had not received the money that by rights was hers. Neither had any other surviving cohabitants.

7

Rites and Rights

In Chapter 6 we discussed discrimination. It is unlawful to discriminate against people on the grounds of their religious beliefs, just as it is unlawful to discriminate against people on many other grounds. In a predominantly secular society, though, the courts have found it particularly difficult to decide what weight should be given to an individual's religious beliefs when these clash with the rights of others.

In 2019, for example, the Court of Appeal was asked to consider the lawfulness of a public spaces protection order that prevented a prayer vigil being held outside an abortion clinic in west London. Counsel for two women challenging the order said, somewhat extravagantly, that as far as they knew this was 'the first time since the reign of Elizabeth I that any kind of public prayer has been subject to potential criminal sanction in English law'. Their appeal was dismissed: the court concluded that, in creating an exclusion zone, the local authority had struck a fair balance between their rights as protestors and the rights of women using the clinic.[1]

The gay cake case

Graham Lee is a gay man who volunteered with QueerSpace, an LGBT self-help organisation that supported the campaign to legalise same-sex marriage in Northern Ireland. Invited by QueerSpace to a reception in 2014, he decided to bring a specially made cake.

Ashers Baking Company runs a bakery with six shops in Northern Ireland. It had a machine that can scan an image and print a copy of it, in edible ink, onto the icing of a cake.

Although Lee had previously visited the company's shop in Belfast, staff at Ashers had no knowledge of his sexual orientation. Equally, he had no idea that the bakery was owned by a Christian family, the McArthurs. Not many people would have picked up the biblical reference to one of Jacob's 12 sons: Asher's blessing was to produce rich bread and delicacies fit for a king.[2]

In May 2014 Lee walked into the shop and ordered a cake, to be decorated with artwork which he provided. This showed a picture of Bert and Ernie, two puppets from the children's show *Sesame Street* who are described by the producers as 'best friends'. It also included the slogan 'Support Gay Marriage'.

Karen McArthur, who served him, raised no objection to Lee's request at the time – partly to avoid embarrassment. But the McArthur family then decided that they could not, in all conscience, produce a cake with a message that conflicted with their religious beliefs. In their view, the only form of marriage consistent with the Bible and acceptable to God was marriage between a man and a woman. They apologised to Lee, refunded his £34 and returned the image. Another bakery made the cake that he wanted in time for the reception.

You might have expected matters to end there. But Northern Ireland, a country that for centuries has been deeply divided on religious and sectarian lines, has a publicly funded Equality Commission whose responsibilities include advising victims of discrimination. Lee felt that he had been discriminated against on the grounds of his sexuality. He sought advice from the commission, which supported his complaint to Ashers.

The McArthur family also felt that they had been left with no alternative. They might have expected help from the Equality Commission too. Instead, they found support from the Christian Institute, a non-denominational charity that, in its own words, is committed to upholding the truths of the Bible. And so one of the most fascinating social conflicts of recent times headed inexorably towards the courts.

Both sides believed that they were in the right, and attempts at compromise proved unsuccessful. But what became known as the 'gay cake case' was treated in a dignified, principled way by all concerned. Lee and Ashers both declined media interviews, limiting their public comments to formal statements made outside court.

Moreover, neither side questioned the other's good faith. Ashers were happy to serve – and employ – gay people. Dr Michael Wardlow, the chief equality commissioner, who supported Lee's complaint, is himself a committed Christian with degrees in theology.

Anti-discrimination law

I summarised the anti-discrimination law of England and Wales in the previous chapter. Although the principles are similar in Northern Ireland, there are some legislative differences. Discrimination in the provision of goods, facilities or services on grounds of sexual orientation is prohibited by what are called the Sexual Orientation Regulations.[3] And there is also a Fair Employment and Treatment Order,[4] which bans discrimination on grounds of political opinion, as well as religious belief.

Lee went to the county court in Northern Ireland and claimed that Ashers had directly discriminated against him on all three grounds. In May 2015 Presiding District Judge Brownlie agreed, and awarded him damages of £500.[5]

The bakery had denied discrimination. Ashers told the judge that they would have been happy to produce a cake for Lee without his chosen graphics – just as they would have refused to sell a cake supporting gay marriage to a heterosexual customer.

The judge did not find otherwise, but she regarded these as false comparisons. As she saw it, Lee had received less favourable treatment than a straight person who ordered a cake supporting opposite-sex marriage. Brownlie applied similar reasoning in deciding that Ashers had discriminated against Lee on political or religious grounds, given that his cake was calling for reforms – opposed by some Christians – to marriage law in Northern Ireland.

The bakery decided to appeal, opting for a curious procedure in which the trial judge was required to put a series of questions to the Northern Ireland Court of Appeal.[6] One of these asked whether Brownlie had been correct, as a matter of law, to conclude that Ashers had directly discriminated against Lee on the grounds of his sexual orientation. The answer to that, said the appeal judges, was 'yes'. For that reason, there was no need to decide whether the judge had been right in holding that the bakery had directly discriminated against their customer on the grounds of his religious belief or political opinions.[7]

So, Ashers lost again. In appeals brought under this procedure in Northern Ireland, the Court of Appeal decision is normally final. But, for reasons that need not trouble us, the UK Supreme Court decided that it could consider the bakery's appeal against all aspects of the Court of Appeal's judgment. It was as if the case was being argued afresh.

Before I tell you how the Supreme Court ruled in 2018, think what you would have decided. This was a case about members of two minority communities whose interests appear to conflict. Gay people had suffered from a great deal of discrimination in the past. This was particularly so in Northern Ireland, where homosexual acts were not decriminalised until 1985 and where the introduction of gay marriage – celebrated in other parts of the UK – had been opposed by political leaders. On the other hand, people whose lives are governed by their faith have long played an active part in the commercial life of Northern Ireland and, as the Court of Appeal said, it is important that there should be no 'chill factor' to their future participation.

Remember, the Supreme Court justices were not being asked which community had a better claim to their sympathy. The question to be decided, as they put it, was 'whether it is unlawful discrimination, either on grounds of sexual orientation or on grounds of religious belief or political opinion, for a bakery to refuse to supply a cake iced with the message "support gay marriage" because of the sincere religious belief of its owners that gay marriage is inconsistent with biblical teaching and therefore unacceptable to God'. What would you say?

The Supreme Court decides

The Supreme Court decision came as something as a surprise – even, I think, to those who had prayed for it. At its heart was a simple but profound point: you don't have to be gay to welcome same-sex marriage.[8] As the court put it, 'people of all sexual orientations, gay, straight or bi-sexual, can and do support gay marriage. Support for gay marriage is not a proxy for any particular sexual orientation.'[9]

The mistake made by the courts in Northern Ireland had been to assume that Ashers acted as they did because of Lee's perceived sexual orientation. But the bakery's objection had been to the message, not the messenger. Lady Hale explained this very clearly in a summary of the judgment that she read out in court:[10]

> As to Mr Lee's claim based on sexual orientation discrimination, the bakers did not refuse to fulfil his order because of his sexual orientation. They would have refused to make such a cake for any customer, irrespective of their sexual orientation. Their objection was to the message on the cake and not to the personal characteristics of Mr Lee, or of anyone else with whom he was associated. The message on the cake would not just be for the benefit of gay people, but also for the benefit of their families and friends and anyone else who recognises the social benefits which the commitment involved in gay marriage can bring. Accordingly, this court holds that there was no discrimination on the ground of the sexual orientation of Mr Lee or anyone else with whom he was associated.

It was clear from her remarks that Hale was associating herself with those who recognise the wider social benefits of gay marriage. That would be entirely consistent with her known views. There is nothing in the earlier judgments to suggest that the Northern Ireland judges shared those opinions – even though, unlike the Supreme Court, they found in Lee's favour. It was certainly not the view of the Northern Ireland Assembly when it voted against marriage reform in 2015.

Hale might have allowed the bakery's appeal simply because she accepted that Lee's sexual orientation was not the reason for its decision.[11] But this may have been a case where the judges' view of society governed their view of what the law was. Judges in Northern Ireland dutifully upheld gay rights but – we may infer – they assumed that these were of benefit mainly to the gay community. Judges based in London – including Lord Kerr, whose home is in Northern Ireland – concluded that gay rights were of benefit to society as a whole.

The Supreme Court went on to deal with the claim based on religious belief or political opinion. Again, the bakery's objection was to the cake, not the consumer. But in this case, said the court, there was a much closer association between the political opinions of the purchaser and the message he wanted to promote. So, there might have been discrimination against Lee on the grounds of his political opinions. As we have seen, though, the Human Rights Act says that all legislation is, so far as it is possible to do so, to be read and given effect in a way which is compatible with human rights.[12] The Supreme Court took the view that the Fair Employment and Equal Treatment Order 'should not be read or given effect in such a way as to compel providers of goods, facilities and services to express a message with which they disagree, unless justification is shown for doing so'. On that 'reading down' there had been no discrimination on these grounds either.

Perhaps ironically, the Supreme Court appeared to show more respect for freedom of belief than had the courts of Northern Ireland, where the Christian faith might be seen as more deeply rooted than it is in other parts of the UK. But, as the justices explained, the freedom of thought, conscience and religion enshrined in article 9 of the European Convention on Human Rights also includes the freedom not to manifest beliefs that one does not hold. The McArthur family enjoyed the right not to express a message with which they deeply disagreed.

What happened next?

Daniel McArthur, general manager of Ashers Baking Company, read a statement to reporters gathered outside the Supreme Court for the ruling:[13]

> I want to start by thanking God. He has been with us during the challenges of the last four years … He is our rock and all His ways are just …
>
> We always knew we hadn't done anything wrong in turning down this order. After more than four years, the Supreme Court has now recognised that and we're very grateful – grateful to the judges and especially grateful to God …

We want to move on from this now, and I'm sure Mr Lee does as well. And let me finish by saying he'll always be welcome in any of our shops.

Gareth Lee, who had not previously given interviews, also spoke to reporters outside court. 'All I wanted was to order a cake in a shop,' he said. 'It was refused, based on the beliefs of the business owners. That made me feel like a second-class citizen. And the judgment today tells me that that's ok.'

In allowing the bakery's appeal, the Supreme Court had a blunt message for the Equality Commission for Northern Ireland:

> It is deeply humiliating, and an affront to human dignity, to deny someone a service because of that person's race, gender, disability, sexual orientation or any of the other protected personal characteristics. But that is not what happened in this case and it does the project of equal treatment no favours to seek to extend it beyond its proper scope.

In response, the commission said it was disappointed: it was also concerned that the judgment might lead to uncertainty in the commercial sphere.[14] Its counsel, the leading discrimination lawyer Robin Allen QC, explained this thinking in a lecture he gave the following month.[15]

The commission, he said, had 'wanted to ensure that, in ordinary, simple commercial dealings, purchasers did not need to be concerned with the personal identities of the providers; and providers should not take into account the personal identities of the purchaser'. This point seemed to have been lost on the Supreme Court, Allen thought. 'Or, to the extent that they took it into account, it was not determinative.'

In the end, said Allen, 'the Supreme Court decided that the conflict between Mr Lee and Mr and Mrs McArthur was to be resolved by reference to the right to freedom of expression – that was the McArthurs' right, not Mr Lee's'. As Allen saw it, Mrs McArthur's conscience turned out to be the trump card.

'It does not take a genius,' he concluded, 'to see that this approach opens a complete can of worms. Not only did this litigation take four-and-a-half years, it has made it almost certain that there will be more disputes in the future. We'll have to see whether anyone has the energy and resources to litigate them.'

Allen's remarks sounded a little ungenerous. It was his client who had started it all. If the Equality Commission had not supported legal action once it became clear that there was no prospect of a compromise, those worms would have remained in their can. There was no reason to think that a clear statement of the law from the highest court in the UK would lead to more disputes in the future.

Mr Lee goes to Europe

In August 2019 new solicitors acting for Gareth Lee announced that, some four months earlier, he had lodged an application at the European Court of Human Rights. This was not an appeal, as such, against the Supreme Court decision and did not require a response from Ashers. Like all cases in the European Court of Human Rights, it was brought against a member state. Lee claimed that the UK government was responsible for a breach of his human rights.

In particular, his lawyers argued, the UK Supreme Court judgment had left him without adequate protection against discrimination on grounds of his political opinion – his support for gay marriage in Northern Ireland. This, he claimed, was a breach of article 8 (respect for his private life); article 9 (freedom of thought); article 10 (freedom to receive and impart ideas); and article 14 (freedom to enjoy these rights without discrimination).

In written submissions to the court Robin Allen QC argued that the UK court had been wrong to assume that the claim engaged the rights of the McArthur family under articles 9 and 10. It should have treated Ashers as a company – which clearly could not have religious beliefs. In law, a company was a separate entity from its owners and directors.

Allen concluded his submissions by accusing Lady Hale's court of judicial activism:

> Overall the UK Supreme Court has overstepped the constitutional limits of the judicial role by failing to give any (or any adequate) weight to the careful balance deliberately struck by the legislature, after much debate,

in ensuring protection against discrimination in this context. It has therefore permitted a violation of Mr Lee's rights under articles 9 and/or 10, by themselves and when taken with article 14.

Lee's claim was effectively overtaken by events. As mentioned in Chapter 4, section 8 of the Northern Ireland (Executive Formation etc) Act 2019 required the secretary of state to make regulations permitting same-sex marriage in Northern Ireland. Local bakeries were expected to bake their first gay wedding cakes in February 2020.

Charlie Gard

Charlie Gard was born in August 2016 with a rare inherited disease called infantile onset encephalomyopathic mitochondrial DNA depletion syndrome. Progressive muscle failure left him blind, deaf and with no brain activity. His condition was irreversible and death could be postponed only by artificial ventilation. When Charlie was about six months old the hospital that was caring for him asked the High Court to declare that withdrawal of ventilation was lawful. In April 2017 Mr Justice Francis said: 'It is with the heaviest of hearts but with complete conviction ... that I find that it is in Charlie's best interests that ... Great Ormond Street Hospital may lawfully withdraw all treatment, save for palliative care, to permit Charlie to die with dignity.'[16]

The move had been opposed by his parents, Connie Yates and Chris Gard. They wanted to try experimental treatment, taking their child to the US if necessary. After a series of appeals they finally agreed in July 2017 that he should be brought to a hospice, where he died.

Should this be a matter for the courts? 'Why can the parents not just make the decision for themselves,' the judge asked rhetorically. 'The answer is that, although the parents have parental responsibility, overriding control is by law vested in the court exercising its independent and objective judgment in the child's best interests.'[17] That seems incontrovertible.

So, it was curious to see this case taken up by Lord Sumption when he delivered his Reith lectures in 2019:[18]

The courts ruled that not only should the hospital be entitled to withdraw therapeutic treatment but the parents should not be permitted to take the chance of a cure elsewhere. It wasn't suggested that moving him to the United States and treating him there would actually worsen his condition, although it would obviously have prolonged it. The parents' judgment seems to have been within the broad range of judgments which responsible and caring parents could make. Yet in law it was ultimately a matter for an organ of the state, namely the family division of the High Court. The parents' decision was, so to speak, nationalised.

Now, I should make it clear that I am not criticising this decision for a moment. I merely point out that it would probably have been a different decision a generation before, even if the question had reached the courts, which it would probably not have done.

I cite this agonising case because although its facts are unusual, it is illustrative of a more general tendency of law. Rules of law and the discretionary powers which the law confers on judges limit the scope for autonomous decision making by individuals. They cut down the area within which citizens take personal responsibility for their own destinies and those of their families.

The first point to make is a factual one. Sumption said that there was no suggestion that transporting Charlie to the US would worsen his position. In the sense that he was bound to die, that was true. But doctors believed that he could probably experience pain, even if he could not react to it in a meaningful way.[19] Travel to the US and treatment there would surely have caused him further pain. How could that be in his best interests if there was no prospect of any benefit for him?

The only benefit could be to his parents, who had persuaded themselves that they were acting in his best interests, and to the clinicians who would be paid to administer therapy that had not been tested, even on mice. How could that be within the broad range of judgments which responsible and caring parents could make?

The second point is a more profound one. Sumption seemed to be harking back to some imaginary golden age when parents could do what they liked with their children. Perhaps the pendulum has swung too far and courts are now too willing to take children into care. But it cannot be right to give parents ultimate power to do as they wish with their living children.

Sumption's reliance on the *Gard* judgment was much criticised. This was Lord Dyson, who overlapped briefly with him in the Supreme Court before becoming master of the rolls:

> I don't understand why Jonathan Sumption gives top billing to the tragic case of Charlie Gard as an example of judicial power; although he does not say it was wrongly decided. It seems to me that this was a classic case, a very sad case where there was a disagreement between parents and the medical authorities as to what was in the child's best interests. Who else can decide on an issue of that kind other than the courts? And the courts made a decision. Although the facts are striking and tragic, I really don't see how that case is illustrative of any expansion of judicial power or judicial overreach.[20]

And this was Patrick O'Connor QC:[21]

> [Sumption] characterises the court's jurisdiction as a 'nationalising' of the parents' decision by an 'organ of the state'. He glosses the clear evidence that the baby was continuously suffering and would be harmed by prolonged survival to no purpose. He suggests gratuitously, and by a casual misreading, that the doctors brought the proceedings to shelter themselves from legal liability. In fact, they had a clear legal obligation to do so, and not unilaterally to overrule parental wishes …
>
> The inherent jurisdiction of the courts over the welfare of children at common law dates back to feudal times and has been on a parallel statutory basis since

at least 1886. There has been no time in recent legal history when any parental prerogative over children was entirely ungoverned.

At no point did Charlie Gard's parents rely on or even disclose any religious affiliations they may have had. Their case was certainly taken up by people of faith – although some Christians who commentated on the case from the US were 'staggeringly ill-informed', according to the columnist Melanie Phillips.[22] Nearly four weeks before Charlie died, a statement from the Vatican said that Pope Francis was following the case 'with affection and sadness' and wanted to express his closeness to Charlie's parents. 'For them he prays, hoping that their desire to accompany and care for their own child to the end is not ignored.'[23]

The family courts frequently have to balance the best interests of children against the religious beliefs of their parents. In Chapter 5 I mentioned the case of conjoined twins, born in Manchester in 2000, whose Catholic parents did not want one twin to die in order to save the life of the other.[24] Lord Justice Ward, whose court overruled their wishes, had taken a similar decision in 1990, ruling that a hospital could give blood products to a boy aged nearly 16 who was being treated for leukaemia. The boy and his family had refused to consent to transfusions because they were devout Jehovah's Witnesses.[25]

In cases such as these, we expect our judges to take the role that believers ascribe to the Almighty.

8

Privacy and the Press

Many of the cases we have discussed so far show the courts in cautious mode, reluctant to usurp the role of parliament. The most that judges have done in these cases is to declare the existing law incompatible with human rights, sending a message to ministers without changing the law; sometimes they have held back even from that. As we shall see in this chapter, though, one area in which the courts have taken a much more activist role is freedom of expression; both limiting the media's right to publish in some cases and, in one famous case, expanding it.

No right to privacy?

For decades, celebrities have been complaining to the courts of England and Wales about media intrusions into their personal privacy. The low point in their campaign for a privacy law came in 1990. Gorden Kaye, a popular television actor, was recovering in hospital from emergency brain surgery after being injured in a road accident. Two men walked into his private ward, ignoring notices saying that visiting was restricted. They turned out to be a reporter and photographer from a notorious Sunday tabloid newspaper.

Attempts to prevent publication of their story proved unsuccessful. 'It is well known that in English law there is no right to privacy,' said Lord Justice Glidewell in the Court of Appeal, 'and accordingly there is no right of action for breach of a person's privacy.'[1]

Could the judges create one? This question was taken up by one of the judges who sat with Glidewell in the Court of Appeal and concurred with his judgment. Lord Justice Bingham noted that the case had highlighted 'the failure of both the common law of England and statute to protect in an effective way the personal privacy of individual citizens'.

Six years later – and just a couple of weeks before he became lord chief justice – Bingham took up the cause in a lecture:

> Should there be a law to protect rights of personal privacy? To a very large extent the law already does protect personal privacy; but to the extent that it does not, it should. The right must be narrowly drawn, to give full effect to the right of free speech and the public's right to know. It should strike only at significant infringements, such as would cause substantial distress to an ordinary phlegmatic person.
>
> My preference would be for legislation, which would mean that the rules which the courts applied would carry the imprimatur of democratic approval. But if, for whatever reason, legislation is not forthcoming, I think it almost inevitable that cases will arise in the courts in which the need to give relief is obvious and pressing; and when such cases do arise, I do not think the courts will be found wanting.[2]

This did not go down well with the politician who might become responsible for introducing legislation. In 1996 Lord Irvine of Lairg QC was Labour's lord chancellor-in-waiting. 'Statements that judges can invent or make a law protecting privacy, where there is no consensus for it, sound to ordinary people uncomfortably like a judicial threat to legislate,' he said during a debate in the House of Lords. Not, of course, that he was against courts developing the law:

> Judges do make law. As Lord Reid once said, you would believe in fairy tales if you thought otherwise. But what is the boundary between legitimate development of the law by judges and what counts as illegitimate legislation by judges? The general understanding of English law is that it does not recognise a generalised right to privacy. Should the judges make one? Only, I would say, if there were a clear community consensus that way. If there is no such consensus – and I am sure

there is none – then I say that if the judges invented a law of privacy, they would seem to be taking sides. The result would be to imperil their major asset: their reputation for impartiality.[3]

In retrospect, this was a strange thing for Irvine to say. The following year he introduced proposals that became the Human Rights Act 1998. Looking back on the Act in 2003, Lord Phillips of Worth Matravers, who was then master of the rolls, suggested that it might be 'a skeleton key which opens the door to the development of a right of privacy by the English judiciary'.[4]

Indeed it was – and Irvine should not have been surprised that his legislation was used in that way. If there was any damage to the judges' reputation for impartiality, the blame was his.

Even without the Human Rights Act, I suspect that the courts would have built a new law of privacy on the foundations of existing confidentiality law. What appeared to stand in their way was the law's need for some sort of relationship between the claimant and defendant: traditionally, the law of confidence applied only to information given 'in confidence' by one person to another.

But that restriction was already beginning to break down. In 2000, shortly after the Human Rights Act took effect, Lord Justice Sedley said that the law no longer needed to 'construct an artificial relationship of confidentiality between intruder and victim: it can recognise privacy itself as a legal principle drawn from the fundamental value of personal autonomy'.[5]

It was some time before Sedley's view became widely accepted: Lord Hoffmann, another leading judge, was still insisting in 2003 that invasion of privacy had not achieved the status of a free-standing 'tort', or civil wrong. In his view, there was a great difference between 'identifying privacy as a value which underlies the existence of a rule of law (and may point the direction in which the law should develop) and privacy as a principle of law in itself'.[6]

Model takes drugs

The issue was resolved in the summer of 2004, when the law lords – who were then the UK's highest court – ruled on an appeal brought by Naomi Campbell, the fashion model. She had sued the *Daily Mirror* for 'breach of confidence and/or unlawful invasion of privacy' after the newspaper had reported in 2001 that she was attending meetings of Narcotics Anonymous 'in a courageous bid to beat her addiction to drink and drugs'. The *Mirror* carried pictures of Campbell, dressed in jeans and a baseball cap, outside one of the self-help group's meetings. Its revelations were particularly damaging, as Campbell had falsely maintained that, unlike other models, she did not take drugs, stimulants or tranquillisers.

In an important concession before the trial began, Campbell's lawyers accepted that the *Mirror* had been entitled to publish the fact that she 'had a drug problem' and was receiving treatment for addiction. By mendaciously asserting to the media that she was not a drug taker, the model had rendered it legitimate for the media to put the record straight. However, Campbell maintained that there was no overriding public interest in publishing details of her therapy or pictures of her leaving a meeting.

In court, the *Mirror* argued that publication of the story was legitimate because the public interest in favour of publication outweighed any public interest in protecting Campbell's rights of confidentiality. That argument was rejected by Mr Justice Morland in the High Court. 'Although many aspects of the private lives of celebrities and public figures will inevitably enter the public domain,' he said, 'it does not follow that even with self-publicists every aspect and detail of their private lives are legitimate quarry for the journalist. They are entitled to some space of privacy.'[7]

Morland's decision was overturned by three judges in the Court of Appeal, headed by Lord Phillips.[8] 'Given that it was legitimate for the [newspaper] to publish the fact that Miss Campbell was a drug addict and that she was receiving treatment,' the appeal judges said, 'it does not seem to us that it was particularly significant to add the fact that the treatment consisted of attendance at meetings of Narcotics Anonymous.' In their view, details published by the newspaper and the photograph of Campbell outside the group's meeting-place 'were a legitimate, if not essential, part of the journalistic package designed to demonstrate that Miss Campbell had been deceiving the public when she said she did not take drugs'.

Campbell then appealed to the law lords. Their judgment, in May 2004, was something of a cliff-hanger. Lords Nicholls and Hoffmann voted to dismiss Campbell's appeal. Lord Hope and

Lady Hale then voted to allow it. All eyes were on Lord Carswell, the newly appointed Northern Ireland judge, who had remained inscrutable during the hearing. 'In my opinion it is a delicately balanced decision,' he said, raising the *Mirror*'s hopes. But then he sided with Hope and Hale. Campbell had won.[9]

Giving his reasons, Hope said that the details of Campbell's treatment for drug addiction were covered by confidentiality. That included photographs of her attending a meeting of Narcotics Anonymous. Her right to keep these private had to be balanced against the newspaper's right to freedom of expression. 'Had it not been for the publication of the photographs and looking to the text only,' said Hope, 'I would have been inclined to regard the balance between these rights as about even.' But the photographs added greatly to the intrusion. Their publication was a 'gross interference with her right to respect for her private life'. It was more than enough to outweigh the newspaper's right to free expression.

Hale said that there was nothing to stop anyone photographing Campbell as she walked down the street: 'readers will obviously be interested to see how she looks if and when she pops out to the shops for a bottle of milk'. But it was not necessary for the press to publish any further information, especially if this might jeopardise the continued success of Campbell's treatment.

The three judges in the majority – Hope, Hale and Carswell – did not disagree with Nicholls and Hoffmann on the law. So the minority judgments can be seen as equally authoritative.

Nicholls, the senior law lord, explained that the case concerned just one aspect of the fast-growing law of privacy – wrongful disclosure of private information. That, in turn, was derived from the law of confidence, which had its origins in the improper use of information that had been disclosed, in confidence, by one person to another. But 'this cause of action has now firmly shaken off the limiting constraint of the need for an initial confidential relationship', Nicholls explained. Now the law imposed a 'duty of confidence' whenever a person received information that he or she knew, or ought to know, was fairly and reasonably to be regarded as confidential. But even that formulation was awkward. We would not normally describe information about someone's private life as 'confidential'. A much better description would therefore be 'misuse of private information'.

As the judge explained, a person's privacy could also be invaded in ways not involving publication of information – a strip-search, for example. 'Essentially, the touchstone of private life is whether in respect of the disclosed facts the person in question had a reasonable expectation of privacy,' Nicholls said. He made it very clear that the judges were developing a new law of privacy. 'The time has come to recognise that the values enshrined in articles 8 and 10 [of the European Convention on Human Rights] are now part of the cause of action for breach of confidence.'

Agreeing with Nicholls, Hoffmann recalled the law lords' decision a year earlier that there was no general tort of invasion of privacy. But there had been 'developments of the law of confidence, typical of the capacity of the common law to adapt itself to the needs of contemporary life'. It was now established that a claim for breach of confidence no longer needed a prior confidential relationship between the parties.

It was illuminating to watch the judges creating a law of privacy in the opening years of the 21st century. They were inspired by the Human Rights Act – while maintaining that they were simply developing the common law, as judges always had.

Entertainer wrongly televised

A decade after Naomi Campbell's victory, key figures in the UK's most influential news organisation appeared not to have grasped its significance. Senior BBC journalists are familiar with the law of libel. They know that they can defend themselves against a claim for defamation by proving the truth of what they report. But what some of them seemed to have forgotten was that in 2004 a newspaper had to pay damages to a public figure even though what it had published was largely true. It was the images and details that had breached Campbell's right to privacy.

Sir Cliff Richard began his singing career in the 1950s, and was still working in 2014 when a police force began investigating allegations against him of involvement in a sex offence involving an under-age boy. It took two years for prosecutors to announce that no charges would be brought against him.

This happened at a time when a number of public figures were having their reputations damaged by allegations that turned out to be entirely false. Some of the complaints were malicious; others were fantastic; and yet suspects had to wait years for their names to be cleared.

But the BBC was also vulnerable to allegations that it had turned a blind eye to unacceptable behaviour by other entertainers, including many who had worked for the broadcaster. In the preceding two years Jimmy Savile had been exposed as a paedophile by a rival broadcaster. Rolf Harris and Stuart Hall had been convicted of indecent assaults. Gary Glitter was facing similar charges.

Responding to the allegations against Richard, South Yorkshire Police decided to search his apartment at a secure gated complex in Sunningdale, Berkshire. It is hard to imagine what evidence the police expected to find, given that they were investigating an incident that was alleged to have taken place in another part of the country nearly 30 years earlier. But the police must have known that their search would attract publicity.

A BBC reporter found out in June 2014 that the entertainer was under investigation and asked South Yorkshire Police about it the following month. The force – which had not been the reporter's source – then agreed to give the BBC advance notice of its search of Richard's home. Although it is standard practice to alert journalists to forthcoming developments, this appears to have been a rare BBC scoop.

When the raid took place in August 2014 the BBC immediately gave it extensive coverage. Advance notice had enabled the BBC's newsgathering team to deploy a helicopter camera. The police had not identified Richard as the owner of the property that was searched – but the BBC did. Other media outlets followed the BBC's lead.

A compelling witness

Richard sued the BBC for invading his privacy.[10] A separate claim against South Yorkshire Police was settled. His case against the BBC was heard in the spring of 2018 by Mr Justice Mann. Richard, then a youthful 77-year-old, gave evidence. The judge found him a 'compelling witness'.

From the evidence given by BBC managers, the judge concluded that the broadcaster's principal concerns were factual accuracy and defamation rather than privacy. A senior editor had been satisfied that reporting the raid was in the public interest but did not 'rationalise the privacy rights side of the matter'.[11]

What Mann had to decide was whether Richard had a 'legitimate expectation of privacy in relation to the fact of the investigation and the fact of the search of his apartment'. If he did, 'was the BBC nonetheless justified in publishing by virtue of its rights of freedom of expression?' The answers to these questions involved striking a balance between the BBC's right to freedom of expression under article 10 of the European Convention on Human Rights, as interpreted by the European Court of Human Rights,[12] and Richard's privacy rights under article 8.

Mann ruled that a suspect has a reasonable expectation of privacy in relation to a police investigation. Even though it might not lead to charges, there was bound to be some stigma attached to an investigation: mud sticks. In some cases – for example, if there was an immediate risk to the public – the expectation of privacy might be displaced and a suspect could be identified. But that was not the case here.

The BBC accepted that Richard had a reasonable expectation of privacy in respect of the investigation itself – but it said that that had come to an end once a search warrant had been issued by a court and executed by the police. Mann, however, was not persuaded that a search, by itself, removed the expectation of privacy that would otherwise exist.

The judge then considered the BBC's rights to freedom of expression. The story certainly contributed to a debate of general public interest, it had argued. And Mann accepted that there was a public debate about how celebrities had used their status to commit sexual abuse. But he was not persuaded that publishing the identity of an individual under investigation contributed to that debate.

People in public life had a reduced expectation of privacy, the judge acknowledged. But they were not fair game for any intrusion. Turning to the way the BBC had obtained its information, Mann accepted that journalistic subterfuge might sometimes be justifiable. But in this case publication started with 'obviously private and sensitive information, obtained from someone who ... ought not to have revealed it, and confirmed and bolstered with a ploy in the form of a perceived threat that ought not to have been made'.

Finally, the judge looked at the content and form of the BBC's broadcasts. They were 'presented with a significant degree of breathless sensationalism', he noted. Mann acknowledged that television relied on pictures but concluded that 'the main purpose of utilising the helicopter was to add sensationalism and emphasis to the scoop of which the BBC was so proud'.

Striking the balance, Mann reached 'the clear conclusion that Sir Cliff's privacy rights were not outweighed by the BBC's rights to freedom of expression'.

The BBC decided not to appeal.[13] This was wise. Prospects of success were slim, while the reputational damage of losing was huge. The case was already thought to have cost the BBC £1.9m. An unsuccessful appeal by the BBC would also have endorsed Mann's ruling, turning it into a binding precedent rather than one that was merely persuasive.

Privacy today

The law of privacy made a giant leap in the 14 years between Gorden Kaye's unsuccessful claim in 1990 and Naomi Campbell's victory over the *Mirror* in 2004. It made equally large strides in the 14 years between 2004 and Cliff Richard's victory in 2018. This was almost entirely the result of judicial activism.

Like most judges, Mann sought to play this down. Gavin Millar QC, for the BBC, had argued at the hearing that the case raised 'issues of great, arguably of constitutional, importance for the freedom of the press in this country'. If Richard's claim were successful, he said, it would undermine the long-standing press freedom to report the truth about police investigations. Any change in the law should be a matter for parliament.

But Mann thought that was overstating the BBC's case. 'I agree that the case is capable of having a significant impact on press reporting,' he said, 'but not to a degree which requires legislative, and not merely judicial, authority.' Parliament had passed the Human Rights Act 20 years earlier, and that had already affected media reporting. 'If the position of the press is now different from what it was,' the judge said, 'that is because of the Human Rights Act and not because of some court-created principle.'

Really? Until Mann delivered his judgment, reporters had thought it safe to report that a named individual was under investigation by the police. We now know that such people have a legitimate expectation of privacy. But journalists believed that this expectation was not breached merely because they reported that a warrant to search the premises of a public figure had been issued or executed. Outside court, Fran Unsworth, the BBC's director of news and current affairs, said the case marked a 'significant shift' against press freedom. She was right; and journalists should thank the BBC for fighting the case in a vain attempt to hold the line.

Of course, *Richard v BBC* deals only with the position of suspects under police investigation. There is no suggestion – at least for now – that it is unlawful for journalists to name defendants once they have been charged. But the case led to much greater caution about the way police investigations are reported by news organisations. Suspects are now less likely to be named.

Many people outside the media will welcome increased privacy rights. As a journalist, I am concerned that the public will be less well informed in future. But that was not my reason for discussing privacy here. It was to demonstrate the huge reach of judge-made law in this area.

Freedom of information

Despite his reputation as a social reformer, Tony Blair always seemed indifferent to the Human Rights Act. Even though the subtle balance inherent in a declaration of incompatibility was the greatest achievement of his first lord chancellor, Lord Irvine of Lairg, the Act rates only a sentence in Blair's 700-page memoir.[14] But the former prime minister had rather more to say about Irvine's other great achievement, the Freedom of Information Act 2000:

> Freedom of Information. Three harmless words. I look at those words as I write them and feel like shaking my head till it drops off my shoulders. You idiot. You naive, foolish, irresponsible nincompoop. There is really no description of stupidity, no matter how vivid, that is adequate. I quake at the imbecility of it …

> Some people might find this shocking. Oh, he wants secret government; he wants to hide the foul misdeeds of the politicians and keep from 'the people' their right to know what is being done in their name. The truth is that the FOI Act isn't used, for the most part, by 'the people'. It's used by journalists … It's used as a weapon.[15]

One journalist Blair might have had in mind was Rob Evans, a reporter on the *Guardian*. In April 2005 he made a request under the Freedom of Information Act to see correspondence between a number of ministers in Tony Blair's government and the Prince of Wales. It was known that Prince Charles wrote regularly to people in public life, urging them to adopt policies or courses of action that he supported. Often, he wrote in his own hand. These missives were known as 'black spider letters', an unjustified reference to the prince's impassioned handwriting.

Government departments refused to disclose letters which the prince had sent, claiming that they were covered by an exemption in the Freedom of Information Act. With his newspaper's support, Evans challenged this. In 2012 the Upper Tribunal – a judicial body with the same status as the High Court – ordered the departments to disclose those letters that could be defined as advocacy correspondence. 'It will generally be in the overall public interest for there to be transparency as to how and when Prince Charles seeks to influence government,' the tribunal explained.

The government did not appeal against this decision.[16] Instead, the attorney general, Dominic Grieve QC, issued what amounted to a veto of the Upper Tribunal's order. Section 53 of the Freedom of Information Act allows a cabinet minister or the attorney general to overturn a decision of the Upper Tribunal by signing a certificate saying that he or she has 'on reasonable grounds formed the opinion' that there was no failure to comply with the duty to disclose information.

In Grieve's view, the advocacy correspondence was part of the prince's 'preparation for kingship'. When he became king he would have, by convention, the right to be consulted, to encourage and to warn the government. In order to prepare for this he had the right to be instructed in the business of government. That instruction had to be confidential if it was to be effective.

The Upper Tribunal had rejected this argument on the basis that Prince Charles would stop writing letters of this kind once he became king. Grieve disagreed, saying that advocacy correspondence fell within the ambit of advising or warning ministers. Rather than test this argument in the courts, Grieve simply imposed the view he preferred by issuing a certificate under section 53 of the Act.

Evans sought judicial review. He was unsuccessful in the High Court, but then the Court of Appeal found in his favour.[17] The attorney general appealed to the Supreme Court. Seven justices sat and judgment was delivered in 2015.[18] What would you have said?

Unprincipled

Lord Neuberger, who gave the leading judgment in the Supreme Court, appeared outraged by what he saw as the government's behaviour:

> A statutory provision which entitles a member of the executive ... to overrule a decision of the judiciary merely because he does not agree with it would not merely be unique in the laws of the United Kingdom. It would cut across two constitutional principles which are also fundamental components of the rule of law.
>
> First, subject to being overruled by a higher court or ... a statute, it is a basic principle that a decision of a court is binding as between the parties, and cannot be ignored or set aside by anyone, including (indeed it may fairly be said, least of all) the executive.
>
> Secondly, it is also fundamental to the rule of law that decisions and actions of the executive are, subject to necessary well-established exceptions ... reviewable by the court at the suit of an interested citizen.
>
> Section 53, as interpreted by the Attorney General's argument in this case, flouts the first principle and stands the second principle on its head.

Over many years, the courts have refused to enforce legislation overriding the rule of law unless it has been expressed in terms that are entirely clear. Neuberger concluded that section 53 of the

Act fell short of this requirement. There was a very strong case for saying that a minister could not issue a certificate 'simply on the ground that, having considered the issue with the benefit of the same facts and arguments as the Upper Tribunal, he has reached a different conclusion'. There needed to be something more.

Lord Kerr and Lord Reed agreed with Neuberger. Lord Mance and Lady Hale said section 53 should be given a wider potential effect. But they agreed that the attorney general would need the 'clearest possible justification' for issuing a veto – which he had not shown in this case. So a majority of five judges dismissed the attorney general's appeal.

Lord Hughes dissented. The rule of law was of the first importance, he accepted, but it was an integral part of the rule of law that courts give should give effect to the intention of parliament. 'The rule of law is not the same as a rule that courts must always prevail, no matter what the statute says,' he added pointedly. And, in this case, parliament had plainly shown its intention to allow a member of the executive to override the decision of a court.

Of course, as Hughes explained, the minister's decision would be subject to judicial review. But, in his view, the attorney general had not acted irrationally in this case.

Lord Wilson also dissented – but in even more striking terms:

> I would have allowed the appeal. How tempting it must have been for the Court of Appeal (indeed how tempting it has proved even for the majority in this court) to seek to maintain the supremacy of the astonishingly detailed, and inevitably unappealed, decision of the Upper Tribunal in favour of disclosure of the prince's correspondence! But the Court of Appeal ought (as, with respect, ought this court) to have resisted the temptation. For, in reaching its decision, the Court of Appeal did not in my view interpret section 53 of the Freedom of Information Act 2000. It re-wrote it. It invoked precious constitutional principles but among the most precious is that of parliamentary sovereignty, emblematic of our democracy.

Wilson said a power of executive override on issues of law would have been an unlawful encroachment on the principle of separation of powers. But issues relating to the evaluation of public interests were entirely different.

The government made no attempt to overturn the court's ruling – although it had already legislated to ensure that, in future, the heir to the throne and the second-in-line would share the unqualified exemption from disclosure enjoyed by the monarch.[19] Within a few weeks, the prince's letters were published.[20] They were interesting rather than earth shattering – not least because they had all been written more than a decade earlier. It is hard to see that they did any damage to the future king.

But what damage did they do to the reputation of the courts? It is one thing to develop a new law of privacy but quite another to disapply an Act of parliament. Surely the *Evans* case was a clear example of judicial overreach?

That was certainly the view of Lord Sumption. Delivering his Reith lectures in 2019, the former Supreme Court justice recalled that his colleagues, by a majority of five to two, had quashed the attorney general's certificate:

> The majority's reason, however dressed up, was that they did not approve of the power that parliament had on the face of it conferred on ministers. Three of the judges thought that it was such a bad idea that parliament could not really have meant what it had plainly said. Two other judges accepted that parliament must have meant it but thought that the Attorney-General had no right to disagree with the tribunal.
>
> For my part, I think that there is no reason why a statute should not say that on an issue like this a minister answerable to parliament is a more appropriate judge of the public interest than a court ... No other modern case reveals so clearly the judges' expansive view of the rule of law.[21]

Sumption was justified in his criticism. But he was also right to say that the judges had not taken such an expansive view of the law in any other recent case.

Lord Dyson, whose decision in the Court of Appeal was upheld by the Supreme Court, criticised Sumption for the 'surprisingly polemical language' he used in his lecture.[22] 'It was a difficult borderline case in which the Supreme Court was split,' Dyson added. 'It seems to me that this is hardly a sound basis for a general complaint of excessive exercise of judicial power at the expense of politics.'

Privacy International

A day after Sumption had delivered his final Reith lecture, the Supreme Court gave judgment on an appeal that brought these issues into sharp focus.[23] Sumption had been one of seven justices who heard an appeal at the end of 2018 by Privacy International, a charity that promotes privacy around the world.

Legislation passed in 2000 had created a special court called the Investigatory Powers Tribunal, whose decisions, the legislation said, 'shall not be subject to appeal or be liable to be questioned in any court'.[24] What did those words mean? Were the tribunal's decisions subject to judicial review? Could a more senior court quash a decision if the tribunal had made an error of law?

On the face of it, parliament's intentions seemed pretty clear. The tribunal had been set up to hear cases involving the UK's security and intelligence services. To protect national security, the legislation contained what was called an 'ouster clause': a provision intended to oust the jurisdiction of the ordinary courts. Since parliament had not created any right of appeal against the tribunal's decisions, it must have wanted the tribunal to have the last word.

Parliament had tried this before. Legislation passed in 1950 said that a 'determination' (or decision) made by a body called the Foreign Compensation Commission 'shall not be called in question in any court of law'.[25] But, said the law lords in 1968, that restriction must apply only to a *valid* determination by the commission. And the only people who could decide whether a determination was valid were the judges. So what purported to be a determination by the commission could be called into question by the courts after all. This was a victory for a company called Anisminic, whose reward – apart from the money involved – was to be immortalised in the law reports.[26]

Parliament was alive to this in 1985, when it created the tribunal's predecessor. So it went further than it had in 1950 and added a phrase to the ouster clause. That was slightly modified when a new tribunal was created in 2000. It now said that 'decisions of the tribunal (including decisions as to whether they have jurisdiction) shall not be subject to appeal or be liable to be questioned in any court'.

Would that wording be sufficient to stop the courts interfering? Did the words in brackets make all the difference? What do you think?

Whose decision is it anyway?

Lord Carnwath gave the first judgment. Lady Hale and Lord Kerr agreed with him. So that was three of the seven justices who sat – not quite a majority.

Carnwath began by tracing the supervisory role of the High Court back to the time of William I – 1066 and all that. Attempts to restrict that role had received a hostile response from the judges ever since the 17th century, he noted. 'In such cases, conventional principles of statutory interpretation, based on the ordinary meaning of the words used by parliament, have yielded to a more fundamental principle that no inferior tribunal or authority can conclusively determine the limits of its own jurisdiction.'

After an unusually lengthy summary of the case law and its development, Carnwath followed the *Anisminic* approach. When the statute referred to decisions of the tribunal, it meant decisions that were legally valid. That applied equally to the word 'decisions' in brackets. 'A decision which is vitiated by error of law, whether "as to jurisdiction" or otherwise, is no decision at all,' he said.[27]

That did not make the words in brackets meaningless. There were circumstances in which they might apply. However, judicial review could be excluded only by the most clear and explicit words. 'If parliament has failed to make its intention sufficiently clear,' said Carnwath, 'it is not for us to stretch the words used beyond their natural meaning. It may well be that the promoters of the 1985 Act thought that their formula would be enough to provide comprehensive protection from jurisdictional review of any kind … But one is entitled to ask why they did not use more explicit wording … The reason for not adopting that course may simply be that … it might not have been expected to survive parliamentary scrutiny.'

As you might expect, Lord Sumption took a different view. The legislation in question simply excluded a challenge to the tribunal's decision on the merits, he said:

> In other words, it excludes judicial review on grounds which would be tantamount to an appeal. The Investigatory Powers Tribunal acts as a court. Its function is to exercise powers of judicial review over (among others) the intelligence services, which would otherwise have been exercisable by the High Court, and to do so on the same basis as the High Court. The purpose of judicial review is to maintain the rule of law. But the rule of law is sufficiently vindicated by the judicial character of the tribunal. It does not require a right of appeal from the decisions of a judicial body of this kind.[28]

Lord Reed agreed with Sumption. Lord Wilson also voted to dismiss Privacy International's appeal, concluding that parliament does indeed 'have power to exclude judicial review of any ordinary errors of law made by the Investigatory Powers Tribunal'.

That left Lord Lloyd-Jones as the swing vote. 'If the jurisdiction of the High Court can be excluded at all,' he said, 'it requires the most clear and explicit words.' He sided with Carnwath, and Privacy International, represented by Dinah Rose QC, won its appeal.

National security

Did that jeopardise national security? That, after all, was what the ouster clause was there to protect.

The case involved computer hacking by the government's eavesdropping centre GCHQ. At issue was whether a secretary of state had power to issue so-called thematic warrants authorising a broad range of interference with property.

For the security and intelligence services to remain effective, their methods and capabilities must remain confidential. It is standard practice neither to confirm nor deny these, a policy known as NCND. And you can see that discussing their actions in the ordinary courts might jeopardise this confidentiality. That's why parliament wanted to confine scrutiny of the security and intelligence agencies to a unique court.

But the common law has developed a way of assessing whether the agencies have behaved lawfully without jeopardising their work or the NCND policy. The tribunal simply assumes that the facts asserted by the claimants are true and proceeds to consider the legal issues in an open hearing. If the agencies are found to have behaved unlawfully on the facts as assumed, the tribunal can then consider the actual facts in closed session.

I cannot see how allowing the ordinary courts to review decisions of the tribunal would threaten the capabilities of the security and intelligence services. Those agencies might see this differently – and, if they do, they would not be able to tell us why. In that event, they might ask parliament to pass beefed-up legislation.

But would it ever be possible for parliament to oust the supervisory jurisdiction of the High Court? And, if so, how?

The Supreme Court was asked to rule on these questions too. Strictly speaking, the case had already been decided in favour of Privacy International. So the justices' comments on this issue were *obiter* – not necessary for the decision and therefore not binding. But that did not stop some of them from having a go.

Carnwath said there were certain fundamental requirements of the rule of law that no form of ouster clause, however clear and explicit, could exclude from the supervision of the courts. These included exceeding or abusing the tribunal's powers. That was not so far from what had happened here. Parliament could not entrust a statutory decision-making process to a particular body and then leave it free to disregard the essential requirements laid down by the rule of law for such a process to be effective. In an earlier case, called *Cart*,[29] the Supreme Court had confirmed that it was ultimately for the courts to set the limits.

This was Carnwath's conclusion, with which only Hale and Kerr agreed:

> I see a strong case for holding that, consistently with the
> rule of law, binding effect cannot be given to a clause

which purports wholly to exclude the supervisory jurisdiction of the High Court to review a decision of an inferior court or tribunal, whether for excess or abuse of jurisdiction, or error of law.

In all cases, regardless of the words used, it should remain ultimately a matter for the court to determine the extent to which such a clause should be upheld, having regard to its purpose and statutory context, and the nature and importance of the legal issue in question; and to determine the level of scrutiny required by the rule of law.

This was strong stuff – but not as strong as the response from some commentators.

Too much judicial power?

I referred in Chapter 1 to the Judicial Power Project, supported by the think-tank Policy Exchange. It issued a statement in the name of Professor Richard Ekins:[30]

> The Supreme Court's decision today, *Privacy International v Investigatory Powers Tribunal*, undermines the rule of law and violates the sovereignty of parliament. A majority of the court (four of seven judges) has chosen to misinterpret an ouster clause – the statutory provision which expressly limits the High Court's jurisdiction to review decisions of the Investigatory Powers Tribunal. Parliament chose to limit judicial review by creating a specialist tribunal to consider complaints against the intelligence services. It is not the Supreme Court's place to unravel this choice by way of implausible and unreasonable statutory interpretation …
>
> It is clear that some Supreme Court judges have a wholly misconceived idea of their place in our constitution. Three of the four judges in the majority also chose to assert that the courts would not be obliged to give effect to an even more clearly worded ouster clause. This assertion was not necessary to resolve the

case – it would not form part of the court's judgment even if supported by a majority – but it is an incredible thing for any judge to say.

These three judges have asserted an intention in the future openly to disobey statute. Any judge who acted on this intention would warrant removal from office in accordance with the terms of the Senior Courts Act 1981.

In reality, Carnwath, Hale and Kerr were not refusing to give effect to a future ouster clause. They were simply predicting that they might not interpret a clause in the way that lawyers such as Ekins were arguing for. Nor were they ignoring the intention of parliament, as other critics had complained.[31] Carnwath's formulation required the courts to take account of a clause's purpose and statutory context.

The *Privacy International* ruling shows a clear division between Carnwath, Hale and Kerr, at the activist end of the spectrum, and their colleagues Sumption, Reed and Wilson, who took a more literal approach to statutory interpretation – with Lloyd-Jones somewhere in the middle.

But the decision attracted very little public attention. In the US there would have been much more interest in the positions taken by individual justices, not least because Reed was being lined up at the time to succeed Hale as president.

9

Access to Justice

In any developed system of law, the courts will not allow government ministers to act unconstitutionally. Most countries have written constitutions, making it relatively easy for ministers to know the extent of their powers. But the UK – like Israel and New Zealand – has an uncodified constitution, one that is largely unwritten. Although that provides ministers with an enviable degree of flexibility, it also gives them much greater responsibility.

Doing the decent thing

Put simply, the British constitution expects ministers to do the decent thing. For centuries, members of the establishment have known how to behave. Until recently, the 'powers that be' used to know how to use the powers they had.

We have already seen in Chapter 2 how Liz Truss, as lord chancellor, failed to speak up for the judges when they were accused of being 'enemies of the people'. But one of her recent predecessors was in post for long enough to make many more misjudgments. He was Chris Grayling, who was secretary of state for justice from September 2012 until the general election of May 2015.

Grayling was the first non-lawyer to have served as lord chancellor for 440 years. Unfamiliar with the responsibilities of an ancient office that was still recovering from Tony Blair's reforms a decade earlier, he started at a disadvantage. Even so, Grayling displayed a remarkable inability to understand the fundamental principle of an uncodified constitution – that just because the law permits you to do something, that doesn't mean you should.

Some of Grayling's failings could be reversed relatively easily by his immediate successor Michael Gove. These included the criminal courts charge – a financial penalty payable by all convicted defendants that led to protest resignations by magistrates. Another of Grayling's policies had severely restricted the possession or acquisition of books that individual prisoners could treat as their own, according to a High Court judge who found the policy to have been unlawful.[1] That, too, was rapidly reversed.

But other decisions – particularly those designed to reduce public spending in a time of austerity – were still causing problems for David Gauke, lord chancellor from January 2018 to July 2019. Shortly before he resigned, I asked him if he hoped his successor would, like him, be a lawyer.

'It was certainly an advantage for me to have come from a legal background,' Gauke said, 'if only in terms of being given the benefit of the doubt by the legal professions. Some of my predecessors won the respect of the legal professions very quickly by their approach. Those who [did not] didn't come from a legal background.'[2]

Gauke would not name names. But the two non-lawyer lord chancellors who won the respect of the legal profession were Gove (2015–16) and David Lidington (2017–18). The two who did not were Grayling (2012–15) and Truss (2016–17).

Gauke was indeed succeeded by a lawyer: his deputy, Robert Buckland QC.

Legal aid

Although the Legal Aid, Sentencing and Punishment of Offenders Act 2012 (known as LASPO) became law before Grayling was appointed lord chancellor, he was responsible for the way it was implemented in April 2013. Its aims included making significant savings in the cost of legal aid; discouraging unnecessary and adversarial litigation at public expense; targeting legal aid at those who needed it the most; and delivering better value for money.

How well had those objectives been met? The government published the report of a post-implementation review in February 2019.[3] It found that the reforms had made significant savings: the cost of legal aid had fallen by more than 20% since April 2013, which was more than had been expected – or, presumably, intended.

But there had been only mixed success in reducing the number of court cases. 'It must be concluded that the changes made by LASPO were not entirely successful at discouraging unnecessary and adversarial litigation at public expense,' the review reported laconically.

Did Grayling's reforms succeed in targeting legal aid at those who needed it the most? 'We think it is impossible to say with certainty if the LASPO changes achieved this objective,' the review team said. And had the reforms delivered better value for money? That, too, was difficult to answer. 'Stakeholders argued that LASPO had simply shifted costs onto other areas of government, including local authorities and the Home Office.' It had also been claimed that the reforms 'caused long-term sustainability issues for the legal aid market' – which means that it was harder for people to get legal aid in the future. Again, more research was needed.

Above all, though, the government made no attempt to contradict six broad concerns put to the review team by lawyers and others working in the legal aid sector:

- Removing many areas of early civil and family legal advice from the scope of legal aid had arguably undermined the reform's value-for-money objective, as relatively minor legal problems were allowed to become more serious.
- Although LASPO did not substantially reform the financial eligibility requirements for legal aid, its operational requirements limited access by those who should have received it.
- The exceptional case funding scheme, intended to ensure that legal aid would be available when an individual's human rights were at risk, was difficult to access.
- Inadequate legal aid fees had affected recruitment and retention of lawyers, potentially limiting the future provision of legal aid.
- Removing funding had increased the number of litigants-in-person, generating more costs for the courts.
- There were more advice deserts – areas of the country where it was difficult or impossible to obtain legal advice.

Although the government did not say so, all these concerns could fairly be blamed on Grayling's implementation of the reforms. David Gauke, his successor, responded with a legal support action plan.[4] But even though spending on legal aid had been reduced from just over £2bn in 2013 to £1.6bn in 2018, Gauke could offer no more than £8m to help put things right. The promised 'comprehensive review of the legal aid eligibility regime' would take 18 months to complete, meaning that any reforms would not take effect before 2021.

Probation

In June 2014, 35 self-governing probation trusts in England and Wales were replaced by a new public-sector National Probation Service and 21 community rehabilitation companies. This was the culmination of a strategy launched by Grayling in January 2013 and known as 'Transforming Rehabilitation'. By transferring most community sentence and rehabilitation work to the private and voluntary sectors, the justice secretary had promised 'lower crime, fewer victims and safer communities'.[5]

'The probation model delivered by Transforming Rehabilitation is irredeemably flawed', Grayling's successor was told by the Chief Inspector of Probation in March 2019. 'To implement government policy,' said Dame Glenys Stacey, 'capable probation leaders were required to deliver change they did not believe in, against the very ethos of the profession. On inspection, we now find probation supervision provided under contract to be substandard, and much of it demonstrably poor. Judicial confidence in community sentencing is now at serious risk.'[6]

The government announced in May 2019 that Grayling's reforms would be reversed. All offender management would be brought under the National Probation Service.[7]

Judicial pensions

New Judicial Pension Regulations were signed by Grayling in 2015 and took effect in April of that year. The regulations, made under the Public Services Pensions Act 2013, created a new pension scheme for full-time judges. Unlike its predecessor, the scheme was registered for tax. That made the new pension much less valuable to those who would receive it.[8] After a detailed investigation, the Review Body on Senior Salaries said it was 'no longer seen to provide a strong incentive to legal professionals who have made adequate provision for their retirement at an early stage'.[9]

Those legal professionals – many of them highly successful QCs – were exactly the people that the judiciary needed to recruit. But, because they had already invested in retirement plans, the barristers would have been worse off financially if they had accepted the pension on offer. No longer the incentive that it once was to lawyers seeking a change of pace, the pension was now a positive disincentive.[10]

'The damage that the pension changes have had on judicial morale was a consistent and forceful message heard throughout our visits', the review body reported in October 2018. 'Pay and pensions were also raised with us as being emblematic of the perceived low value set on the judiciary by the government.'[11]

That made it impossible to recruit enough judges to fill vacancies in the High Court. And that, in turn, jeopardised the international reputation of the High Court, which, as the lord chief justice said on several occasions during 2018, was vital to investment in the UK.[12] The new pension scheme was yet another of Grayling's false economies.

Was it also unconstitutional? Judges' salaries have not been reduced since 1832.[13] The principle that ministers cannot reduce judges' pay is enshrined in statute[14] and helps to buttress the judges' independence. Michael Beloff QC, a distinguished member of the bar, has argued that 'it is unconstitutional to cut the salary of an individual judge of a superior court during the currency of his or her commission'. As Beloff pointed out, 'the principle that judicial salaries may be increased by administrative action but may not be reduced except, presumably, by Act of parliament has its origins in the Act of Settlement 1701 and has been linked with immunity from removal as one of the guarantors of [judicial] independence'.[15]

It must surely be appropriate for these purposes to treat pension benefits as deferred pay. Grayling could argue that the pension changes applied only to new recruits and were made under powers granted by parliament. But the reforms were clearly damaging to judicial independence. In principle, a judge is just as vulnerable to improper pressure from a cut in pension as from a cut in pay.[16]

Shortly before standing down as lord chancellor in July 2019, David Gauke secured a temporary recruitment and retention allowance from the Treasury of 25% for High Court judges and 15% for Circuit and Upper Tribunal judges who were covered by the new pension scheme.[17] The pay rises affected only about a quarter of the salaried judiciary and were intended to resolve the immediate recruitment issue until a long-term solution could be put in place.

Judges judging judges

By the time the Treasury had agreed to the recruitment and retention allowance, it was clear that Grayling's pension scheme was unlawful and would have to be replaced. That was established in unprecedented legal action brought on behalf of some 230 serving judges, including half a dozen in the High Court.[18]

These judges, all appointed before April 2012, had been members of the old pension scheme established in 1993. They were required to join the new scheme when it was set up in 2015. As we have seen, this scheme was less valuable than its predecessor. But, to reduce the disadvantage to those approaching retirement at the age of 70, a number of concessions were made. Judges born before April 1957, who would have been at least 58 in April 2015, were fully protected from the reforms. Those born after August 1960 received no protection. Those born between the two dates had limited relief.

This was, of course, direct discrimination against judges who were too young to qualify for the full protection given to those born before April 1957. It was also illogical: the people who benefitted from the concession were those least likely to need it. The lord chancellor accepted that his transitional provisions were discriminatory but asserted that they were a proportionate means of achieving a legitimate aim – which was to protect those closest to retirement from the financial effects of pension reform.

That argument was rejected by an employment tribunal in January 2017.[19] An appeal by the lord chancellor to the Employment Appeal Tribunal was dismissed in January 2018.[20] The government lost a further appeal to the Court of Appeal in December 2018,[21] but it was not until June 2019 that the Supreme Court refused the government permission to appeal one more time, effectively endorsing the original employment tribunal ruling in the judges' favour.

It is unusual for judges to bring legal action against the lord chancellor, and there seems to have been some concern that the case might have attracted adverse publicity. Perhaps for this reason only two of the 230 claimants were named in the published judgments. One was Victoria McCloud, who was born in 1969 and appointed a Queen's Bench Master – a junior judge – in 2010. Master McCloud was referred to coyly as 'Ms V McCloud' in the Employment Appeal Tribunal judgment. The other was Mr Justice Mostyn, who was born in July 1957 and therefore fell into the intermediate group of judges. Sir Nicholas Mostyn, who became a judge of the High Court family division in 2010, was referred to even more coyly as 'Mr N Mostyn'. The Court of Appeal went further still and dropped their honorifics.

In the event, the case attracted little publicity. Care was taken to ensure that the judges who heard the challenges were not personally affected by them: most had already retired (and were therefore sitting as part-time, fee-paid judges), while one was nearing retirement.

The effect of the pension changes is best explained through the example of a High Court judge born in 1961 and appointed in 2008. A judge in that position faced a tax bill of £26,000 as a result of the pension changes. The new recruitment and retention allowance was worth £25,000, leaving the judge no more than £1,000 out of pocket. As a result of the litigation, that judge can expect to forego the £25,000 and join the old pension scheme.

Tribunal fees

Chris Grayling's prison, probation and pension policies were merely dry runs for the case that forms the centrepiece of this chapter. In 2017 seven justices in the Supreme Court found that an order issued in his name 'effectively prevents access to justice and is therefore unlawful'.[22]

Two years earlier Grayling had led national celebrations to mark the 800th anniversary of Magna Carta. Now he was found to have breached its best-known surviving principles.

But did the Supreme Court get it right? A highly experienced lawyer accused it of claiming the right 'to second-guess and overturn political policy decisions' by reference to how they had turned out in practice.

Grayling might have thought he was simply exercising powers granted to him by parliament in accordance with his political judgment. So, was he the unlucky victim of judicial overreach? Or were the courts simply upholding the rule of law?

Before you make up your own mind on the question that lies at the heart of this book, I need to tell you more about the *Unison* case, as it is called. It involved applications to employment tribunals, many of them brought by people who claimed they had been unlawfully sacked by their employers.

In July 2013 a junior minister in Grayling's department signed a fees order 'by authority of the lord chancellor'.[23] This order required claimants in employment tribunals and the employment appeal tribunal to pay fees, for the first time.

Charging fees is not, itself controversial: users should contribute to the cost of running the courts if they can afford to do so. If Grayling had introduced fees in line with those charged by comparable courts, he would not have been open to challenge.

Instead, the lord chancellor decided that claimants in all but the simplest employment cases should pay a total of £1,200 before their claims were heard by a tribunal. If the claimants lost and wanted a hearing before the appeal tribunal, a further £1,600 was payable. So, those court users – inevitably including some who had recently lost their jobs – would have to pay £2,800 in addition to their own legal fees and other expenses.

There were exceptions for people with little or no money. But these fee remissions were not available if the claimant or the claimant's partner had £3,000 or more in the bank. And it was not uncommon for someone challenging a redundancy decision to have received a payment of that order.

As anybody but Grayling would have expected, the huge increase in court fees produced a 'dramatic and persistent fall in the number of claims brought in employment tribunals'. The long-term reduction, according to the Supreme Court, was 'of the order of 66–70%'.

One reason for this was that the proportion of claimants paying reduced fees – or no fees at all – was far lower than Grayling had expected. In 2012 the government estimated that at least 24% of the pre-fees population of claimants would receive full remission, and that a further 53% would receive partial remission (making a total of 77% who would not have to pay full fees). In reality, the proportion receiving full or partial remission was initially very low, and by 2016 had increased only to about 29%.

The main aim of introducing fees had been to raise money – about 33% of the cost of providing the tribunals. Because fewer claims than expected were being brought, the amount raised turned out to be less than 20%.

A further aim of Grayling's reforms was to deter claims that had no merit. In fact, the proportion of unsuccessful claims turned out to be much higher than before. Another aim was to encourage settlements. In reality, the proportion of settlements was slightly lower – it is thought because some employers were delaying negotiations to see whether the claimant could afford the hearing fee.

The trade union Unison challenged the fees order on the ground that it breached EU principles of effectiveness and equality. It was also said to be discriminatory. These claims were rejected by the High Court and Unison's appeal was dismissed by the Court of Appeal. The union, represented by Dinah Rose QC, appealed to the Supreme Court.

Access to the courts

Lord Reed, with whom the other justices agreed, began his judgment by looking at the legislation under which Grayling had made the fees order. In interpreting that legislation, he said, a court must consider the constitutional principles that underlie the text. One of those principles was access to justice:

> The constitutional right of access to the courts is inherent in the rule of law. The importance of the rule of law is not always understood. Indications of a lack of understanding include the assumption that the administration of justice is merely a public service like any other, that courts and tribunals are providers of services to the 'users' who appear before them, and that the provision of those services is of value only to the users themselves and to those who are remunerated for their participation in the proceedings.

This lesson was aimed squarely at the government. Reed patiently explained to ministers and officials why access to justice matters to us all:

> At the heart of the concept of the rule of law is the idea that society is governed by law. Parliament exists primarily in order to make laws for society in this country ... Courts exist in order to ensure that the laws made by parliament, and the common law created by the courts themselves, are applied and enforced.
>
> That role includes ensuring that the executive branch of government carries out its functions in accordance with the law. In order for the courts to perform that role, people must in principle have unimpeded access to them.
>
> Without such access, laws are liable to become a dead letter, the work done by parliament may be rendered nugatory, and the democratic election of members of parliament may become a meaningless charade. That is why the courts do not merely provide a public service like any other.

In English law, said Reed, the right of access to the courts went back to Magna Carta. He cited chapter 29 of the version confirmed by Edward I, which found its way onto the first Statute Roll in 1297: 'We will sell to no man, we will not deny or defer to any man either justice or right.' This provision is still on the statute book.[24] As Reed explained, it does not prohibit court fees – but it does guarantee access to courts that administer justice promptly and fairly.

'In order for the fees to be lawful,' explained Reed, 'they have to be set at a level that everyone can afford, taking into account the availability of full or partial remission. The evidence now before the court, considered realistically and as a whole, leads to the conclusion that that requirement is not met.'

The government immediately repealed the unlawful fees order and made costly arrangements to refund all fees that had been paid under it. Claims more than doubled and, in June 2018, the Judicial Appointments Commission announced that it was seeking to recruit 54 full-time judges to serve on employment tribunals. After the fees order was introduced in 2013, many experienced employment judges had, ironically but unsurprisingly, found themselves out of work.

Richard Heaton, the senior civil servant at the Ministry of Justice, told MPs in November 2018 that he thought a fee system would be reintroduced – 'but we have not finalised it yet and there are no immediate plans to introduce one'. As he explained, 'you have to get the fee levels right, and then you have to get the rebate scheme right'.[25]

Nothing more was heard of it.

Second-guessing the judiciary

From what Heaton told MPs in 2018, we can see that the Ministry of Justice thought it would be possible to introduce a fee system that was consistent with access to justice. The real problem seemed to be that employment tribunal fees were more trouble than they were worth.

But that's not how it looked to a former civil servant, writing earlier that year for the Judicial Power Project.[26] Sir Stephen Laws had retired as first parliamentary counsel in 2012. In a fine example of nominative determinism, he had spent more than 35 years drafting legislation. Laws accused the Supreme Court of claiming the right 'to second-guess and overturn political policy decisions' by reference to how they had turned out in practice.

There had certainly been a much sharper reduction in the use of employment tribunals than ministers had expected. But why, he asked, should the lawfulness of the fees order have depended on the minister's ability to predict the future? 'The court applied a retrospective test to the fees order which it was impossible, in practical terms, for the person making the order to have been sure of satisfying when doing so.' It was not possible, in his view, to make a fee order that would have complied with the government's objectives and the court's tests.

This argument is unconvincing. If Grayling had introduced modest fees, there is every chance that any challenge would have been unsuccessful. The Supreme Court quoted the fees charged for small claims in the county court. 'For claims issued online, they begin at £50 for claims up to £300, and rise in stages to £745 for claims between £5,000 and £10,000. The fee structure has thus been designed in a way which is likely to have a less deterrent effect on the bringing of small claims.' Though Reed did not say this, we can infer that he regarded the county court fee structure as lawful. Judges may not be much good at building fee structures, but they know when one is so lop-sided that it needs to be demolished.

Laws was on stronger ground when he criticised Reed's analysis of parliament's constitutional position. In a paragraph which I quoted earlier, Reed said that 'parliament exists primarily in order to make laws for society in this country'. This view, said Laws, 'totally disregards the significance both of the executive's role in legislation and of parliament's functions of scrutinising the non-legislative policies and actions of government and of calling ministers to account for the carrying out of executive functions'.

It is true that the executive – which means the government – has a role in legislation. Most legislation is proposed by the government of the day and enacted thanks to the government's supporters in parliament. 'In the real-world constitution,' Laws argued, 'the main function of parliament is to bestow constitutional legitimacy on the policy and other actions of the executive.' It does that, he said, by calling ministers to account. No help is needed by the courts.

Given this collaborative relationship, Laws continued, it was hard to believe that parliament intended to give the secretary of state a power to fix fees that was either impossible or impracticable to exercise.

But the power to set fees could certainly have been used lawfully. The only way of knowing what parliament intended is to draw inferences from the legislation it has passed. And how can the judges be sure that parliament did not mean what it said?

Let's give the last word on this to Lord Sumption. In his Reith lectures he expressed concern that the judges had 'inched their way towards a notion of fundamental law overriding ordinary processes of political decision making. These things have carried them into the realms of legislative and ministerial policy.'[27]

Sumption gave two examples. One of them was the *Unison* case:[28]

> The government had a general statutory power to charge fees but in 2017 the Supreme Court held that the language of the Act was not clear enough to authorise

fees so large that many employees would be unable to enforce their rights in court. This decision has been criticised but I think it was perfectly orthodox. MPs looking at the words of the bill as it went through parliament would not have suspected that the power to charge fees would be used to stifle people's employment rights.

This time, not even Sumption thought his colleagues had gone too far.

10

Friends, Actually

Do the judges have too much power? Are they unaccountable activists, usurping the role of an elected parliament? Have they become enemies of the people?

That's certainly what some supporters of the Judicial Power Project seem to think. And support for their views can be found in the Reith lectures delivered by Lord Sumption in the spring of 2019. But I profoundly disagree.

Judicial power

The Judicial Power Project's central thesis is that 'the decisions of parliament ought not to be called into question by the courts and that the executive ought to be free from undue judicial interference which fails to respect political judgment and discretion'.[1] When the project was set up, that executive was led by a Conservative prime minister.

An inevitable inference is that the Judicial Power Project regards judges as standing to the left of the Conservatives. If that is so, they must have moved across the political spectrum in little more than half a century – as Sir Mark Potter, a former president of the High Court family division, imagined in 2011:

> Any judge who started life in the law, as I did, as a barrister in the early 1960s, was appointed in the late 1980s, and has only recently retired, will have seen the stereotype of the High Court judge transformed in certain organs of the press from that of a portsoaked reactionary, still secretly resentful of the abolition of

the birch and hostile to liberal influences of any kind, to that of an unashamedly progressive member of the chattering classes, spiritually if not actually resident in Islington or Hampstead, out of touch with 'ordinary people', and diligently engaged in frustrating the intentions of parliament with politically correct notions of human rights.[2]

Neither caricature is accurate, of course. In recent decades the judges have followed largely the same approach, keeping ministers in check regardless of the governing party.

Crossing the Finnis line

The Judicial Power Project was launched in October 2015 with a lecture by John Finnis, Professor Emeritus of Law and Legal Philosophy at the University of Oxford. His lecture, delivered at Gray's Inn, was introduced by Michael Gove, who was then lord chancellor. Finnis gave a second lecture at Lincoln's Inn in December 2016. A book based on the lectures, with added comments, was published in 2018.[3]

Lord Burnett of Maldon, lord chief justice of England and Wales, described Finnis in the book's preface as 'one of the most distinguished legal philosophers of our age', an academic who has spent 'more than half a century thinking and writing about the concept of judicial power'.

But Finnis has never had to exercise that power himself. Without revealing his own position, Burnett noted that 'all judges called on to decide cases that occupy the intersection between judicial power and that of parliament and the executive must work out for themselves where in the spectrum of judicial activism they lie'.

In his first lecture Finnis complained about 'decisions that confuse the rule of law and legality with the rule of judges'. To say that the common law was declared rather than made was not a fairy tale, as Lord Reid had suggested in the early 1970s: it was a statement of judicial responsibility. Judicial efforts to reform the common law were often counter-productive, he argued. Legislatures were better designed to do this than were the courts.

In the printed version of his first lecture Finnis discussed a number of cases that he would have decided differently himself if he had been the judge. He maintained, plausibly enough, that our courts have sometimes come up with the wrong answer. But, as the former appeal judge Sir Patrick Elias pointed out in a response published alongside Finnis's lecture, getting it wrong does not demonstrate an improper exercise of judicial power – merely a deficient one. 'I am not persuaded the judges can fairly be criticised for usurping the legislative role in the development of the common law,' Elias wrote.

Cutting through the philosopher's arguments, Elias inferred that Finnis's ideal judge was essentially a conservative figure, amending and developing the common law only when it was out of line with principles in analogous areas, and not merely because judges thought the law would be better served by altering established principles.

But who is to say when the Finnis line has been crossed? An obvious difficulty with his analysis, as Elias pointed out, is that the distinction between legitimate dispute resolution and illegitimate rule making may be extremely difficult to draw in any particular case.

As an academic, Finnis could view the law as he would like it to be; a judge, as Elias was, must deal with the law as it is. Finnis had questioned whether courts hearing judicial review claims should have to apply the proportionality test discussed in Chapter 1, describing it as 'a power that is inherently legislative, not judicial'. Elias had considerable sympathy for that view. But the judges had no choice: parliament had told them that they must take rulings by the European Court of Human Rights into account. 'Much as Professor Finnis might wish it were otherwise, the courts cannot ignore that injunction.'

As Burnett said in his introduction, 'reading this collection of essays is likely to clarify, perhaps lead to the evolution of, the views the reader started with'. In other words, Finnis was unlikely to win anybody over.

Working a Sumption

Lord Sumption is one of only seven people to have been appointed directly from the bar to the highest court in the land.[4] Some months after his retirement from the Supreme Court at the end of 2018, he delivered the BBC's prestigious Reith lectures. They were called *Law and the Decline of Politics*.

Sumption's thesis, as I read it, is that the judges are acting politically rather than judicially, both in the way that they use their common law powers when construing statutes – or deciding judicial review claims – and in the way that they use their powers under the Human Rights Act.

'Judges have always made law,' Sumption acknowledged in the second of his lectures.[5] 'In order to decide disputes between litigants, they have to fill gaps, supplying answers which are not to be found in existing legal sources. They have to be prepared to change existing judge–made rules if they are mistaken, redundant or outdated. The common law, which has grown up organically through the decisions of judges, remains a major source of our law.'

So far, so uncontroversial. But the former judge then argued that his erstwhile colleagues had gone too far – that they had, in effect, overreached themselves:

> In the last three decades … there has been a noticeable change of judicial mood. The courts have developed a broader concept of the rule of law which greatly enlarges their own constitutional role. They have claimed a wider supervisory authority over other organs of the state. They have inched their way towards a notion of fundamental law overriding the ordinary processes of political decision making and these things have inevitably carried them into the realms of legislative and ministerial policy. To adapt the famous dictum of the German military theorist Clausewitz about war, law is now the continuation of politics by other means.

That assessment was highly contentious. For what it is worth, the Clausewitz quip had twice been dismissed, in court, by appeal judges. 'Judicial review is not, and should not be regarded as, politics by another means,' they had said earlier in 2019.[6]

Confusingly, Sumption also seemed to think the judges were not very good at overreaching themselves. They were too weak to protect us from 'majoritarian tyranny', he said in a subsequent lecture:[7]

> Law can protect minorities identified by some personal characteristic, such as gender, race or sexual orientation, from discrimination. But the courts cannot parry the broader threat that legislative majorities may act oppressively, unless they assume legislative powers for themselves. The only effective constraints on the abuse of democratic power are political.

The principle of legitimacy

What was Sumption's justification for accusing judges of inching towards a notion of fundamental law? It was a principle that they themselves had developed. Judges described it as the principle of legality; he preferred to call it the principle of legitimacy. It required ministers who proposed inherently illegitimate legislation to 'squarely declare what they are doing and take the political heat'.[8] He continued:

> The principle of legitimacy is a very valuable technique for ascertaining what parliament really intended. But it puts great power in the hands of judges. Judges decide what are the norms by which to identify particular actions as illegitimate. Judges decide what language is clear enough. These are elastic concepts. There are usually no clear legal principles to shape them. The answer depends on a subjective judgment in which a judge's personal opinion is always influential and often decisive. Yet the assertion by judges of a power to give legal effect to their opinions and values: what is that, if not a claim to political power?[9]

Sumption then referred to the case of the Prince of Wales's letters, discussed in Chapter 8, and rightly said that 'no other modern case reveals so clearly the judges' expansive view of the rule of law'. But he went on to argue that the same technique had been applied more discreetly to other, more sensitive issues of social policy:

Examples over the past half century include education,[10] subsidised fares on public transport,[11] social security benefits,[12] the use of overseas development funds,[13] statutory defences to murder,[14] the establishment of public inquiries,[15] and many, many others.[16]

Sumption's examples were challenged at a conference of administrative lawyers some weeks later by Lord Falconer of Thoroton, who served from 2003 to 2007 as Tony Blair's lord chancellor.[17]

'What the courts have done over the last 40 or 50 years,' said Falconer, 'is to hold the executive to standards of decency, honesty, competence, non-discrimination, sticking by their word, and where they create an expectation abiding by it.'

He continued:

> Those principles are not the making of policy. They are holding the executive to account in the courts in a way that the politicians either do not or cannot ... The greater and greater assertion of the courts' willingness to hold the executive to account since the early 1960s is, in my view, a reflection of the public's view that we should hold the executive to higher standards.

Public support

In his Reith lectures, Sumption offered another area where he thought the judges had taken an expansive view:

> On immigration and penal policy, the courts have for many years applied values of their own which are at odds with the harsher policies adopted, with strong public support, by parliament and successive governments.

Sumption is probably right to suppose that public enthusiasm for wide-ranging immigration restrictions is not shared by judges who have to apply those laws when dealing with individual asylum-seekers. But he produced no evidence of public support for harsher sentences. In the Sally Challen case, discussed in Chapter 3, the

Court of Appeal found a way of reducing a remarkably harsh minimum term set by parliament for a premeditated domestic murder.[18] The court's decision was widely welcomed – as was an equally sensitive decision, also discussed in Chapter 3, that maintained John Radford's sentence while keeping him in prison.

Sumption's overriding concern was that allowing the judges to circumvent statutes or review the merits of policy decisions conferred 'vast discretionary power' on people who were 'not constitutionally accountable'. It also undermined what he saw as the single biggest advantage of the political process, which was to accommodate the divergent interests and opinions of citizens.

'It is true that politics do not always perform that function very well', he said – something of an understatement in the year of the Brexit crisis. 'But judges will never be able to perform it.' That, he explained, was because judges had to make clear choices and politicians could reach messy compromises.

Again, I find this unconvincing. A judge must make a clear choice in an individual case. But when a different case comes along, another judge may take a different decision. The entire law of homicide is a messy compromise between murder and manslaughter. That's how the common law works.

Far from undermining the political process, the judges buttress it by providing an essential safety valve. We saw this with Gina Miller's twin Brexit challenges. On both occasions, the justices upheld the rule of law.

And what does Sumption imply by saying the judges are not constitutionally accountable? That they are not subject to approval by politicians or removal by the electorate? Would he prefer something closer to the US system of appointments? Clearly not: we know that he is 'passionately opposed to any suggestion that there should be political vetting of judges or confirmation hearings or anything of the sort'.[19]

Judges decide cases in public, with few exceptions, and are accountable to the public they serve. As a former president of the Israeli Supreme Court was fond of saying, when judges try cases they themselves are on trial.[20]

Human rights

Shortly after David Cameron became prime minister in 2010 he told MPs: 'It makes me physically ill even to contemplate having to give the vote to anyone who is in prison.'[21] He was referring to a ruling five years earlier in a case called *Hirst*: the European Court of Human Rights had ruled that the UK's 'blanket', or automatic, ban on convicted prisoners voting at elections was a breach of the European Convention on Human Rights.[22]

Seven years after Cameron's fit of the vapours, the lord chancellor David Lidington told MPs that offenders who had been released on temporary licence would be allowed to vote, provided they were registered at a home address. This change, which was expected to affect no more than 100 offenders on home leave at any one time, could be implemented simply by issuing new guidance to prison governors.[23] In response to concerns raised by the European Court of Human Rights, warrants of committal issued when defendants were sent to prison were amended to make it clear that the prisoners were now disenfranchised. These changes, which did not require parliamentary approval, were brought into effect in the summer of 2018.[24]

Although Lidington's reforms were so minimalist as to be almost homeopathic, they were enough of a fig leaf to satisfy the committee of ministers of the Council of Europe that the UK had complied with the *Hirst* ruling. In September 2018 the case was closed.[25]

Lord Sumption drew attention to the issue of prisoners' votes in his Reith lectures[26] – but made no mention of the fact that it had been resolved some six months earlier. As Sumption saw it, the European Court of Human Rights in Strasbourg had rejected the authority of parliament. Not at all: the court had asked the government to consider deficiencies in the law, and these had been resolved by ministers consistently with their parliamentary responsibilities.

Good judgment

On the whole, successive governments have repaired the human rights breaches identified by the courts. And, these days, ministers do not criticise individual judges – certainly not to the extent chronicled in my book *Trial of Strength*, published in 1997.[27]

The reason is not hard to see. It is because, with few exceptions, judges in the UK have shown good judgment.[28] Unlike their counterparts in some other countries, they have not tried to undermine the government of the day for reasons of party politics. Far from thwarting the will of parliament, judges have taken steps to uphold its sovereignty. Occasionally, the courts have delivered questionable decisions: I have made it clear that I prefer the minority view in *Evans*, the case about the Prince of Wales's letters. But nobody can doubt the judges' honesty, integrity and good faith. They develop the law when the law needs it. On the whole, they know just how far to go.

But is that what they should be doing? 'Parliamentary scrutiny is generally perfectly adequate for the purpose of protecting the public interest in the area of policy-making,' said Lord Sumption in 2011. 'It is also the only way of doing so that carries any democratic legitimacy.'[29]

Really? Parliamentary scrutiny is not enough to ensure that statutes are properly drafted, internally consistent and fair in their application. And it is certainly not enough to ensure that parliament is not prorogued unlawfully. Ministers sometimes take broad powers and use them to make contentious decisions. When these are improper, we rely on the judges to put them right.

Cases that reach the Supreme Court are likely to involve issues that have simply not been contemplated by parliament, and courts are a vital part of the democratic process.

Mission creep

Sumption's main concern about human rights was what he called mission creep – the Strasbourg judges' development of the European convention in directions that had never been contemplated by those who drafted it. For him, article 8 of the convention was the worst offender:

> Article 8 protects the human right to private and family life, the privacy of the home and personal correspondence. It was designed as a protection against

the surveillance state in totalitarian regimes. But the Strasbourg court has developed it into what it calls a 'principle of personal autonomy'. Acting on this principle, it has extended article 8 so that it potentially covers anything that intrudes upon a person's autonomy unless the court considers it to be justified …

They include the legal status of illegitimate children, immigration and deportation, extradition, criminal sentencing, the recording of crime, abortion, artificial insemination, homosexuality and same-sex unions, child abduction, the policing of public demonstrations, employment and social security rights, environmental and planning law, noise abatement, eviction for non-payment of rent and a great deal else besides …

None of them is to be found in the language of the convention. None of them is a natural implication from its terms. None of them has been agreed by the signatory states. They are all extensions of the text which rest on the sole authority of the judges of the Strasbourg court. This is, in reality, a form of non-consensual legislation.[30]

Is it? The European Court of Human Rights has certainly extended the reach of article 8 – much further than anybody might have imagined when it was drafted in 1950. But at what point do judicial decisions cease to be proper development of the law and start to become legislation? And how can law making be characterised as non-consensual when parliament agreed to it, instructing judges in the UK to give effect to legislation compatibly with decisions of the European Court of Human Rights? Successive UK governments have always complied with the court's rulings, although – as we saw in the *Hirst* case – they sometimes take as long as they can to do as little as they can get away with.

Speaking at a lawyers' conference in July 2019, Lord Dyson, a former Supreme Court justice, reminded Sumption that parliament had gone into this with its eyes wide open.[31] Tony Blair's government, which introduced the Human Rights Act, knew perfectly well that the Strasbourg court would continue to develop convention rights. Dyson quoted from the government's proposals, published in 1997:[32]

The convention is often described as a 'living instrument' because it is interpreted by the European court in the light of present-day conditions and therefore reflects changing social attitudes and the changes in the circumstances of society. In future our judges will be able to contribute to this dynamic and evolving interpretation of the convention.

But, as Sumption explained, his main argument was with the way the legislation had been drafted:

The Human Rights Act 1998 empowers the British courts to strike down any rule of common law, regulation or government decision which is found to be incompatible with the human rights convention. Even an Act of parliament can be declared incompatible with the convention, which is a signal to parliament to repeal or amend it. Crucially, the Human Rights Act requires the British courts to take account of rulings of the European Court of Human Rights.[33]

Does the Act really empower the courts to 'strike down' common law rules, regulations or government decisions? Not quite.

Section 6 makes it unlawful for a public authority to act in a way which is incompatible with a convention right, unless primary legislation means that it could not have acted differently. The courts can, where necessary, declare that. They are also public authorities themselves. But judges can already quash ministerial regulations under well-established common law principles – as the Supreme Court did in the *Unison* case, when it decided that a ministerial order setting employment tribunal fees was outside the lord chancellor's powers and therefore unlawful.[34]

Section 3 goes further, saying that primary legislation and subordinate legislation must be read and given effect in a way which is compatible with convention rights. In Chapter 1 I mentioned the *Godin-Mendoza* ruling, in which the survivor of a gay couple was treated as a surviving spouse so that he could continue to live in a rented flat.[35] But that was not 'striking down' or ignoring legislation. It was respecting it and building it up.

The flexibility and pragmatic development of the common law is its great merit, as Patrick O'Connor QC pointed out in a response to Sumption's lectures.[36] 'Nobody suggests that the 1991 House of Lords judgment abolishing the common law marital rape exemption[37] was judicial overreach,' O'Connor wrote. 'Many ancient common law rights have kept pace with the times. It would be anomalous and unworkable for those rights to be interpreted according to living, flexible and pragmatic criteria, whilst European convention rights are tied to a rigid originalist approach.'

Sumption answers back

To his credit, Lord Sumption agreed to face his critics in July 2019 at a conference of lawyers practising administrative law.[38] He was deftly cross-examined by Sir Rabinder Singh, a well-regarded Court of Appeal judge.

Singh first got Sumption to agree that judicial review has a fundamental role in restraining excesses of power by the executive. The former justice also said it was very difficult to draw the line between questions of policy that belonged to the realm of politics and questions of law that belonged to the courts. But, he insisted, 'the fact that it is difficult to draw a line does not mean to say that such a line doesn't exist'.

Sumption conceded that the judges were becoming more deferential: 'that there is some evidence that the up-and-coming generation of judges are more circumspect in their regard for what is properly part of the political domain than their predecessors were'. That was true of the human rights judges in Strasbourg too, he thought.

Singh then suggested to Sumption that parliament seemed relatively content to let the courts develop common law principles of judicial review. Parliament could have limited the grounds of review if it believed the courts had gone too far.

'I'm not sure that it's sensible to ask whether parliament is content,' Sumption retorted. 'We are entitled to be concerned about something even if we find that parliament is not concerned about it.'

Turning to the Human Rights Act, Singh suggested that parliament had been fully entitled to give the higher courts the power to declare legislation incompatible with the convention.

Sumption side-stepped the question, complaining instead that parliament had given an 'essentially legislative power' to a court in Strasbourg that was not amenable to democratic input. He made no mention of the Council of Europe, whose parliamentary assembly – comprising national parliamentarians – selects the human rights judges and whose committee of ministers – representing each of the member states – supervises enforcement of judgments from the European Court of Human Rights.

Singh accepted that the European Convention on Human Rights imposed limitations, in international law, on the powers of democratic legislatures. But surely increased protection for minorities, developed by the European Court of Human Rights over the years, had been a desirable outcome?[39]

Many outcomes were desirable, Sumption acknowledged, but the ends did not justify the means. Take privacy. 'How much privacy are we as a society prepared to sacrifice in order to be better protected against crime?' This was a matter for legislators to decide, not courts.

But the Strasbourg court had always been sensitive to these issues, Singh responded. It allowed national parliaments what it called a margin of appreciation – in effect, room for manoeuvre.

Yes, Sumption replied, but that degree of discretion should have been very much greater. If courts in the UK were required to take decisions that were essentially political, then people would demand political vetting of judges – as we saw with Senate confirmation hearings in the US. And no lawyer in the UK wanted to go down that road.

There had been no pressure to introduce political vetting of judges in the 19 years since the Human Rights Act had come into force, Singh reminded him. Perhaps that was because the judges had applied the Act in a way that was 'conscientious, sensible and balanced'.

'Well it comes and goes,' Sumption replied airily. 'There have been pressures from some parts of the press and from some parts of the House of Commons for some kind of confirmation hearings … They haven't acquired much traction but the pressure is there and it is liable to grow over time.'

Sumption: the verdict

Less than a week after Sumption's conversation with Sir Rabinder Singh, Theresa May announced that Lord Reed would become president of the Supreme Court from 2020 and that he would be joined by three new justices, one of whom had never been a full-time judge.[40] It was a busy news day – May resigned as prime minister a few hours later – but nobody took any notice of the announcement or suggested that the new justices should face confirmation hearings.

That changed after the Supreme Court ruled in September 2019 that Boris Johnson's attempt to prorogue parliament had been unlawful. Critics of the ruling argued that the senior judiciary had behaved in a way that was political and should therefore face some sort of political vetting. But wiser heads prevailed.

Just before Singh interviewed Sumption, Lord Dyson had pointed out a contradiction in the former justice's position. Why was Sumption happy for judges to make some laws but not others? Once he accepted that the judges could develop the law, the only question was how far they should go.

In reality, said Dyson, we needed judges to interpret statutes and decide whether the executive had acted lawfully:

> I accept that, in recent years, judges have been exercising power in areas where they didn't do before … But the increase in judicial power should not be overstated and presented as some sort of revolution. Most judges, I believe, tend to be cautious. In judicial review, they are aware of the need for deference, or to allow a generous area of judgment to the decision maker.

There were areas of policy in which the courts still refused to interfere – rightly, in Dyson's view:

> I accept, of course, as Lord Sumption says, that judges do have their prejudices and subjective values – but so does everybody else … [He] does not identify a principle by which one should distinguish between those political issues which fall outside the proper domain of the law

or indeed a mechanism by which such issues can be decided.

I say: leave well alone.

We should certainly leave the judges to continue making law. But we are still entitled to consider how activist they are – or should be.

Active or asleep?

Perhaps not surprisingly, 'activism' is not a term the judges like. It can be used pejoratively. 'The word has no jurisprudential meaning,' wrote Sir Stephen Sedley. 'A judge is either active or asleep.'[41]

Lord Bingham argued that the term 'activist', if used at all, should be confined to cases where the courts had unexpectedly declined a claim. The law lords had held in 1999 that the parents of a normal and healthy child, born to a mother following allegedly negligent advice on the effect of a vasectomy performed on her husband, could not recover as damages the cost of bringing up the child.[42] 'The ingredients of a successful claim were there,' Bingham said. Although the judges 'had good reasons for declining to regard a human life as no more than a financial liability ... it was an exercise in creative decision making'.[43]

Lord Dyson said in 2013 that temperament had a lot to do with it:

> It is an inescapable fact that some judges are more conservative than others. Some are cautious and prefer to paddle in the warm and safe shallows of clear precedent. Others are more adventurous and are prepared to give it a go in the more treacherous waters of the open sea. Fortunately for them, the worst fate that they can suffer is to be overturned, unless they are in the Supreme Court. But history has shown that the product of today's buccaneer sometimes becomes tomorrow's orthodoxy.[44]

And Lord Reed, speaking as deputy president of the UK Supreme Court in 2019, explained how his court took account of different views:

Unlike the Court of Appeal, we are not bound by precedent, and so an important aspect of our role is the development of the law through our consideration of the cases raising the most important questions. The performance of that function requires a sense of the coherence of the law as a whole, an awareness of how it has developed over time, and an understanding of how it needs to develop now so as to respond to the evolving needs of our society. In order to meet those requirements, we have larger panels than in the lower court: at least five justices, and sometimes seven or more. That larger panel also tends to even out the differences in judicial outlook and temperament which can be more significant on a smaller court.[45]

Lord Neuberger, who was president of the UK Supreme Court from 2012 to 2017, gave a remarkably frank interview in 2018 to Claire Foster-Gilbert, director of the Westminster Abbey Institute, for the Radio 4 *Sunday* programme.[46] How did it feel, she asked him, to have the responsibility of setting precedent?

Some judges don't have many doubts. Some judges are plagued by doubts. And I was closer to the latter category. I do worry. I wanted to get it right; but I think I probably worried whether I was making the law or interpreting the law: whether it was interpreting a statute or making it. I tended to be something of a swing vote.

You could say in favour of a judge like me that obviously I take decision making very seriously and appreciate both sides and weigh them up; or you could say I'm an indecisive character: it depends on your taste.

Hale to the chief

Lady Hale was president of the UK Supreme Court from 2017 until the end of 2019. Although she had worked part time as a barrister,[47] most of her career before becoming a judge was spent as an academic. That may explain why she was seen as more radical and activist than some of her colleagues. Lord Sumption accepted that he had been more 'cautious' than she was. 'But has she ever overstepped the mark? No, I don't think I can think of a single case when she has.'[48]

Lord Hope, who had been a law lord since 1996, was more apprehensive about Hale's arrival in 2004 than he was about those appointed alongside her. 'Simon [Lord Brown of Eaton-under-Heywood] will keep up the spirit of good humour,' he told his diary at the time. 'Bob [Lord Carswell] will drop neatly into Brian's [Lord Hutton's] shoes as our man from Northern Ireland.' And Hale? 'Brenda will be a source of some anxiety until we adjust to the very different contribution that she will make.'[49]

When Lord Phillips of Worth Matravers retired as president of the Supreme Court in 2012, Hale had every reason to expect that she would succeed him. Instead, the 'anyone but Brenda' campaign alighted on Lord Neuberger, less than three years into his post as master of the rolls. Lord Judge, the lord chief justice of England and Wales, had concluded that Neuberger 'was the obvious person' to succeed Phillips, and wanted Lord Dyson, who was then a fairly new member of the Supreme Court, to succeed Neuberger.[50] When Neuberger retired from the Supreme Court in 2017, Hale was left with little more than two years to make her mark.[51]

The new president was not the radical activist that some had expected – though she was determined to improve the Supreme Court's gender balance. She worked tirelessly to encourage more women to become lawyers and judges, celebrating both the tenth anniversary of the Supreme Court and the hundredth anniversary of women in the law[52] before reaching mandatory retirement age.[53]

Her greatest achievement was to produce a unanimous judgment in September 2019 on the prorogation of parliament cases.[54] To an outsider, this might not have seemed particularly unusual. But it was the first time that 11 judges had sat in a UK court and delivered a single judgment on which they all agreed.

What is a person?

To what extent did Hale see it as her role to develop the law? There was a difference between statute law and case-based law, she told me in January 2019:[55]

The common law of England and Wales, of Scotland, of Northern Ireland has proceeded on a gradual incremental development of principle from one case to the next – hopefully, keeping up with developments in society and in the general zeitgeist to reflect modern life. So, in common law cases it is the role of the court, in that very cautious incremental way, to develop the law to meet new situations. As far as statutory interpretation is concerned, generally of course the statute is the statute and it's our job to work out what it means.

But meanings could change – particularly in the field of family law. What, she asked me, did I think parliament had meant by the word 'person' in the 1880s?

That question had come before the law lords in 1908, Hale recalled, in an appeal brought by five women who had graduated from the University of Edinburgh.[56] That made them members of the university's general council. And under the Representation of the People (Scotland) Act 1868, 'every person' registered on the council could vote to elect a university member of parliament.[57] But the five women were refused voting papers – and that refusal was upheld by the Scottish courts. They appealed to the House of Lords.

The leading judgment was given by Lord Loreburn, the lord chancellor. 'It is notorious that this right of voting has ... been confined to men ... from the earliest times down to this day,' he said. 'If this legal disability is to be removed, it must be done by Act of parliament.'

Lord Ashbourne added that when the statute was passed 'the legislature could only have had male persons in contemplation, as women could not then be graduates'. He therefore had no doubt that 'person' meant 'male person'. The other judges agreed that the appeals should be dismissed. For these purposes, at least, woman was not a person.

Little more than 20 years later, the law lords – sitting as the judicial committee of the privy council to hear an appeal from Canada – were asked to think again.[58] Under the British North America Act 1867, passed a year earlier than the voting legislation, 'qualified persons' could be made senators. Did the word 'persons' include 'female persons'? The Supreme Court of Canada thought not. Again, five distinguished women appealed to London.

This time, they were successful. After an exhaustive analysis of the legislation five judges, led by Lord Sankey, the lord chancellor, ruled that females could indeed be appointed. So 'persons' now included women.[59]

This was a clear change in what the courts understood the wording to mean. The same term had been used by parliament at almost exactly the same time. But the social context had changed hugely between 1908 and 1929.

Are some judges more activist?

Do the judges' backgrounds affect the way they decide cases? I asked Hale whether it mattered whether a case was decided by a man or a woman.[60]

> We all bring our experience of life to the business of deciding particular cases; and that will include things in our background like, possibly, our gender, our upbringing, our education, our experience of professional life, our experience of life generally and our values and attitudes to the law. We bring all of those things, men or women, to the business of judging. And the theory is that if you have five, seven, or nine different legal minds – all trying to get the right answer to the particular problem – what they come up with will actually be better than what any individual would have come up with, because something greater will be forged out of the deliberation, the discussion, the attrition of diverse minds.

On the other hand, Hale added, individual judges were not particularly predictable in the way they might decide a case. 'We are all capable of surprising one another.'

But how far did Hale think the judges should go? 'The law has to move with the times – up to a point,' she said in a subsequent lecture.[61] 'When designing the Supreme Court of the United Kingdom, we deliberately put the library at the heart of the building, surrounded by the three court rooms: one on top, one to one side and one to the other. It contains, of course, centuries of legislation and law reports. It symbolises an important truth: we are not making it up as we go along but building on those centuries of legal learning.'

What, then, should guide the judges when they put another brick in the wall? Principle or pragmatism? Doctrine or policy? 'Generally speaking,' said Hale, 'the incremental approach from established principle is to be preferred to imposing the court's own choices, which are clearly based upon practical or policy considerations rather than on principle.'

A conservative court?

Until the week before its tenth anniversary the UK Supreme Court had been seen as pretty conservative. That was certainly the view of its incoming president, Lord Reed – himself a pretty conservative judge.[62] In March 2019 Reed observed that his court's approach to human rights cases had been criticised as being 'excessively deferential' towards the assessments made by government and parliament.[63] Examples discussed in this book included challenge to the law on assisted suicide – in *Nicklinson* and *Conway*[64] – and the challenge to abortion law in Northern Ireland. 'The challenge to the benefit cap was also rejected,' he said, 'on the basis that the government's assessment of proportionality was not manifestly without a reasonable foundation.'[65]

Reed's conclusion was stark. Referring to a major constitutional ruling that had limited the power of the 18th-century state, he suspected that 'the government of the day was more dismayed by the case of *Entick v Carrington*[66] than present-day Whitehall has been by the decisions of the Supreme Court.'

Six months later, everything changed. Citing *Entick v Carrington*, Hale and Reed – sitting with nine other justices – delivered a judgment that drew heavily on Reed's judgment in the *Unison* case[67] and dismayed Whitehall very much indeed.

Miller and Cherry

I explained in Chapter 2 how Gina Miller and Joanna Cherry launched parallel claims in England and Scotland challenging Boris Johnson's decision to prorogue parliament in the run-up to Brexit. Both claims were dismissed in September 2019 by the judges who heard them first.

But then the Supreme Court ruled in favour of the two campaigners.[68] The issue was justiciable – meaning that the courts would consider whether the prime minister's advice had been lawful. Proroguing parliament for five weeks shortly before the expected date of Brexit was not lawful because it had stopped parliament holding the government to account – and the prime minister had shown the court no reasonable justification. So, it was as if parliament had not been prorogued after all.

Among the 11 justices who sat was Lord Sales; three years earlier, as Lord Justice Sales, he had been traduced as an enemy of the people. He and his colleagues knew exactly what to expect when they ruled against Boris Johnson in a case that, despite all their protestations, was ultimately about Brexit.

Nobody had predicted a unanimous ruling. Many legal commentators had thought the case too close to call – although Lord Sumption, a newcomer to our ranks, said at the outset that victory for Miller and Cherry was 'a very, very long shot'.[69] After that shot had reached home, he supported his former colleagues' decision – perhaps indicating how even a 'cautious' judge, as he had been, could have been won over:

> The objection to judicial interference in politics is that it undermines the democratic legitimacy of public decision making. The problem that we have here is that the government itself has sought to undermine the democratic legitimacy of public decision making by dispensing with a central feature of our constitution: that ministers are answerable to parliament. What the Supreme Court has done is to invent a brand-new ... constitutional rule, the effect of which is to reinstate parliament at the heart of the decision making process. That is not undermining democracy at all; nor is

it a coup. It is simply replacing what ought to have
happened [through constitutional] convention by law
– in circumstances where the government has tried to
kick away the conventions.[70]

I myself had not expected the justices to be quite so bold. Not that
I was doubting their personal courage. They had enhanced security
in the courtroom, but none when they walked out of the building.
Sitting without wigs and gowns, they were easily recognisable to
anyone who watched the broadcast hearings. But what concerned
me was that the more the judges are seen as entering the political
arena, the less respect the public will have for their rulings. It was
not that the judges were undermining the legitimacy of decision
making by ministers; it was that ministers, in stretching their
constitutional powers to breaking-point, were undermining the
legitimacy of decision making by judges.

Gina Miller's first victory in 2016, and her second success in
2019, did not involve power-grabs by the judiciary. In both cases
the Supreme Court handed power back to parliament that the prime
minister of the day had wrongly sought to exercise. It is shameful
that some news outlets sought to obscure these fundamental truths.

But what these cases also show is the immense respect that both
the executive and the legislature have for the courts. If judges say
that legislation is needed to trigger Brexit, ministers will seek
legislation. And if judges say there is nothing to stop parliament
sitting, then it will sit.

As the Supreme Court said, this case was a 'one-off' – in
circumstances that have never arisen before and are unlikely to
arise again. But, the justices added, 'our law is used to rising to
such challenges and supplies us with the legal tools to enable us to
reason to a solution'.

The day after the Supreme Court's prorogation ruling one senior
legal figure asked me what had changed. His point was that the
courts had been ensuring for centuries that rulers did not exceed
their powers. For decades, they had been reviewing the decisions
of ministers. This, he thought, was just another area in which the
courts would ensure that powers were properly exercised.

He was right: the justices were not creating a new area of law.
And the outcome – as advocated by Lord Pannick and agreed by

the court – seemed so simple, so obvious. It was a classic example of what one of the lawyers involved in the case told me immediately after the judgment: 'the thing about great cases is that what once seemed impossible now seems inevitable'.

Until this ruling, the most senior member of the UK government had few constitutional responsibilities. The prime minister appoints and dismisses other ministers; chairs the cabinet; and advises the monarch. But prime ministers used to be regarded as no more than first among equals. The Supreme Court made it clear that, in advising the monarch on prorogation, the prime minister now has a 'constitutional responsibility, as the only person with power to do so, to have regard to all relevant interests, including the interests of parliament'.[71] As the legal commentator David Allen Green pointed out, that means 'the prime minister has a special responsibility above the selfish political interests of the government'.[72]

I suggested in Chapter 9 that the British constitution would not work properly unless the 'powers that be' made proper use of the powers they had. This case was an example of a prime minister ignoring a long-standing constitutional convention and misusing his powers. What the Supreme Court did was to restore the balance of power between the legislature and the executive. At the same time, the judiciary reinforced its own role as a separate but equal power.

By judicial standards this was an unusually concise ruling – perhaps because there was little time to write it. Even though it was the product of more than one hand, it was remarkably clear and easy to read. It marked the Supreme Court's coming-of-age after ten years; it showed that the justices could hold their heads high as a modern constitutional court; and it marked the pinnacle of Lady Hale's career as a pioneering judge. Above all, it brought together activist and conservative members of a court who were determined to resist the arbitrary use of power. We have no need to codify the British constitution when it is to be found in the hearts and minds of judges such as these.

Not enemies at all

The judges are not the public's elected representatives and it is not for them to make political decisions. But there can be no justification for the incendiary reporting of judicial decisions epitomised by the

Daily Mail's notorious headline in 2016 and some of the reaction to the *Miller* and *Cherry* cases three years later. The judges are simply being true to the oaths they took on appointment.

Commenting on Lord Sumption's Reith lectures in July 2019,[73] the former lord chancellor Lord Falconer helpfully answered the question I posed at the beginning of this book. He thought it would be 'disastrous' if Sumption's view – that the courts have gone too far – were to gain currency:

> I can see a lot of politicians who would think: let's go with that route. It's an absolute gift for those who saw the courts as the enemies of the people.
>
> The courts are not the enemies of the people. The courts have proved themselves to be the upholders of standards that almost everybody would agree with. And, in the UK, we have done it without there being a revolutionary moment. We've done it without taking on the politicians and we've done it successfully in a way that has not caused any constitutional disaster.
>
> So, I applaud the judges in the way they've been over the last 50 years and ultimately deprecate the conclusions that Lord Sumption reached in the Reith lectures.

Ultimately, the British constitution relies on a delicate balance between the executive, the legislature and the judiciary: all three powers of the state must demonstrate good judgment if we are to be governed under the rule of law.

The Brexit referendum of 2016 knocked that balance off course, weakening the executive and putting greater demands on the legislature. We cannot expect constitutional equilibrium to be restored overnight. In the meantime, the judicial function is more important than ever.

Far from being enemies of the people, judges are just about the only friends we have.

Notes

Preface

1 *R (Miller) v Secretary of State for Exiting the European Union* [2016] EWHC 2768 (Admin).

2 *R (Miller) v Prime Minister; Cherry v Advocate General* [2019] UKSC 41, paragraph 69.

3 Adam Benforado, *Unfair: The New Science of Criminal Injustice*, Broadway Books, 2016, p 158.

4 'Judges and justices are servants of the law, not the other way around. Judges are like umpires. Umpires don't make the rules; they apply them. The role of an umpire and a judge is critical. They make sure everybody plays by the rules. But it is a limited role. Nobody ever went to a ball game to see the umpire.' Judge John Roberts, Senate Judiciary Committee, 12 September 2005, http://edition.cnn.com/2005/POLITICS/09/12/roberts.statement.

5 Lady Hale, *Judges, Power and Accountability*, Constitutional Law Summer School, Belfast, 11 August 2017, https://www.supremecourt.uk/docs/speech-170811.pdf.

6 Lord Reid, 'The judge as law maker', *Journal of the Society of Public Teachers of Law*, vol 12 (1972), p 22. And see Chapter 1.

7 Lord Lloyd-Jones, *General Principles of Law in International and Common Law*, lecture to the Conseil d'État, Paris, 16 February 2018, https://www.supremecourt.uk/docs/speech-180216.pdf.

8 Jonathan Sumption, *Judicial and Political Decision Making: The Uncertain Boundary*, F.A. Mann Lecture, 9 November 2011, https://www.scribd.com/document/72814968/Sumption-Mann-Lecture-Final.

9 Jonathan Sumption, *In Praise of Politics*, BBC Reith Lectures 2019, lecture 2, 28 May 2019, https://www.bbc.co.uk/programmes/b00729d9/episodes/player.

10 See Chapter 10.

11 www.bailii.org.

Chapter 1

1   Joshua Rozenberg, 'Is this new statute untouchable?', *Telegraph*, 16 September 2004, https://www.telegraph.co.uk/news/uknews/1471841/Is-this-new-statute-untouchable.html. The term 'Queen-in-Parliament' refers jointly to the House of Commons, the House of Lords and the monarch. But royal assent to legislation is never refused and, in practice, the Lords does not block legislation that has the clear support of the Commons. So law making is in the hands of MPs.

2   '*Le parlement peut tout, excepté faire une femme d'un homme, &* vice versa', Jean-Louis De Lolme, *Constitution de l'Angleterre*, 1789 edn, p 126, fn 1, https://archive.org/details/constitutiondela00lolm/page/n165.

3   See Gender Recognition Act 2004.

4   'Parliament has no right to plot a Brexit coup', *The Times*, 23 August 2019, https://www.thetimes.co.uk/article/parliament-has-no-right-to-plot-a-brexit-coup-jf0k8r89t.

5   *R (Miller) v Prime Minister; Cherry v Advocate General* [2019] UKSC 41.

6   Rt Hon Peter Lilley, 'Who is sovereign – people or parliament?', *The Article*, 31 August 2019, https://www.thearticle.com/who-is-sovereign-people-or-parliament.

7   Suicide Act 1961, section 1.

8   For example, the War Damage Act 1965, which retroactively revoked *Burmah Oil v Lord Advocate* [1965] AC 75 (HL).

9   *R v Home Secretary ex parte Fire Brigades Union* [1995] 2 AC 513 at 567.

10 *R (Miller) v Prime Minister; Cherry v Advocate General* [2019] UKSC 41, paragraphs 28, 34.

11 The Benn Act – as it was called – required the prime minister to seek a three-month extension to the Brexit deadline on 19 October 2019 unless, by then, MPs had approved a deal or agreed to leave the EU without a deal. Boris Johnson complied with it.

12 See, for example, Joshua Rozenberg, *Trial of Strength*, Richard Cohen Books, 1997, p ix.

13 *M v Home Office* [1992] QB 270 at 314, adopting a submission by Stephen Sedley QC.

14 Tom Bingham, *The Rule of Law*, Allen Lane, 2010. The core of the principle, he wrote (p 8), was that 'all persons and authorities within the state, whether public or private, should be bound by and entitled to the benefit of laws publicly made, taking effect (generally) in the future and publicly administered in the courts'.

15 Section 17(1).

16 The office of lord chancellor goes back to at least the 11th century, if not before. Since 2007 it has been combined with the office of secretary of state for justice (or justice secretary). I have used the terms interchangeably. The holder is now a cabinet minister, not a judge.

17 'Parliament having recognised this "existing constitutional principle", and provided no definition, there is nothing controversial in the proposition that it is for the courts, and ultimately the Supreme Court (created by the same Act), to determine its content and limits.' *R (Privacy International) v Investigatory Powers Tribunal* [2019] UKSC 22, paragraph 121.

18 [1993] AC 593 (HL).

19 For examples, see Rozenberg, *Trial of Strength*, pp 94–8.

20 *R v Secretary of State for the Home Department Ex p Simms* [2000] 2 AC 115, 131.

21 Jonathan Sumption, *In Praise of Politics*, BBC Reith Lectures 2019, lecture 2, 28 May 2019, https://www.bbc.co.uk/programmes/b00729d9/episodes/player.

22 Section 3(1).

23 *Donoghue v Stevenson* [1932] AC 562, the case of the (alleged) snail in the ginger-beer bottle, is the one that all law students know, just as 1066 is the one date that all history students can remember.

24 Lord Reid, 'The judge as law maker', *Journal of the Society of Public Teachers of Law*, vol 12 (1972), p 22.

25 *Blackstone's Criminal Practice*, Oxford University Press, 2020, paragraph B1.1.

26 In simple terms, 'the offence of murder involves the perpetrator killing a person when intending either to kill or to inflict grievous bodily harm'. *R (Nicklinson) v Ministry of Justice* [2014] UKSC 38, paragraph 15 (Lord Neuberger).

27 3 Co Inst 47. The original wording reads: 'Murder is when a man of sound memory, and of the age of discretion, unlawfully killeth within any county of the realm any reasonable creature in rerum natura under the king's peace, with malice fore-thought, either expressed by the party, or implied by the law, so as the party wounded, or hurt, etc die of the wound, or hurt, etc within a year and a day after the same.'

28 Offences against the Person Act 1861, section 9.

29 See Law Reform (Year and a Day Rule) Act 1996.

30 Stephen Sedley, *The Common Law and the Constitution*, Radcliffe Lecture, University of Warwick, 14 November 1996.

31 The reference is to the ruler of a desert island, laying down the law without regard to settled principles.

32 *Magor and St Mellons RDC v Newport Corporation* [1950] 2 All ER 1226, 1236 (CA).

33 *Magor and St Mellons RDC v Newport Corporation* [1952] AC 189, 191. His approach was more than a little hypocritical, as we shall see in Chapter 3.

34 Quoted in Michael Zander, *The Law-Making Process*, 7th edn, Hart Publishing, 2015, p 365.

35 Practice Statement (Judicial Precedent) [1966] 1 WLR 1234.

36 P.J. Fitzgerald, *Salmond on Jurisprudence*, 12th edn, Sweet & Maxwell, 1966.

37 *Salmond on Jurisprudence*, Preface. Sir Henry Fisher is best remembered for his decision – considered shocking at the time – to resign from the High Court bench in 1970 after less than three years and become a merchant banker. It was said that he did not find the work of a judge intellectually challenging.

38 At that time, the House of Lords; since 2009, the Supreme Court.

39 *R v Jogee* [2016] UKSC 8; *Knauer v Ministry of Justice* [2016] UKSC 9; *Patel v Mirza* [2016] UKSC 42.

40 J.A.G. Griffith, *The Politics of the Judiciary*, 5th edn, Fontana, 1977, p 52 (emphasis in original).

41 Sir Stephen Sedley said: 'Griffith was being led by his own radicalism to applaud, or at least not to criticise, a number of decisions in which a now self-confident judiciary was standing up to authoritarian acts of a Conservative government'. Sedley, *Lions under the Throne*, Cambridge, 2015, p 110.

42 Griffith, *The Politics of the Judiciary*, p 57.

43 'Precedent is a Jewish mother. You don't have to do what it tells you, but it makes you feel terrible about not doing it.' Sir Stephen Sedley, Atkin Lecture, 6 November 2001, Reform Club, reprinted in Sedley, *Ashes and Sparks*, Cambridge, 2011, p 203.

44 In this context I am distinguishing civil law from common law. The term is more frequently used as the antithesis of criminal law: civil law governs the relationships between individuals (or groups) while criminal law deals with the relationship between individuals (or groups) and the state. The term Civil Law is sometimes used as a synonym for Roman Law.

45 Gaps.

46 'The Judge as Lawmaker: an English Perspective', reprinted in Tom Bingham, *The Business of Judging*, Oxford University Press, 2000, p 28.

47   *Ras Behari Lal v King-Emperor* [1933] UKPC 60.

48   Atkin Lecture, 6 November 2001, Reform Club, reprinted in Stephen Sedley, *Ashes and Sparks*, Cambridge, 2011, p 205.

49   *Woolwich Equitable Building Society Respondents v Inland Revenue Commissioners* [1993] AC 70, 173.

50   They included the Northern Ireland (Executive Formation etc) Act 2019, discussed in Chapter 4.

51   The term used in legislation is 'British Islands': see schedule 1 of the Interpretation Act 1978.

52   In the United States, the Secretary of State is the minister responsible for foreign affairs and the State Department is the foreign ministry.

53   A protocol, in this context, is a subsequent treaty adding to or amending the original convention.

54   Lord Irvine of Lairg, the lord chancellor who devised the legislation, never received the credit he deserved for it.

55   Human Rights Act 1998, section 4.

56   Lord Neuberger of Abbotsbury, *The Supreme Court Yearbook Volume 8*, 2018, p 3.

57   *Ghaidan v Godin-Mendoza* [2004] UKHL 30.

58   Interestingly, the government supported that position. See Lady Hale, British Institute of Human Rights Annual Lecture 2018, https://www.supremecourt.uk/docs/speech-181107.pdf.

59   Lady Hale, *Human Rights and Family Life in the United Kingdom and Islands*, Caroline Weatherill Memorial Lecture 2018, Isle of Man Law Society, 5 December 2018, https://www.supremecourt.uk/docs/speech-181205.pdf.

60   Rules of the Supreme Court (Amendment No 3) 1977, rule 5, creating a new Order 53: '(1) An application for … an order of mandamus, prohibition or certiorari … shall be made by way of an application for judicial review …'

61   *R (Countryside Alliance) v Attorney General* [2008] 1 AC 719, paragraph 45.

62   The legislation was passed, under the Parliament Acts, without the agreement of the House of Lords.

63   There may be a 'rolled-up' hearing, in which the application for permission and the claim itself are decided at the same time.

64   The mayor of London, in *R (DSD and NBV) v Parole Board* [2018] EWHC 694.

65   The master of the rolls deals mainly with civil cases and is second in seniority only to the lord chief justice of England and Wales.

66 *Associated Provincial Picture Houses Ltd v Wednesbury Corporation* [1948] 1 KB 223 at 229.

67 Sedley, *Ashes and Sparks*, p 64. He argued that the council had unjustifiably excluded parents of young children from a leisure activity on the one day they were free to enjoy it.

68 In *Your Rights and the Law* (with Nicola Watkins), Dent, 1986.

69 Known as the GCHQ case: *Council of Civil Service Unions v Minister for the Civil Service* [1985] AC 374 at 410.

70 *R v Parliamentary Commissioner for Administration Ex p Balchin (No 1)* [1998] 1 PLR 1, paragraph 27.

71 Lord Dyson MR, Sultan Azlan Shah Lecture, Malaysia, November 2015, https://www.judiciary.uk/wp-content/uploads/2015/12/is-judicial-review-a-threat-to-democracy-mr.pdf.

72 *R v Ministry of Defence ex p Smith* [1996] QB 517 at 554.

73 *R (ABCIFER) v Secretary of State for Defence* [2003] EWCA Civ 473, paras 34/5.

74 *R (Q) v Secretary of State for the Home Department* [2003] EWCA Civ 364, para 112.

75 *Smith and Grady v UK* (2000) 29 EHRR 493.

76 Human Rights Act 1998, section 2.

77 *R (SB) v Governors of Denbigh High School* [2006] UKHL 15.

78 Lord Lloyd-Jones, *General Principles of Law in International and Common Law*, Conseil d'État, Paris, 16 February 2018, https://www.supremecourt.uk/docs/speech-180216.pdf.

79 http://judicialpowerproject.org.uk/about.

80 Lord Lloyd-Jones, *General Principles of Law in International and Common Law*, Conseil d'État, Paris, 16 February 2018, https://www.supremecourt.uk/docs/speech-180216.pdf.

81 http://judicialpowerproject.org.uk/about.

82 Lord Reed, interviewed 29 January 2019 for *Law in Action*, BBC Radio 4.

83 Owen J, Leicester Crown Court, 30 July 1990 [1991] 1 All ER 747 (text unreported).

84 *Owens v Owens* [2018] UKSC 41, paragraph 46.

85 *R (Nicklinson) v Ministry of Justice* [2014] UKSC 38, paragraph 116.

86 *Re McLaughlin's Application for Judicial Review* [2018] UKSC 48, paragraph 116.

87 Hale, *Judges, Power and Accountability*.

Chapter 2

1   'It wouldn't just have been hard for me to deliver a policy I didn't believe in – I wouldn't have been able to do so.' David Cameron, *For the Record*, William Collins, 2019, p 680.

2   This says, in part:
    1. Any Member State may decide to withdraw from the Union in accordance with its own constitutional requirements.
    2. A Member State which decides to withdraw shall notify the European Council of its intention …

3   https://www.gov.uk/government/speeches/eu-referendum-outcome-pm-statement-24-june-2016.

4   https://www.gov.uk/government/speeches/pm-commons-statement-on-eu-reform-and-referendum-22-february-2016.

5   https://www.theguardian.com/commentisfree/2016/jun/24/brexit-won-vote-remain-eu-article-50-lisbon-treaty-referendum-david-cameron.

6   https://ukconstitutionallaw.org/2016/06/27/nick-barber-tom-hickman-and-jeff-king-pulling-the-article-50-trigger-parliaments-indispensable-role.

7   'Exercise of ministers' prerogative powers must … be consistent both with the common law as laid down by the courts and with statutes as enacted by parliament.' *R (Miller) v Secretary of State for Exiting the European Union* [2017] UKSC 5, paragraph 50.

8   https://ukconstitutionallaw.org/2016/06/27/nick-barber-tom-hickman-and-jeff-king-pulling-the-article-50-trigger-parliaments-indispensable-role.

9   See Gina Miller, *Rise: Life Lessons in Speaking Out, Standing Tall and Leading the Way*, Canongate, 2018, p 12. Two other clients withdrew when they saw the abuse Miller had received.

10 There were other claimants too. One of them had filed proceedings earlier, contrary to the 'pre-action protocol', because of fears that Brexit might be triggered precipitately. But Miller was made the 'lead claimant' by a senior judge in order to ensure that the lead argument would be put by her counsel, Lord Pannick QC, the leading advocate of his generation in this area of law.

11 *R (Miller) v Secretary of State for Exiting the European Union* [2016] EWHC 2768 (Admin). As normally happens in judicial review claims, the judges were sitting as a divisional court of the Queen's Bench division.

12 Or more, as it turned out: like Superman, prime ministers could stop – or at least delay – a speeding bullet. And in December 2018 the Court of Justice of the European Union decided that

the UK could revoke Brexit unilaterally if certain conditions were met: https://eur-lex.europa.eu/legal-content/EN/TXT/?uri=CELEX:62018CJ0621.

13 Mark Elliott, *Prospect*, 31 July 2018, https://www.prospectmagazine.co.uk/politics/britains-constitution-is-buckling-under-the-weight-of-brexit.

14 *Daily Mail*, 4 November 2016. The wording changed slightly between editions.

15 Lord Burnett of Maldon, *Becoming Stronger Together*, speech to Commonwealth Judges' and Magistrates' annual conference, Brisbane, 10 September 2018, para 30, https://www.judiciary.uk/announcements/speech-by-the-right-hon-the-lord-burnett-of-maldon-becoming-stronger-together.

16 Martin Fletcher, 'The humbling of Britain', *New Statesman*, 27 March 2019, https://www.newstatesman.com/politics/uk/2019/03/humbling-britain.

17 In the House of Lords – at that time, the UK's highest court – on 30 July 1987, Lord Ackner, Lord Brandon of Oakbrook and Lord Templeman held that *Spycatcher* could not be reported in England and Wales even though the book, a memoir by a former MI5 officer, had been widely published in other parts of the world. Lord Bridge of Harwich and Lord Oliver of Aylmerton dissented. See *Attorney-General v Guardian Newspapers* [1987] 1 WLR 1248.

18 Sir Philip Sales, *Legalism in Constitutional Law: Judging in a Democracy*, Neill Lecture, All Souls College, 26 January 2018, reprinted in *Public Law*, October 2018 [2018] PL 687.

19 *The Guardian*, 5 November 2016, https://www.theguardian.com/law/2016/nov/05/barristers-urge-liz-truss-to-condemn-attacks-on-brexit-ruling-judges.

20 BBC interview, 6 November 2016, quoted in *The Guardian*, https://www.theguardian.com/commentisfree/2016/nov/08/liz-truss-defend-judges-article-50-stood-by.

21 Interview with Paddy O'Connell, *Broadcasting House*, BBC Radio 4, 13 January 2019, https://www.bbc.co.uk/sounds/play/m000203h.

22 Constitutional Reform Act 2005, section 7.

23 Putney Debates 2019, https://www.youtube.com/watch?v=o-rEhi36z9A at 53.23.

24 Under the Constitutional Reform Act 2005, section 3.

25 John Dyson, *A Judge's Journey*, Hart Publishing, 2019, p 174.

26 Lord Mayor's banquet, 3 July 2019, https://www.gov.uk/government/speeches/lord-mayors-banquet-2019-david-gaukes-speech.

27 He remained editor-in-chief, but a newspaper can have only one editor.

28 See Dan Sabbagh, 'New Daily Mail editor: we want the least damaging Brexit', *The Observer*, 12 August 2018, https://www.theguardian.com/media/2018/aug/11/new-daily-mail-editor-will-strike-tolerant-brexit-note.

29 Email, 24 September 2019.

30 See Jim Waterson, 'Daily Mail backs May's Brexit plan and brands rebel Tories "traitors"', *The Guardian*, 13 September 2018, https://www.theguardian.com/media/2018/sep/13/daily-mail-backs-theresa-may-brexit-plan-conservative-mps-traitors.

31 'BORIS BLASTS: WHO RUNS BRITAIN?', 25 September 2019, in response to the prorogation ruling discussed later in this chapter, https://www.theguardian.com/media/2019/sep/25/who-runs-britain-papers-divided-over-courts-damning-indictment-of-pm.

32 https://www.societyofeditors.org/soe_news/brexit-hating-media-is-a-problem-in-restoring-public-trust-says-paul-dacre/.

33 Ibsen's play is *An Enemy of the People*. The title is ironic.

34 *R (Miller) v Secretary of State for Exiting the European Union* [2017] UKSC 5, 24 January 2017. The court's membership was one down on its normal complement of 12 – which allowed all its members to sit without the risk of a tie.

35 25 January 2017, www.dailymail.co.uk/debate/article-4154526/DAILY-MAIL-COMMENT-not-good-day-democracy.html.

36 Lord Reed, interviewed 29 January 2019 for *Law in Action*, BBC Radio 4.

37 Address at Temple Church, 27 March 2019.

38 House of Lords Select Committee on the Constitution, 1 March 2017, https://www.parliament.uk/documents/lords-committees/constitution/Annual-evidence-2016-17/CC010317lordchancellor.pdf. I covered the press conference on 3 November 1987 at which Lord Mackay of Clashfern, the lord chancellor, declared that 'if a person has been appointed as a judge … I think he should be able to decide what to do if he is approached by the media'. Truss was aged 12 at the time.

39 House of Lords Select Committee on the Constitution, 22 March 2017, http://data.parliament.uk/writtenevidence/

committeeevidence.svc/evidencedocument/constitution-committee/lord-chief-justice/oral/49312.html.

40 Law Society *Gazette*, 24 April 2017, https://www.lawgazette.co.uk/commentary-and-opinion/will-liz-truss-be-shuffled/5060734.article.

41 Review Body on Senior Salaries, *Major Review of the Judicial Salary Structure*, October 2018, https://www.gov.uk/government/publications/major-review-of-the-judicial-salary-structure-2018.

42 'Government acts urgently to protect judicial recruitment', 5 June 2019, https://www.gov.uk/government/news/government-acts-urgently-to-protect-judicial-recruitment.

43 Gauke received a standing ovation at the Lord Mayor's banquet on 3 July 2019.

44 Author's sources. I shall have more to say about pay and pensions in Chapter 9.

45 Personal statement, *Hansard*, House of Lords, 25 October 2018.

46 Frances Gibb, *The Times*, 31 October 2018, https://www.thetimes.co.uk/article/lord-hain-disrespected-our-laws-by-outing-sir-philip-green-says-justice-chief-david-gauke-rr0c9t5j2.

47 Lord Hodge, speech at Gray's Inn, 27 February 2018, unpublished.

48 Lord Sumption, keynote speech, Bar Conference, 24 November 2018, https://www.supremecourt.uk/docs/speech-181124.pdf.

49 This is an apparent reference to the *Daily Telegraph*: see Gordon Rayner, 'Four judges to rule on Brexit have previous ties to Europe', 4 November 2016, https://www.telegraph.co.uk/news/2016/11/04/Four-judges-to-rule-on-Brexit-have-previous-ties-to-Europe/. The four were Lord Carnwath, Lord Reed, Lord Kerr and Lord Mance. In the event, two of them found for the government and two for Miller.

50 Lord Reed, *The Supreme Court Ten Years On*, Bentham Association Lecture, University College London, 6 March 2019, https://www.supremecourt.uk/docs/speech-190306.pdf.

51 Lord Burnett of Maldon, *Becoming Stronger Together*, para 31.

52 The order, made on 28 August 2019, had allowed for prorogation to start on a date between 9 and 12 September.

53 *R (Miller) v Prime Minister* [2019] EWHC 2381 (QB).

54 *Cherry v Advocate General* [2019] CSIH 49.

55 Interview with Andrew Neil, 11 September 2019, https://www.bbc.co.uk/news/uk-politics-49670901.

56 https://twitter.com/RobertBuckland/status/1171743709148454913.

57 On 12 September 2019 *The Scotsman*, in a parody of the *Daily Mail*, called them 'Heroes of the People'.

58 *The Times*, 18 September 2019.

59 Johnson's counsel had submitted that there were no 'judicial or manageable standards by reference to which the court could review or control an exercise of the prerogative power' to prorogue and that it would be 'constitutionally inappropriate for the courts to enter the territory'.

60 *R (Miller) v Prime Minister; Cherry v Advocate General* [2019] UKSC 41.

61 *R (Miller) v Prime Minister; Cherry v Advocate General* [2019] UKSC 41, paragraph 50.

62 Quentin Letts, 'Judges blew their hallowed status with the Supreme Court ruling and will now be fair game for public scrutiny', *The Sun*, 25 September 2019, https://www.thesun.co.uk/news/9998887/judges-supreme-court-public-scrutiny.

63 *R (Miller) v Prime Minister; Cherry v Advocate General* [2019] UKSC 41, paragraph 58, emphasis in original.

64 'Who runs this country?', *Daily Mail*, 25 September 2019, https://www.dailymail.co.uk/news/article-7500691/Boris-blasts-runs-Britain-PM-Johnsons-allies-declare-war-judiciary.html.

65 *Hansard*, Commons, 25 September 2019, columns 652, 655, http://bit.ly/2mTBzt3.

66 Letter to *The Times*, 26 September 2019.

Chapter 3

1 *R v Jones and others* [2006] UKHL 16.

2 *Shaw v DPP* [1962] AC 220. Presumably the draftsman thought that using archaic language would conceal the fact that he had made it all up.

3 *R v Delaval* (1763) 97 ER 913.

4 *R v Callaghan (Hugh)*, (1989) 88 Cr App R 40, 28 January 1988, Lord Lane CJ, Sir Stephen Brown P, O'Connor LJ.

5 *R v McIlkenny* [1992] 2 All ER 417, 27 March 1991, Lloyd, Mustill and Farquharson LJJ.

6 *R v Brown* [1992] 1 QB 491, Lord Lane CJ, Rose and Potts JJ.

7 *R v Brown* [1994] 1 AC 212, Lords Templeman, Jauncey of Tullichettle, Lowry, Mustill and Slynn of Hadley.

8 *Laskey, Jaggard and Brown v the United Kingdom*, http://hudoc.echr.coe.int/eng?i=001-58021, 19 February 1997. The court found that 'the national authorities were entitled to consider that the prosecution and conviction of the applicants were necessary in a

democratic society for the protection of health within the meaning of Article 8 para 2 of the convention'.

9 *R v BM* [2018] EWCA Crim 560.

10 https://www.bbc.co.uk/news/uk-england-birmingham-47658303.

11 *R v R* [1992] 1 AC 599, Lord Lane CJ, Sir Stephen Brown P, Watkins, Neill and Russell LJ.

12 *R v R* [1992] 1 AC 599 at 612, Lords Keith of Kinkel, Brandon of Oakbrook, Griffiths, Ackner and Lowry.

13 *CR v UK* [1996] 21 EHRR 363.

14 Under the Murder (Abolition of Death Penalty) Act 1965; the death penalty for murder survived in Northern Ireland until 1973.

15 Criminal Justice Act 2003, schedule 21, paragraph 6.

16 Criminal Justice Act 2003, schedule 21, paragraph 4.

17 Until the new minimum terms were approved by parliament, most lifers spent between 8 and 14 years in prison. It was recognised that the changes would lead to a substantial rise in the long-term prison population.

18 *R v Ahluwalia* [1993] 96 Cr App R 133.

19 *R v Thornton (No 2)* [1996] 1 WLR 1174.

20 Coroners and Justice Act 2009, sections 54–6, in effect from October 2010.

21 Serious Crime Act 2015, section 76, which took effect on 29 December 2015.

22 *Law in Action*, BBC Radio 4, 14 June 2016, https://www.bbc.co.uk/programmes/b07ffxsy.

23 *Law in Action*, BBC Radio 4, 26 February 2019, https://www.bbc.co.uk/programmes/m0002r4m.

24 See *DSD and NBV v Commissioner of Police of the Metropolis* [2014] EWHC 436, para 6, and [2015] EWCA Civ 646, para 2.

25 Dated, implausibly, 26 December 2017.

26 Crime (Sentences) Act 1997, section 28(6).

27 The government announced that it would change the law in the light of this case. The prohibition on disclosure of information about the board's proceedings would be removed. See: https://assets.publishing.service.gov.uk/government/uploads/system/uploads/attachment_data/file/703534/review-of-the-law_policy-and-procedure-relating-to-parole-board-decisions.pdf. The government also proposed what amounts to an internal appeal process: a decision (either to release or not to release a prisoner) could be challenged within a limited period and reconsidered by the Parole Board if it met the required threshold.

See https://consult.justice.gov.uk/digital-communications/ reconsideration-of-parole-board-decisions/supporting_ documents/ReconsiderationofParoleBoardDecisionsconsultation. pdf.

28   *R (DSD and NBV) v Parole Board* [2018] EWHC 694 (Admin): Sir Brian Leveson PQBD, Jay and Garnham JJ.

29   https://www.bbc.co.uk/news/uk-england-london-46265924.

30   When the changes were introduced in July 2019, it became clear that challenges by victims would be indirect.

Chapter 4

1   Lord Reed, *The Supreme Court Ten Years On*, Bentham Association Lecture, University College London, 6 March 2019, https://www. supremecourt.uk/docs/speech-190306.pdf.

2   *Roe v Wade,* 410 US 959 [1973]; *Obergefell v Hodges* 135 S Ct 2584 [2015].

3   *Stack v Dowden* [2007] 2 AC 432. See also Joshua Rozenberg, 'Ruling denies cohabitors rights of spouses', *Daily Telegraph*, 26 April 2007, https://www.telegraph.co.uk/news/uknews/1549703/ Ruling-denies-cohabitors-rights-of-spouses.html.

4   *The Ground for Divorce*, Law Com 192, https://www.lawcom.gov. uk/project/family-law-the-ground-for-divorce/, summarised in Lady Hale, speech at Resolution's 30th National Conference, Bristol, 20 April 2018, https://www.supremecourt.uk/docs/ speech-180420.pdf. As Brenda Hoggett QC, Hale was the Law Commissioner responsible for family law.

5   Lady Hale, speech at Resolution's 30th National Conference, Bristol, 20 April 2018, https://www.supremecourt.uk/docs/ speech-180420.pdf.

6   See Stephen Cretney, *Family Law in the Twentieth Century: A History*, Oxford University Press, 2003, chapter 5, on the origins of the Matrimonial Causes Act 1857. Adultery remained the only ground for divorce for the next 80 years.

7   Matrimonial Causes Act 1973, section 1.

8   Of the 114,000 petitions filed in 2016, around 17 were defended in the courts. See [2018] UKSC 41, paragraph 15, based on [2017] EWCA Civ 182, paragraph 98.

9   Judge Tolson QC, Central Family Court.

10   *Owens v Owens* [2017] EWCA Civ 182, Sir James Munby P, Hallett and Macur LJJ.

11   *Owens v Owens* [2018] UKSC 41, Lady Hale, Lords Mance, Wilson and Hodge, Lady Black.

12 *Owens v Owens* [2018] UKSC 41, paragraph 54.

13 David Allen Green, 'Law and justice, and divorce', *Financial Times*, 27 July 2018, https://www.ft.com/content/ce122e1e-9189-11e8-b639-7680cedcc421.

14 Lord Burnett of Maldon, *Becoming Stronger Together*, speech to Commonwealth Judges' and Magistrates' annual conference, Brisbane, 10 September 2018, https://www.judiciary.uk/announcements/speech-by-the-right-hon-the-lord-burnett-of-maldon-becoming-stronger-together.

15 https://consult.justice.gov.uk/digital-communications/reform-of-the-legal-requirements-for-divorce.

16 The bill was reintroduced in January 2020.

17 These periods could be adjusted in future, although the total could not be more than 26 weeks.

18 *Hansard*, Commons, 25 June 2019, column 588.

19 Civil Partnership Act 2004, section 3.

20 *Steinfeld and Keidan v Secretary of State for Education* [2016] EWHC 128 (Admin), paragraph 2, Andrews J.

21 *R (Steinfeld and Keidan) v Secretary of State for Education* [2017] EWCA Civ 81, paragraph 5, Arden, Beatson, Briggs LJJ.

22 *R (Steinfeld and Keidan) v Secretary of State for International Development* [2018] UKSC 32, Lady Hale, Lords Reed, Kerr and Wilson, Lady Black, paragraph 6.

23 [2017] EWCA Civ 81, paragraph 5.

24 13 March 2014 in the case of England and Wales.

25 In *M v Secretary of State for Work and Pensions* [2006] UKHL 11, paragraph 5.

26 The second most senior sits at the right hand of the presiding judge and the third most senior sits at the presiding judge's left hand. If there are more than three, the right/left pattern is repeated so that the most junior judges are at the furthest extremes of the bench.

27 Known as 'wingers'.

28 *The Future Operation of Civil Partnership: Gathering Further Information*, 10 May 2018, https://www.gov.uk/government/publications/the-future-operation-of-civil-partnership-gathering-further-information.

29 *R (Steinfeld and Keidan) v Secretary of State for International Development* [2018] UKSC 32, Lady Hale, Lords Reed, Kerr and Wilson, Lady Black.

30 See *Bellinger v Bellinger* [2003] UKHL 21, paragraph 53: 'It may … be that there are circumstances where maintaining an offending

law in operation for a reasonable period pending enactment of corrective legislation is justifiable.' (Lord Nicholls of Birkenhead)

31 Explained in Chapter 1.

32 *R (Nicklinson) v Ministry of Justice* [2014] UKSC 38, para 343.

33 Lord Neuberger in conversation with Claire Foster-Gilbert, *Sunday*, BBC Radio 4, 18 November 2018, https://www.bbc. co.uk/sounds/play/p06s4fp3.

34 Lady Hale, *What Is a 21st Century Family?*, speech to International Centre for Family Law, Policy and Practice, 1 July 2019, https:// www.supremecourt.uk/docs/speech-190701.pdf.

35 *Evening Standard*, 2 October 2018, https://www.standard. co.uk/news/uk/straight-couples-to-be-allowed-to-enter-civil- partnerships-theresa-may-reveals-a3950956.html.

36 *Implementing Opposite-Sex Civil Partnerships: Next Steps*, https:// assets.publishing.service.gov.uk/government/uploads/system/ uploads/attachment_data/file/815741/Civil_Partnerships_-_ Next_Steps_and_Consultation_on_Conversion.pdf.

37 *Northern Ireland Human Rights Commission's Application for Judicial Review* [2018] UKSC 27.

38 The four justices regarded the law as incompatible to the extent that it prohibited abortion in cases of (a) fatal foetal abnormality, (b) pregnancy as a result of rape and (c) pregnancy as a result of incest. Lady Black agreed on (a) but not on (b) or (c). So, five justices, in all, found the ban on abortion in cases of fatal foetal abnormality incompatible with article 8.

39 Paragraph 202.

40 *Moral Courage in the Law*, The Worcester Lecture 2019, Worcester Cathedral, 21 February 2019, https://www.supremecourt.uk/ docs/speech-190221.pdf.

41 Letter to Les Allamby, 13 November 2018, https://www. parliament.uk/documents/commons-committees/women-and- equalities/Correspondence/181113-NI-SoS-NI-Human-Rights- Commission-legal-cases.pdf.

42 Karen Bradley, oral evidence to Commons Women and Equalities Committee, 27 February 2019, Q481, http://data.parliament.uk/ writtenevidence/committeeevidence.svc/evidencedocument/ women-and-equalities-committee/abortion-law-in-northern- ireland/oral/97489.html.

43 European Union (Withdrawal Agreement) bill 2019, schedule 3, paragraph 5. When enacted, this will allow the commission to bring proceedings without being required to show that there would be an actual or potential victim.

44 Lord Kerr of Tonaghmore, *Striking the Balance between Common Sense and Legal Reasoning*, Barnards Inn Reading, 20 June 2019, https://www.gresham.ac.uk/lectures-and-events/grays-inn-reading-2019.
45 In response to a question I put after he had delivered the lecture referred to in the previous note.
46 'Supreme Pragmatism', *New Law Journal*, 15 June 2018, https://www.newlawjournal.co.uk/content/supreme-pragmatism.
47 Interview recorded 29 January 2019 for *Law in Action*, BBC Radio 4, 26 February 2019, https://www.bbc.co.uk/programmes/m0002r4m.

Chapter 5
1 Suicide Act 1961, section 1.
2 (1884) 14 QBD 273.
3 A.W. Brian Simpson, *Cannibalism and the Common Law*, University of Chicago Press, 1984; Penguin Books, 1986.
4 *In Re A (Children) (Conjoined Twins: Surgical Separation)* [2001] Fam 147.
5 *Airedale NHS Trust Respondents v Bland* [1993] AC 789.
6 *An NHS Trust v Y (by his litigation friend, the Official Solicitor)* [2018] UKSC 46, paragraph 19.
7 *An NHS Trust v Y (by his litigation friend, the Official Solicitor)* [2018] UKSC 46.
8 *R (Nicklinson) v Ministry of Justice* [2014] UKSC 38, paragraph 98.
9 *R (Nicklinson) v Ministry of Justice* [2012] EWHC 2381 (Admin).
10 *R (Nicklinson) v Ministry of Justice* [2013] EWCA Civ 961.
11 John Dyson, *A Judge's Journey*, Hart Publishing, 2019, p 188.
12 [2002] 1 AC 800.
13 *R (Nicklinson) v Ministry of Justice* [2014] UKSC 38, paragraph 116.
14 Lady Hale, *Celebrating 70 Years of the Universal Declaration and 20 Years of the Human Rights Act*, British Institute of Human Rights Annual Lecture 2018, 7 November 2018, https://www.supremecourt.uk/docs/speech-181107.pdf.
15 *R (Nicklinson) v Ministry of Justice* [2014] UKSC 38, paragraph 230.
16 Jonathan Sumption, *Human Rights and Wrongs*, BBC Reith Lectures 2019, lecture 3, 4 June 2019, https://www.bbc.co.uk/programmes/b00729d9/episodes/player.
17 'Assisted dying: couple tell of anguish over police inquiry', *The Guardian*, 7 February 2019, https://www.theguardian.com/society/2019/feb/07/assisted-dying-couple-tell-of-anguish-over-police-inquiry-dignitas.

18 Jonathan Sumption, *Law's Expanding Empire*, BBC Reith Lectures 2019, lecture 1, 21 May 2019, https://www.bbc.co.uk/programmes/b00729d9/episodes/player.

19 Serious Crime Act 2007, section 44. Encouraging or assisting another person to commit suicide carries a maximum penalty of 14 years (Suicide Act 1961, sections 2 and 2A). Intentionally encouraging a person to assist in a suicide carries the same maximum penalty.

20 Stephen Sedley, 'A boundary where there is none', *London Review of Books*, 12 September 2019.

21 *R (Conway) v Secretary of State for Justice* [2017] EWHC 640 (Admin), paragraph 4.

22 *R (Conway) v Secretary of State for Justice* [2017] EWCA (Civ) 275, paragraph 38.

23 *R (Conway) v Secretary of State for Justice* [2017] EWHC 2447 (Admin), paragraph 12, and *Nicklinson v United Kingdom* (2015) 61 EHRR SE7.

24 *R (Conway) v Secretary of State for Justice* [2017] EWHC 2447 (Admin), paragraphs 107, 108.

25 *R (Conway) v Secretary of State for Justice* [2018] EWCA Civ 16, Sir Ernest Ryder SPT and Underhill LJ.

26 *R (Conway) v Secretary of State for Justice* [2018] EWCA Civ 1431.

27 22 November 2018. A video recording of the hearing can be viewed here: https://www.supremecourt.uk/watch/uksc-2016-0168/221118.html.

28 *R (Conway) v Secretary of State for Justice*, https://www.supremecourt.uk/docs/r-on-the-application-of-conway-v-secretary-of-state-for-justice-court-order.pdf.

29 Letter before claim from Bindmans LLP representing Philippe Newby to Government Legal Department, 21 May 2019, para 37, https://crowdjustice.s3-eu-west-1.amazonaws.com/download/documents/2019.05.21+NEWBY+LBC+4th+draft++(2).docx_2121577_1+(2)+(1).pdf.

Chapter 6

1 I shall explain what that means later in this chapter.
2 See Equality Act 2010, section 29(7) and section 20 (duty to make adjustments).
3 *Paulley v FirstGroup plc* [2014] EWCA Civ 1573.
4 *Paulley v FirstGroup plc* [2017] UKSC 4.

5   But only after more than a decade of campaigning and arguing: see generally Sir Bob Hepple QC, *Equality, the Legal Framework*, Hart Publishing, 2nd edn, 2014.

6   The others are harassment and victimisation.

7   Equality Act 2010, section 13(1).

8   The concept comes from the US Supreme Court case *Griggs v Duke Power*, 401 US 424 (1971).

9   *Homer v Chief Constable of West Yorkshire Police* [2012] UKSC 15, paragraph 17.

10 Equality Act 2010, section 19(1).

11 Equality Act 2010, section 19(2).

12 See Malcolm Sargeant, *Discrimination and the Law*, Routledge, 2nd edn, 2018, chapter 1, section 6.

13 Human Rights Act 1998, section 3. This applies only to the rights listed in section 1.

14 Widowed parent's allowance and bereavement benefits were replaced by bereavement support payments for deaths occurring after 5 April 2017.

15 *Re McLaughlin's Application for Judicial Review* [2016] NIQB 11.

16 *Re McLaughlin's Application for Judicial Review* [2016] NICA 53.

17 See *Re McLaughlin's Application for Judicial Review* [2018] UKSC 48, paragraph 15.

18 *McLaughlin's Application for Judicial Review* [2018] UKSC 48.

19 See *Re McLaughlin's Application for Judicial Review* [2018] UKSC 48, paragraph 81.

20 *Brown v Allen*, 344 US 443 (1953) at 540, https://supreme.justia.com/cases/federal/us/344/443/#532.

21 British Institute of Human Rights Annual Lecture 2018, 7 November 2018, https://www.supremecourt.uk/docs/speech-181107.pdf.

22 Will Quince MP, oral evidence to the Work and Pensions Select Committee, 17 July 2019, Q137, http://data.parliament.uk/writtenevidence/committeeevidence.svc/evidencedocument/work-and-pensions-committee/support-for-the-bereaved/oral/103885.html.

Chapter 7

1   *Dulgheriu and Orthova v London Borough of Ealing* [2019] EWCA Civ 1490.

2   Genesis 49: 20. The Hebrew word for 'bread' can refer to food in general. The adjective translated as 'rich' also means 'fat'. Asher's

inheritance was a particularly fertile area of the upper Galilee (see Joshua 19: 24–31).

3   Equality Act (Sexual Orientation) Regulations (Northern Ireland) 2006 (SI 2006/439).

4   Fair Employment and Treatment (Northern Ireland) Order 1998 (SI 1998/3162 (NI 21)).

5   *Lee v Ashers Baking Co Ltd* [2015] NICty 2, https://www.bailii. org/nie/cases/Misc/2015/NICty_2.html. That figure had been agreed, subject to liability, on the basis that Lee suffered only from temporary injury to his feelings.

6   This is called an appeal by way of case stated.

7   *Lee v Ashers Baking Co Ltd* [2016] NICA 39.

8   Iconic advertisements for a Brooklyn bakery in the 1960s featured photographs of conspicuously non-Jewish New Yorkers with the slogan 'You don't have to be Jewish to love Levy's real Jewish Rye'.

9   *Lee v Ashers Baking Co Ltd* [2018] UKSC 49, paragraph 25.

10   https://www.supremecourt.uk/watch/uksc-2017-0020/judgment.html.

11   Compare *Bull v Hall* [2013] UKSC 73, the case about Christian hoteliers who refused a double-bedded room to two civil partners. The hotel keepers' reason was not, as they had argued, that the couple were unmarried but that they were both men. This was unlawful discrimination on grounds of sexual orientation.

12   Human Rights Act 1998, section 3(1). This is known as 'reading down'.

13   https://www.christian.org.uk/wp-content/uploads/ashers-press-statement-daniel-mcarthur-10102018.pdf.

14   https://www.equalityni.org/Footer-Links/News/Individuals/Commission-disappointed-about-Supreme-Court-Judgme.

15   Hamlyn Lecture, Middle Temple Hall, 5 November 2018.

16   *Great Ormond Street Hospital v Yates* [2017] EWHC 972 (Fam).

17   *Great Ormond Street Hospital v Yates* [2017] EWHC 972 (Fam), paragraph 11.

18   *Law's Expanding Empire*, BBC Reith Lectures 2019, lecture 1, 21 May 2019, https://www.bbc.co.uk/programmes/b00729d9/episodes/player.

19   *Great Ormond Street Hospital v Yates* [2017] EWHC 972 (Fam), paragraph 22.

20   Lord Dyson, Administrative Law Bar Association conference, 20 July 2019.

21   In *Counsel* magazine, 'Judicial overreach: a response to Sumption', August 2019.

22　In whom I declare an interest. See *A Cruel and Ignorant Campaign*, 26 July 2017, https://www.melaniephillips.com/cruel-ignorant-campaign.

23　*Charlie Gard: Pope and Trump offer parents support*, BBC News, 3 July 2017, https://www.bbc.co.uk/news/uk-england-london-40479074.

24　*In Re A (Children) (Conjoined Twins: Surgical Separation)* [2001] Fam 147.

25　*Re E (A Minor) (Wardship: Medical Treatment)* [1993] 1 FLR 386. The story was lightly fictionalised by Ian McEwan in his novel *The Children Act*, published in 2014, and a film released in 2017.

Chapter 8

1　*Kaye v Robertson* [1991] FSR 62. For a fuller account, see Joshua Rozenberg, *Privacy and the Press*, Oxford University Press, 2004, p 19.

2　Lord Bingham of Cornhill, *Should there Be a Law to Protect Rights of Personal Privacy?*, lecture to the Society of Liberal Democrat Lawyers, 21 May 1996, reprinted in *The Business of Judging*, Oxford University Press, 2000, p 153.

3　*Hansard*, House of Lords, 5 June 1996, column 1259.

4　Lord Phillips of Worth Matravers, Bentham Club Presidential Lecture, University College London, March 2003.

5　*Douglas v Hello! Ltd (No 1)* (CA) [2001] QB 967, paragraph 126.

6　*Wainwright v Home Office* [2003] UKHL 53, paragraph 31.

7　*Campbell v MGN Ltd* [2002] EWHC 499 (QB), paragraph 66.

8　*Campbell v MGN Ltd* [2002] EWCA Civ 1373.

9　*Campbell v MGN Ltd* [2004] UKHL 22.

10　*Richard v BBC* [2018] EWHC 1837 (Ch).

11　*Richard v BBC*, paragraphs 111, 114.

12　In *Axel Springer AG v Germany* [2012] EMLR 15.

13　https://www.bbc.co.uk/news/uk-45183421.

14　Tony Blair, *A Journey*, Hutchinson, 2010, p 26.

15　Blair, *A Journey*, pp 516–17.

16　According to Lord Wilson, it had no grounds to do so: see *R (Evans) v Attorney General* [2014] EWCA Civ 254, paragraph 178.

17　*R (Evans) v Attorney General* [2014] EWCA Civ 254.

18　*R (Evans) v Attorney General* [2015] UKSC 21.

19　With effect from 19 January 2011: see Freedom of Information Act 2000, section 37(1), as amended by Constitutional Reform and Governance Act 2010, schedule 7, paragraph 3.

20   https://www.theguardian.com/uk-news/ng-interactive/2015/
     may/13/read-the-prince-charles-black-spider-memos-in-full.

21   Jonathan Sumption, *In Praise of Politics*, BBC Reith Lectures 2019,
     lecture 2, 28 May 2019, https://www.bbc.co.uk/programmes/
     b00729d9/episodes/player.

22   Administrative Law Bar Association conference, 20 July 2019.

23   *R (Privacy International) v Investigatory Powers Tribunal* [2019] UKSC
     22.

24   Regulation of Investigatory Powers Act 2000, section 67(8).

25   Foreign Compensation Act 1950, section 4(4).

26   *Anisminic Ltd v Foreign Compensation Commission* [1969] 2 AC 147.
     The company was previously called Sinai Mining Co Ltd. 'Anis'
     is 'Sina' backwards and 'minic' is an abbreviation of 'mining co'.

27   *R (Privacy International) v Investigatory Powers Tribunal* [2019] UKSC
     22, paragraph 109.

28   *R (Privacy International) v Investigatory Powers Tribunal* [2019] UKSC
     22, paragraph 172.

29   *R (Cart) v Upper Tribunal* [2012] 1 AC 663.

30   Email to the author from Rupert Reid, director of research
     and strategy, Policy Exchange, 15 May 2019. I cannot find this
     statement published on any Policy Exchange website.

31   Qureshi, Tench, Hopkins, *Supreme Court: Parliament's 'ouster' of
     High Court Judicial Review Powers Is not Binding*, 21 May 2019,
     www.cms-lawnow.com/ealerts/2019/05/supreme-court-
     parliaments-ouster-of-high-court-judicial-review-powers-is-not-
     binding.

Chapter 9

1   *R (Gordon-Jones) v Justice Secretary* [2014] EWHC 3997 (Admin),
    Collins J.

2   Media briefing, 18 July 2019.

3   *Post-Implementation Review of Part 1 of LASPO*, https://www.gov.
    uk/government/publications/post-implementation-review-of-
    part-1-of-laspo, paragraphs 1138-68.

4   *Legal Support: The Way Ahead*, https://www.gov.uk/government/
    publications/legal-support-action-plan.

5   *Transforming Rehabilitation*, p 6, https://consult.justice.gov.uk/
    digital-communications/transforming-rehabilitation/supporting_
    documents/transformingrehabilitation.pdf.

6   *Report of the Chief Inspector of Probation*, March 2019, https://www.
    justiceinspectorates.gov.uk/hmiprobation/inspections/report-of-
    the-chief-inspector-of-probation.

7   *Justice Secretary announces new model for probation,* press notice, 16 May 2019, https://www.gov.uk/government/news/justice-secretary-announces-new-model-for-probation.

8   The new scheme is 'subject to the restrictions on accrual of benefits imposed by the Finance Act 2004 by means of the annual allowance and lifetime allowance rules. This is significantly disadvantageous to members of the new judicial pension scheme as there is the risk of a substantial increase in tax applied to lump sum and/or pension payments.' Sir Alan Wilkie, sitting as a judge of the Employment Appeal Tribunal, *McCloud v Lord Chancellor* [2018] 3 All ER 208, paragraph 19.

9   Review Body on Senior Salaries, *Major Review of the Judicial Salary Structure,* October 2018, paragraph 2.26, https://www.gov.uk/government/publications/major-review-of-the-judicial-salary-structure-2018.

10   A similar problem had been avoided in 2006 when the then lord chancellor, Lord Falconer of Thoroton, found £9m a year from his departmental budget to satisfy the Treasury's demands. See Joshua Rozenberg, 'Counting the cost of recruiting judges', *Daily Telegraph,* 26 January 2006, https://www.telegraph.co.uk/news/uknews/1508816/Counting-the-cost-of-recruiting-judges.html.

11   Review Body on Senior Salaries, *Major Review of the Judicial Salary Structure,* paragraphs 2.53–2.54.

12   'An efficient and functioning court service is absolutely crucial to stability and to prosperity and … there is an increasing recognition that a functioning, efficient court service which maintains the rule of law is absolutely vital for inward investment … People choose to litigate in London when they could choose to litigate elsewhere. That generates billions of pounds a year for the legal profession, for the professions which are allied to the legal profession, support services and so on. And maintaining the international reputation of the High Court is vital, as I see it, to the continuing prosperity of legal UK' (Lord Burnett of Maldon, press conference, 14 December 2018).

13   Judges' salaries were set at £5,500 in 1825 – an immense sum for those days – and reduced in 1832 to £5,000. They remained unaltered until 1954. See Robert Stevens, *The English Judges,* Hart, 2005, p 81 and R.M. Jackson, *The Machinery of Justice in England,* 5th edn, Cambridge University Press, 1967, p 291.

14   'Any salary payable under this section may be increased, but not reduced, by a determination … under this section' (Senior Courts Act 1981, section 12(3)).

15　Michael Beloff, '*Paying* judges: why, who, whom, how much?', Neill Lecture, 2006, 18 *Denning Law Journal* (2006), pp 35, 2.

16　This argument was put to the Court of Appeal by Michael Beloff QC in the case described in the next section. He won the case on other grounds.

17　Ministry of Justice, *Government acts urgently to protect judicial recruitment*, 5 June 2019, https://www.gov.uk/government/news/government-acts-urgently-to-protect-judicial-recruitment.

18　Mostyn, Newton, Moor, Theis, Arnold, Singh JJ.

19　*McCloud v Lord Chancellor* [2017] 1 WLUK 166, Stuart Williams, retired regional employment judge.

20　*McCloud v Lord Chancellor* [2018] 3 All ER 208, Sir Alan Wilkie, retired High Court judge.

21　*McCloud v Lord Chancellor* [2018] EWCA Civ 2844, Longmore LJ, Sir Colin Rimer and Sir Patrick Elias (retired appeal judges). 'Judge Williams did accord the [Lord Chancellor] a margin of discretion … He just did not consider that the aims relied on stood up to scrutiny, whatever margin of discretion was to be afforded to government. His conclusions … betray no error of law and cannot be successfully impeached' (paragraph 89).

22　*R (UNISON) v Lord Chancellor* [2017] UKSC 51, paragraph 98.

23　Employment Tribunals and the Employment Appeal Tribunal Fees Order 2013/1893, made under section 42(1) of the Tribunals, Courts and Enforcement Act 2007.

24　www.legislation.gov.uk/aep/Edw1cc1929/25/9/section/XXIX.

25　Richard Heaton, oral evidence to Commons Justice Committee, 6 November 2018, http://data.parliament.uk/writtenevidence/committeeevidence.svc/evidencedocument/justice-committee/ministry-of-justice-annual-report-and-accounts-201718/oral/92339.html Q56.

26　*Second-guessing Policy Changes*, Judicial Power Project, Policy Exchange, https://policyexchange.org.uk/wp-content/uploads/2018/03/Second-guessing-policy-choices-2.pdf.

27　Jonathan Sumption, *In Praise of Politics*, BBC Reith Lectures 2019, lecture 2, 28 May 2019, https://www.bbc.co.uk/programmes/b00729d9/episodes/player.

28　The other was the Prince of Wales letters case discussed in Chapter 8.

Chapter 10

1   https://judicialpowerproject.org.uk/about.

2   Sir Mark Potter, *Do the Media Influence the Judiciary?* Foundation for Law, Justice and Society, 2011, www.fljs.org/content/do-media-influence-judiciary.

3   *Judicial Power and the Balance of Our Constitution*, edited by Richard Ekins, Policy Exchange, 2018.

4   Two were Scottish advocates: Lord Macmillan in 1930 and Lord Reid in 1948. The others included Lord Macnaghten (1887), Lord Carson (1921) and Lord Radcliffe (1949). All became law lords; Sumption was the first barrister to be appointed direct to the Supreme Court. His appointment was not popular among judges who had worked their way up to the Court of Appeal, only to be passed over for promotion. I detected no such resentment in 2019 when it was announced that Professor Andrew Burrows QC (hon), a distinguished academic and part-time judge, would be joining the Supreme Court the following year.

5   Jonathan Sumption, *In Praise of Politics*, BBC Reith Lectures 2019, lecture 2, 28 May 2019, https://www.bbc.co.uk/programmes/b00729d9/episodes/player.

6   Singh LJ, Carr J, in *R (Hoareau and Bancoult) v Secretary of State for Foreign and Commonwealth Affairs* [2019] EWHC (Admin) 221 paragraph 326, cited by Hickinbottom and Haddon-Cave LJJ in *R (Wilson) v Prime Minister* [2019] EWCA (Civ) 304 paragraph 56.

7   Jonathan Sumption, *Rights and the Ideal Constitution*, BBC Reith lectures 2019, lecture 4, 11 June 2019, https://www.bbc.co.uk/programmes/b00729d9/episodes/player.

8   See Chapter 1.

9   Sumption, *In Praise of Politics*.

10 Presumably a reference to *Secretary of State for Education v Tameside MBC* [1977] AC 1014, in which a Labour education secretary was not allowed to stop a newly elected Conservative council retaining grammar schools.

11 Presumably *Bromley LBC v GLC* [1983] 1 AC 768, the Fares Fair case, in which a Conservative borough council successfully challenged a decision of the Labour-controlled Greater London Council requiring all London councils to finance the cost of reducing transport fares across London by a quarter.

12 Perhaps *Re McLaughlin's Application for Judicial Review* [2018] UKSC 48, discussed in Chapter 6.

13 Clearly *R v Secretary of State for Foreign and Commonwealth Affairs ex p World Development Movement* [1995] 1 WLR 386, the Pergau Dam case, in which the foreign secretary was not allowed to spend funds intended for overseas development on building an 'economically unsound' hydro-electric power station.

14 Perhaps *R v Ahluwalia* [1993] 96 Cr App R 133, discussed in Chapter 3.

15 Possibly *R (Litvinenko) v Home Secretary* [2014] EWHC 194 (Admin).

16 No citations were given for any of the cases referred to in this paragraph.

17 In unscripted remarks to the Administrative Law Bar Association annual conference, 20 July 2019, https://audioboom.com/posts/7327950-ep-88-reith-lecture-series-part-1-a-response-to-lord-sumption.

18 If a murder is carried out using a weapon that the offender deliberately took to the scene of the crime, the starting point is life imprisonment with a minimum of 25 years in custody. On appeal, Challen's minimum term was set at 18 years. By reducing her conviction from murder to manslaughter, the Court of Appeal allowed for a shorter minimum term.

19 Interview with Lord Justice Singh, Administrative Law Bar Association annual conference, 20 July 2019, https://audioboom.com/posts/7327951-ep-89-reith-lectures-series-part-2-lord-sumption-s-response.

20 Aharon Barak, 'As I sit at trial, I stand on trial', my paraphrase. See, for example, Barak, 'Some reflections on the Israeli legal system and its judiciary', *Electronic Journal of Comparative Law*, vol 6.1, April 2002, final sentence, https://www.ejcl.org/61/art61-1.html.

21 *Hansard*, Commons, 3 November 2010, column 921.

22 *Hirst (No 2) v UK*, 6 October 2005, in which the Court's Grand Chamber found a violation of Article 3 of Protocol No 1 (right to free elections). Other cases followed.

23 *Hansard*, Commons, 2 November 2017, column 1007.

24 House of Commons briefing note, March 2019, https://researchbriefings.parliament.uk/ResearchBriefing/Summary/CBP-7461.

25 Committee of Minsters report, 7 September 2018, http://hudoc.exec.coe.int/eng?i=DH-DD(2018)843E.

26 Jonathan Sumption, *Human Rights and Wrongs*.

27 Published by Richard Cohen Books.

28 One exception was Sir Peter Smith: see Joshua Rozenberg, 'Look out for a retirement announcement from the High Court's Mr Justice Peter Smith', *Legal Cheek*, 11 April 2017, https://www.legalcheek.com/2017/04/joshua-rozenberg-look-out-for-a-retirement-announcement-from-mr-justice-peter-smith and other pieces by the author online. Smith finally retired on 28 October 2017.

29 Jonathan Sumption, *Judicial and Political Decision Making: The Uncertain Boundary*, F.A. Mann lecture, 9 November 2011, https://www.scribd.com/document/72814968/Sumption-Mann-Lecture-Final.

30 Sumption, *Human Rights and Wrongs*.

31 At the Administrative Law Bar Association annual conference, 20 July 2019, https://audioboom.com/posts/7327950-ep-88-reith-lecture-series-part-1-a-response-to-lord-sumption.

32 *Rights Brought Home: The Human Rights Bill*, Lord Chancellor's Department, 1997, Cm 3782, paragraph 2.5, https://www.gov.uk/government/publications/the-human-rights-bill.

33 Sumption, *Human Rights and Wrongs*.

34 *R (UNISON) v Lord Chancellor* [2017] UKSC 51, paragraph 98.

35 *Ghaidan v Godin-Mendoza* [2004] UKHL 30.

36 'Judicial overreach: a response to Sumption', *Counsel* magazine, August 2019.

37 See Chapter 3.

38 Administrative Law Bar Association annual conference, 20 July 2019, https://audioboom.com/posts/7327951-ep-89-reith-lectures-series-part-2-lord-sumption-s-response.

39 And not just minorities: individuals who had been ill treated, murdered or driven to suicide. See the examples cited by Baroness Kennedy of The Shaws QC in Helena Kennedy and Jonathan Sumption, 'Are our human rights working?', *Prospect*, 12 July 2019, https://www.prospectmagazine.co.uk/magazine/helena-kennedy-vs-jonathan-sumption-are-our-human-rights-laws-working.

40 Joshua Rozenberg, 'All change at the top', *Law Society Gazette*, 5 August 2019, https://www.lawgazette.co.uk/commentary-and-opinion/all-change-at-the-top/5071208.article.

41 Stephen Sedley, *Lions under the Throne*, Cambridge, 2015, p 124fn.

42 *McFarlane v Tayside Health Board* [2000] 2 AC 59.

43 Tom Bingham, *The Judges: Active or Passive*, 2005, reprinted in Tom Bingham, *Lives of the Law*, Oxford University Press, 2011, p 136.

44 John Dyson, *Are the Judges too Powerful?*, 2013, reprinted in John Dyson, *Justice: Continuity and Change*, Hart, 2018, p 56.

45 *The Supreme Court Ten Years On*, Bentham Association Lecture, University College London, 6 March 2019, https://www.supremecourt.uk/docs/speech-190306.pdf.

46 Broadcast 18 November 2018. This extract is taken from a longer version of the interview, available online, https://www.bbc.co.uk/sounds/play/p06s4fp3.

47 As Brenda Hoggett, taking the name of her first husband.

48 *Profile*, BBC Radio 4, 28 September 2019, https://www.bbc.co.uk/sounds/play/m0008xb8.

49 Lord Hope of Craighead, *House of Lords 1996–2009*, Avizandum Publishing, 2018, p 207.

50 This account is taken from John Dyson, *A Judge's Journey*, Hart Publishing, 2019, p 139.

51 Lord Neuberger, who first became a judge in 1996 and so had to leave office at the age of 70, famously retired to make way for an older woman.

52 The Sex Disqualification (Removal) Act 1919 was in force from 23 December 1919 until 1 October 2010, when it was replaced by the Equality Act. It said that 'a person shall not be disqualified by sex or marriage from … entering or assuming or carrying on any civil profession or vocation'. The day after the Act was passed, Helena Normanton joined Middle Temple as a student. She began practising in 1922, the year in which Carrie Morrison became the first woman solicitor in England and Wales.

53 In her case it was 75 – because she was first appointed to the judiciary before April 1995, when the retirement age was reduced to 70 for new appointments.

54 *R (Miller) v Prime Minister; Cherry v Advocate General* [2019] UKSC 41.

55 In an interview for *Law in Action*, BBC Radio 4. Extracts were broadcast on 26 February 2019.

56 *Nairn v University of St Andrews* [1909] AC 147.

57 Until 1950 universities in the UK elected their own Members of Parliament. The system originated in Scotland before the union with England.

58 *Edwards v AG for Canada* [1930] AC 124.

59 Strictly speaking, decisions of the Judicial Committee of the Privy Council are not binding on courts in the UK; they are merely persuasive. None of the 'famous five', as they were called, became senators. See Erika Rackley and Rosemary Auchmuty (eds), *Women's Legal Landmarks*, Hart Publishing, 2019, chapter 29.

60 In an interview for *Law in Action*, BBC Radio 4. Extracts were broadcast on 26 February 2019.

61 *Principle and Pragmatism in Developing Private Law*, Cambridge Freshfields Lecture 2019, 7 March 2019, https://www.supremecourt.uk/docs/speech-190307.pdf.

62 See Chapter 4, in which Lord Reed told me: 'I'm much more inclined – and I think more inclined than some of my colleagues – to stand back and leave it to the political branches of government to decide on the appropriate policy.'

63 *The Supreme Court Ten Years On*, Bentham Association Lecture, University College London, 6 March 2019, https://www.supremecourt.uk/docs/speech-190306.pdf.

64 See Chapter 5.

65 *R (SG and others) v Secretary of State for Work and Pensions* [2015] UKSC 16. Imposing a cap on social security benefits affected women more than men. That was because most of the non-working households that received the highest levels of benefits were single-parent households and most single parents are women. Lord Reed, for the majority, said that opinions differed on benefits levels. 'It is not the function of the courts to determine how much public expenditure should be devoted to welfare benefits,' he said. Unless manifestly without reasonable foundation, the assessment of democratically elected institutions should be respected by the court.

66 (1765) 19 State Trials 1030. The king's messengers were not allowed to invade private property without lawful authority.

67 *R (UNISON) v Lord Chancellor* [2017] UKSC 51, discussed in Chapter 9.

68 *R (Miller) v Prime Minister; Cherry v Advocate General* [2019] UKSC 41.

69 BBC *Newsnight*, 28 August 2019, quoted on UK Human Rights Blog: https://ukhumanrightsblog.com/2019/08/28/judicial-review-against-prorogation-of-parliament-launched.

70 *Today*, BBC Radio 4, 25 September 2019.

71 *R (Miller) v Prime Minister; Cherry v Advocate General* [2019] UKSC 41, paragraph 30.

72 *That was the constitutional week that was*, 29 September 2019, https://davidallengreen.com/2019/09/that-was-the-constitutional-week-that-was.

73 At the Administrative Law Bar Association annual conference, 20 July 2019, https://audioboom.com/posts/7327950-ep-88-reith-lecture-series-part-1-a-response-to-lord-sumption.

Index

and access to justice 165–6
and assisted suicide 96, 97–8
and discrimination 110–11
and European Court of Human
    Rights 175–6
faces critics 178–9
and freedom of information 147
and Gard, Charlie 130–3
and Hale, Lady 183
and Human Rights Act 1998 177,
    178–9
and judicial power vi, 5–6, 165–6,
    169–73, 175–80, 190
and judicial review 170, 178
and parliamentary scrutiny 175
and principle of legitimacy 5–6
and prisoners' right to vote 174
and privacy 148, 150, 153
and proroguing parliament 187–8
and value of judges' work 39
Sun 31, 47
Supreme Court
    and abortion in Northern Ireland
        84–8
    and access to justice 162–3, 164–6
    and accommodating different
        views 181–2
    and Article 50 36–7
    and assisted suicide 94–7, 103–5
    and civil partnerships 75, 79–80
    conservatism of 88–9, 186–9
    and discrimination 109–11,
        115–19, 125–30
    and divorce 70–3
    and freedom of information
        145–7
    and judges acting politically 180,
        188
    and privacy 149–50, 151–3
    and proroguing parliament 43–8,
        187–9
    and religious beliefs 125–30
    and wheelchairs on buses 109–11
    and withdrawal of life support
        91–2
Supreme Court of Canada 184–5

T

Templeman, Lord 52–3
Thomas of Cwmgiedd, Lord 29,
    31, 34, 37–8
Times, The 32
Tombs, Robert 1
Toulson, Lord 110
Transforming Rehabilitation 157
Treacy, Mr Justice 114
tribunal fees 160–6
Truss, Liz 33–5, 36, 37–8

U

Underhill, Lord Justice 109
Unison case 161–6, 186
United States, Supreme Court v–vi,
    66, 119
Unsworth, Fran 143
Upper Tribunal 144–5

V

voluntary euthanasia 93
voting rights 174, 184

W

Wallwyn-James, Hugh 16–17
Ward, Lord Justice 91, 133
Wardlow, Michael 124
Wednesbury principle 19, 21, 62–3
Whaley, Ann 97–8
wheelchairs on buses 107–11
widowed parent's allowance
    114–21
Wilson, Lord
    and assisted suicide 96
    and family law 70–1, 84, 85, 88
    and freedom of information
        146–7
    and privacy 150, 153
Wistrich, Harriet 58
Worboys, John 59–65

Y

Yates, Connie 130–3